The Ethics of the
New Economy:
Restructuring and Beyond

"I downsized our staff so effectively,
they promoted me to Executive Vice President.
They also made me custodian, receptionist
and parking garage attendant."

The Ethics of the
New Economy:
Restructuring and Beyond

Edited by Leo Groarke

Wilfrid Laurier University Press

WLU

This book has been published with the help of a grant from the Social Sciences and Humanities Research Council of Canada.

We acknowledge the financial support of the Government of Canada through the Book Publishing Industry Development Program for our publishing activities.

Canadian Cataloguing in Publication Data

The ethics of the new economy : restructuring and beyond

Includes bibliographical references and index.
ISBN 0-88920-311-3

1. Downsizing of organizations – Moral and ethical aspects. 2. Downsizing of organizations – Canada – Moral and ethical aspects. 3. Economic history – 1990-
4. Canada – Economic conditions – 1991-   I. Groarke, Leo.

HD58.85.E83 1998   174'.4   C98-932401-X

Copyright © 1998
WILFRID LAURIER UNIVERSITY PRESS
Waterloo, Ontario, Canada   N2L 3C5

Cover design by Leslie Macredie. Interlocking block construction by Scott Reaume, Jazz Groarke and Kate Reaume. Photograph by Sandra Woolfrey.

Printed in Canada

Dedicated to my father, John Cuthbert Groarke,
in the hope that the independent spirit
that infused his work as the editor of
small town newspapers is to some extent
mirrored in the make up of this book.

Contents

Acknowledgments ix

Part I: Introduction 1

1. Editor's Introduction 3
   Leo Groarke
2. What Are the University's Obligations in the New Economy? 9
   A. Scott Carson
3. The Ethics of Restructuring 25
   Barry Hoffmaster

Part II: The Case Against Restructuring 41

4. Restructuring the Welfare State: Leaner,
   Meaner, and Inequitable 43
   Ken Hanly

Part III: Responsible and Irresponsible Restructuring 59

5. Responsible Restructuring in the Private Sector 61
   Wayne F. Cascio
6. Corporate Judo 75
   Todd J. Hostager, David T. Bastien, and Henry H. Miles

Part IV: Methods of Restructuring 93

7. Cause-Related Marketing: A Restructuring Alternative? 95
   Peggy Cunningham and Pamela J. Cushing
8. Realism, Restructuring, and Amalgamation: What Can We
   Learn from the Mega-mess in Toronto? 111
   Leo Groarke
9. Ethics and Regional Health Boards 125
   Michael Yeo, John R. Williams, and Wayne Hooper
10. Downsizing, Change, and Ownership 143
    Vincent Di Norcia

Part V: The Process of Restructuring 155

11. What Restructuring Can Learn from EBDM 157
    Sharon Dewey and Leo Groarke
12. Discharging Employer Responsibilities to Employees
    during Major Organizational Change 167
    David Drinkwalter
13. Fair Change: Employment Equity and Restructuring 179
    Norma J. MacRae

Part VI: Pitfalls of Restructuring 187

14. Managing Risks in the Restructured Corporation: The Case of
    Dow Corning and Silicone Breast Implants....................................... 189
    Conrad G. Brunk
15. De-Professionalization in Health Care: Flattening the Hierarchy 203
    Andrea Baumann and Barbara Silverman

Part VII: The Restructuring Economy... 211

16. Underemployment and the New Economy 213
    Louis Groarke and Nebojsa Kujundzic
17. Losing Community.. 231
    Robert C. Evans
18. Restructuring beyond the First World.. 239
    Darryl Reed

Part VIII: Case Studies 245

19. Rebuilding the Province of New Brunswick....................................... 247
    The Honourable Edmond P. Blanchard, QC
20. Community Health at the Willett Hospital....................................... 255
    Mary Sylver
21. Alberta Education: Retooling through Deschooling............................ 261
    J.L. Kachur and Derek Briton
22. Bell Canada—from the Bottom Up: An Employee's Perspective 273
    Monica Collins
23. The Banking Sector: Avoiding the Pitfalls of Restructuring................. 279
    Sylvia D. Chrominska

Part IX: Overview 285

24. Ethics and Restructuring: Obstacles, Challenges,
    and Opportunities... 287
    Wesley Cragg

List of Contributors 301

Notes 303

Bibliography... 309

Index 329

Acknowledgments

The present book is a collaborative project which has involved many authors over an extended period of time. As editor, I am grateful to the various contributors for their patience and their willingness to rewrite and rework their initial contributions in order to make this collection a unified whole. We are all grateful to the two anonymous academic referees, whose comments and initial criticisms played an essential role in the reworking of the book. On behalf of all contributors, I would like to thank Sandra Woolfrey, our copy editor Windsor Viney, and the staff at WLU Press for their commitment to academic publishing.

Both the book and the conference from which some of the papers are derived ("Ethics and Restructuring: The First Laurier Conference on Business and Professional Ethics," October 24–25, 1996) were possible thanks to the generous support of the Social Sciences and Humanities Research Council of Canada, the Research Office at Wilfrid Laurier University, and the Office of the Vice President Academic at Wilfrid Laurier. I speak for all contributors when I say that we are grateful for their support.

–L.G.

PART I
Introduction

I

Editor's Introduction

Leo Groarke

Restructuring and its effects surround us. The driver of the Airways Transit van on a recent trip from the airport told me that he had, one-and-a-half years earlier, been the CEO of a publishing company that employed sixty people. "For fourteen years I gave one hundred and fifty percent. I put on overalls and helped in the stockroom when they could not keep up with orders. I knew the families of all my workers."

One day he was told the company was restructuring. He was replaced by a new CEO who had no experience in publishing and was given three months' salary as a severance package. During the six months that followed he tried to adjust to life without his six-figure salary. In the process, he lost his house, his wife divorced him, and he searched unsuccessfully for a new position. His participation in a government retraining plan was cancelled because of technicalities surrounding his eligibility. After a great deal of effort on his part the eligibility issue was resolved, but by then the program had ceased to operate. A year and a half after losing his position, he drives airport vans for minimum wage and lives in a condo which he shares with his twenty-two-year-old son—a young man trained in architectural design who works as a manual labourer in two part-time jobs.

This is a very personal snapshot of the negative side of a new economy that is characterized by the restructuring of private and public enterprise, by the consequences of this restructuring, and by the new economic order it creates. Within this new economy, decisions to downsize, lay-offs, government cutbacks, and the closing or merger of businesses, hospitals, boards of education, schools, and health care services are the order of the day. The fundamental changes this implies have been fuelled by many forces: most obviously, by technological "advances" which continually reduce the need for human workers, by government attempts to eliminate their budget deficits and reduce their debt load,

3

and by the competitive pressures of a globalized economy. The new economy which results is characterized by change rather than stability, by continual restructuring, by ever-increasing competition in the marketplace, and by a social safety net that is increasingly threadbare.

Despite its human costs, opinions about restructuring and the economy it produces are divided. Many argue that economic sacrifices are necessary—if bitter—medicine for an ailing economy that is behind the times and too frequently characterized by inefficiencies and outmoded modes of operation. This economy needs, such commentators argue, to be overhauled in order to create more responsible government, more competitive private enterprise, and a brighter future with more and better jobs. Their opponents answer by decrying restructuring and its effects, and by arguing that restructuring serves primarily as a way to widen the gap between the rich and poor.

The radically divergent views of restructuring this debate implies have sparked many heated exchanges in the popular press but, peculiarly, relatively little discussion among those who study ethics and the ethical issues that arise in business, health, and education. The present collection is an attempt to change this, both in the context of short-term questions about the process of restructuring and in the context of longer-term questions about the economy it produces. The questions discussed include:

- When is restructuring justified, and when is it not?
- What are the ethical concerns which characterize the new economy that restructuring produces?
- What are an employer's obligations to employees during the kinds of major transformational change that characterize restructuring?
- What can past experience teach us about responsible restructuring, and how does it affect "the bottom line"?
- How can the negative social consequences of the restructuring economy be minimized?
- How can the increasingly competitive world economy that restructuring produces be made to promote ethical behaviour in public and private enterprise?
- How does restructuring affect local, national and international communities, and what should be done in this regard?

The answers to these questions which are found in the essays that follow are intended for students and academics, for policy makers, for professionals and business people who must deal with ethical issues, and for everyone affected by restructuring. Though the book is designed to be easily employable as a textbook or a training manual, its aim is a much broader understanding and discussion that—like the issues it discusses—transcends the classroom.

Because this collection is a contribution to applied ethics, it is important to say something about the vision of applied ethics that informs it, especially as the collection represents a notable departure from some traditional conceptions of ethical inquiry. One can better understand this departure by distinguishing two different kinds of questions that applied ethicists typically address. On the one hand, they investigate and discuss questions about the values we should or do adopt in making particular kinds of policy decisions. In dealing with concrete ethical issues, they must also address empirical questions about social, historical, political, and scientific matters that are relevant to the analysis and assessment of particular ethical issues. In discussing employment equity, for example, one might address the theoretical questions it raises about the moral status of discrimination and reverse discrimination, and/or empirical questions about the extent to which discrimination continues to exist and persist, and is likely to be affected by particular social policies. A comprehensive account of the issue must address questions about both "facts" and "values."

This means that applied ethics departs in some significant ways from traditional ethical inquiry, which has tended to emphasize the value side of the value–fact equation. In the context of applied ethics, it is important to say that it remains a central ethical concern, but also that an emphasis on concrete ethical issues means that "applied" ethical inquiry must frequently incorporate a detailed investigation of empirical issues that must inform conclusions about what is right and wrong, and questionable or not questionable in some real-life situation. Discussions of the greenhouse effect and what should or should not be done about it must, for example, be founded on a proper understanding of the science of climate change, including an understanding of the controversial issues of prediction it implies.

While applied ethicists generally agree that empirical considerations have a role to play in practical moral reasoning, the extent to which they should play a central role in applied ethics remains a matter of controversy. A number of commentators have questioned ethics' traditional emphasis on questions of value (see, for example, Hoffmaster 1991, Groarke and Scholz 1996), but others continue to take it to be the heart of ethical inquiry. While this is not the place for a detailed discussion of this issue, it is important to say that the present book adopts a very broad view of applied ethics which includes within its compass empirical inquiries that address key issues that must inform responsible decisions about practical ethical issues. Among other things, this conception of applied ethics suggests that it can, in the context of restructuring, usefully include historical, political, and empirical studies, and should not be narrowly restricted to the study of the moral values that inform restructuring decisions. Moral values do have an important role to play, but they are not the only grist for the applied ethics mill.

This broad conception of ethical inquiry, and applied ethics in particular, has been assumed for a variety of reasons: because there are theoretical reasons why it is difficult, in the realm of ethical inquiry, to usefully separate moral and empirical questions; because empirical disagreements frequently lie at the heart of conflicting conclusions about the ethical concerns raised by restructuring and other practical issues; and because a very broad conception of applied ethics allows a broader variety of stakeholders to state what they themselves take to be the morally most relevant features of restructuring. The broad conception of applied ethics that this implies is, it is worth noting, reflected in other applied ethics anthologies which include selections explicitly designed to address historical, political, and empirical dimensions of ethical issues (see, for example, Coward and Hurka 1993, Shaw 1996, and Cragg and Koggel 1996).

In the context of restructuring and the new economy, the notion that applied ethics should encompass whatever kinds of considerations are important to an ethical assessment of concrete issues makes applied ethics a very interdisciplinary enterprise. In the case of the present book, it means that contributions have come from fields as disparate as business, philosophy, economics, and medicine. The book's interdisciplinary leanings also incorporate an attempt to discuss, compare, and contrast (implicitly as well as explicitly) three different sectors of the economy—business, health, and education. This is useful because the institutions, corporations, and organizations that work in these different sectors are in many cases faced with similar restructuring issues. Even when they are not, comparisons can usefully highlight the differences that characterize different economic sectors.

One final interdisciplinary aspect of this book which merits mention is found in the attempt to include contributions from those who must grapple with ethical issues and the consequences of restructuring in the course of their business and professional lives. It has not been possible to include a representative of every relevant group of stakeholders in one volume, but there has been a concerted attempt to include a variety of voices which are reflected in a number of articles that serve as reports from the front line of the new economy.

Inevitably, the mix of interests and perspectives included in a collection like the present one implies very diverse and often conflicting opinions, interests, and agendas. A number of authors offer critiques of restructuring and the restructuring economy. No one defends the ethics of "slash and burn" downsizing (because it is very difficult to justify from an ethical point of view), but a number of authors do argue that restructuring can be a positive experience, provides a useful opportunity to change a flawed status quo, or is an unavoidable economic reality that must be accepted. A variety of authors suggest that attention to the ethical concerns raised by restructuring can create better corporations, governments, educational institutions, etc., from both a moral and an economic point of view. By including articles that promote responsible restructuring along with others that more universally reject restructuring, the book tries to present an informed account of different sides of the restructuring debate.

Whatever one's attitude to restructuring and the new economy, the ethical issues that they raise cannot be avoided, if only because financial circumstances and/or government policies often force restructuring, requiring that one choose between different restructuring options. In many cases, the result is managers and administrators who are not sympathetic to restructuring, but must nevertheless direct it. To do so responsibly, they must question how restructuring can—even when it is unwelcome—be conducted in as fair a way as possible. Once one takes this question seriously, it becomes clear that different approaches to restructuring and the new economy are not equal from an ethical (or an economic) point of view. This will be obvious if one considers the matter, for one cannot equate fair and unfair severance packages, outplacement services and a lack of concern about the welfare of laid-off workers, the necessary use of contract workers and policies that exploit them to the fullest, more efficient operations and corporate "anorexia," and so on.

The articles in the book have been arranged so that they discuss these kinds of distinctions from both a theoretical and a practical point of view. Though the distinction is not hard and fast, articles are more general and more theoretical in the earlier sections of the book. The discussion begins with this introduction, and with two articles designed to prepare the way for other contributions to the book. Subsequent sections present:

- the case against the restructuring economy;
- discussions of the distinction between responsible and irresponsible restructuring;
- accounts of alternative methods of restructuring;
- perspectives on the obligations created by the process of restructuring;
- examples of the pitfalls of restructuring;
- analyses of the ethical issues raised by the consequences of a restructuring economy;
- case studies of particular restructuring experiences; and
- a final overview and conclusion.

It goes without saying that the divisions between the different parts of the book are necessarily imprecise, and that most articles are usually relevant to issues discussed in a number of sections in the book. It is especially notable that articles which address general issues often do so on the basis of a detailed look at particular cases of restructuring or its consequences.

In the two articles included in the first section of the book, A. Scott Carson and Barry Hoffmaster set the stage for a detailed ethical investigation of restructuring. In "What Are the University's Obligations in the New Economy?" Carson argues that universities and their faculty have an obligation to address the issues that restructuring and the new economy raises. His article places the discussion which follows within the context of a view of university education that welcomes rather than derides an engagement with practical affairs, and stresses its importance both to the well being of the university, and to the society it serves. All the contributions to the present volume are very much in keeping with this view of university education.

In his article, Hoffmaster introduces a discussion of the ethics of restructuring, underscoring the substantial moral issues that it raises. In the process, he emphasizes the importance of a broader view of ethics and corporate responsibility which recognizes restructuring as a moral and not merely an economic issue. Having established this context, he compares the theory and practice of restructuring, especially in the guise of management philosophies like Total Quality Management (TQM). Taking health care as an example, he emphasizes the danger that restructuring may in practice mean that broad moral values are replaced by narrow economic ones which make economic measures the sole arbiter of institutional behaviour. Looked at from this perspective, restructuring is a fundamental challenge to the attempt to place more rather than less emphasis on ethics in the pursuit of business, health, and education.

2

What Are the University's Obligations in the New Economy?

A. Scott Carson

No one in Canada should be surprised to hear that the economy is in transition. Knowledge-based industries are growing rapidly and manufacturing sectors that emphasize manual rather than technological skills are in decline. Characteristic of this economic transition is the *restructuring* of the public and private sectors. In the public sector, restructuring is driven by the goals of debt reduction and fiscal austerity. In the private sector, the changes encompass not only businesses but whole industries. Many of these changes—a greater use of technology, the dislocation of labour, the "flattening" of the institutional hierarchy, and so on—are discussed in the papers in this volume.

In this article, I want to consider the implications of restructuring for Canadian universities. Not for their budgets or their fiscal plans, but for their teaching and their research goals and aspirations. One might put my topic as a question: To what extent are universities obliged to discuss, debate, and teach about restructuring, and to what extent are they obligated to prepare students vocationally for the new, restructured economy? I will note in passing that this is a more fundamental question than the question *how* universities might go about fulfilling such an obligation.

It is from the outset important to note that the question whether universities should prepare students vocationally for a restructured economy is especially controversial. On the one hand, there is immense and growing public pressure on universities to prepare students for the new economic order. Governments in British Columbia, Alberta, Manitoba,

Ontario, and Nova Scotia are pushing for a greater orientation to the needs of the marketplace. Much has already changed in universities, and especially in business schools, but there remains a high degree of resistance to changes in the university community overall.

Peter Emberley has, for example, complained that "increasingly universities are being required to see themselves as 'engines of economic growth,' 'training centres,' as the 'cutting edge of research and development'" (1996, 21–22). Emberley believes that universities should not be involved in preparing students for the workplace and therefore recommends that professional schools be moved out of academe and into polytechnics. Universities would "remain places where the culture of scholarship could proceed undisturbed, and where primary attention would be paid to frontier research, to cultivating critical reason and imagination and to fostering political citizenship and public service" (1996, 262; see also Wolff 1969, 12 and Bloom 1987, 339–340).

Clearly, the vision of a university reflected in the writing of authors like Emberley is not compatible with the notion that universities should—in their curriculum and research—place much emphasis on new social realities like restructuring. In the pages that follow, I examine the case for and against the notion that the university is obliged to address concrete economic and political issues like restructuring, both by preparing students for careers in a restructured economy and, more broadly, by making a concerted attempt to intellectually address the issues that it poses. I will argue that restructuring should in this way be accommodated within academe. One implication of this conclusion is that books like the present one should be written.

One cannot responsibly address questions about the university's obligations in the context of restructuring without considering three standard accounts of the university and its role. The first is the *research-based institution* model which is generally credited to the late-eighteenth-century Germanic conception of the university. Espoused by Humboldt, and with the University of Berlin as a model, it maintains that the proper role of the university is to pursue truth and advance the knowledge of society by research. This ideal travelled to North America through the establishment of universities such as Johns Hopkins and Clarke, which are substantially research-based. Although major institutions such as Harvard, Yale, Stanford, McGill, Toronto, Michigan, and Wisconsin are also centres of research, they corrupt the ideal research model to the extent that they engage in professional programs, athletic endeavours, and other non-research functions.

A second conception of what a university should be is the *classical college*. Cardinal Newman is usually credited with providing the best account of this conception in *The Idea of a University*. Newman's university was less focused on hard research than on educating students. Central to this was the intertwining of the intellectual and moral aspects of human life. The setting, or the educational environment, is an important component of this image of education. The ideal college should be small and removed from the daily affairs of society. It is a place where dialogue, free enquiry, and the study of classical texts is the means of tutoring students. Plato's Academy and Aristotle's Lyceum would be ancient models. Oxford and Yale in the early 1880s are later exemplars. In the ideal, it is teaching, generalist knowledge, and a commitment to a particular environment that sets this model of the university apart from the research institution model.

A third model is the *scholarly community*. This model combines elements of the other two, but moves beyond the research mission and the physical learning environment to concentrate on the nature of the scholarly life. The scholarly community is self-governed and based on the essential elements of reading and conversation. To this Emberley adds that "The purpose of the university is to sustain and enrich the scholarly culture in particular and the wider culture in general" (1996, 262).

The research and college models represent two competing functions in modern universities. The internal debate is often whether research or teaching should have primacy. The scholarly culture model seems to bring them together. It highlights the love of knowledge and truth which unifies the academic purpose. Importantly, as well, it promotes a form of education that is compatible with both, namely "liberal education." The research and college models do place greater weighting on different aspects of what we understand to be liberal education, but they both fit under its umbrella.

I do not have sufficient space to provide a full analysis of liberal education. But Plato is a useful reference point because of the richness and breadth of his position on education. He sees education as a way to guide students toward clarity and truth, as a way to develop in the learner a love for the *principles* that form the basis of human knowledge, and as a way to instill a passion for *order and symmetry*. A student, on Plato's account, learns how to use reason to impose harmony on desires. The education of a human personality is, therefore, broadly concerned with both reason and desire—an *integration* of the whole self. Plato proposes different educational processes for different stages in the learner's development. Most important for us are the later stages when educational activities are directed toward harnessing the senses, emotions, and intellectual virtues to develop a sensitivity to the "forms of the good" and a grasp of the harmony that unites them.

Some of the salient points of Plato's theory are central to our discussion. First, we can see how very different Plato's conception of "education" is from the "skill training." For Plato, what should be learned is what has *inherent value*. Though the knowledge an educated person acquires might turn out to have practical uses, it needs no instrumental justification. Second, Plato emphasizes not just breadth of knowledge but depth as well. Education therefore entails some understanding of the theoretical principles that underlie knowledge and provide coherence and cohesion. Someone who has at their command disparate facts and figures without a sense of what makes them come together is, from this point of view, well informed but not really educated. Finally, Plato understands an educated person to be someone who possess intellectual virtues such as the desire for clarity, impartiality, etc.

Plato's account of liberal education has, of course, been adapted and moulded in different ways by various modern commentators. For our purposes I think we can allow the points made above to stand as a working set of parameters. Whether breadth is ultimately more important than depth, or the intellectual virtues more crucial than the means by which they are developed, is less important to us than recognizing that each is a part of what most people would agree is necessary (in some measure) to the nature of a liberally educated person. So we will take breadth, depth, underlying principles, consistency and coherence, rational autonomy, and development of the intellectual virtues as being key conditions for a liberal education. I leave as an open question the relationship between such education and knowledge that has inherent as opposed to instrumental worth (I deal with this question below, p. 22).

Given this analysis, we can ask how liberal educators should regard the attempt to address contemporary economic realities like restructuring educationally. Certainly some would say that a concern with such realities ties the university too closely to the here and now, not allowing the freedom that is crucial for the theoretical investigation of inherently valuable knowledge. According to Bloom, vocational training is especially problematic because it is too directed and does not allow the student sufficient freedom to radically question and reevaluate their life and goals (1987, 370). For Bloom, the very idea that as educators we ought to look to the transitory state of the Canadian economy and use this as a basis for deciding what ought to be taught in a university, would be anathema.

This, then, is the first argument against the claim that the university has an obligation to address restructuring both vocationally and more broadly, and that academics need to address restructuring issues. It claims that academe is centrally concerned with liberal education and that this is not compatible with an emphasis on timely social, political and economic issues, and is in particular incompatible with professional, careerist education and with other forms of education which prepare students for economic life.

A second argument against the attempt to address the issues raised by restructuring maintains that the university simply cannot meet the demands this would impose. Emberley, for example, writes that universities asked to take on too many other non-scholarly tasks—tasks like attending to the economic needs of society—are unable to cope with the range of competing and incompatible demands. "The university cannot simultaneously be an engine of economic growth, a social welfare agency, a laboratory for a new consciousness, a training centre, and a home for the scholarly culture. Something has to give" (1996, 258).

Here, then, we have two purported reasons why the universities should divorce themselves from immediate social, political and economic concerns like restructuring and the economy it produces. First, because to do so would not be in keeping with their mission of liberal education, and second, because doing so places too many demands on universities, which are already stretched to the breaking point.

What is to be said in answer to these objections? I think we need to begin by recognizing another role of the university: its role as social critic. This is a role that is as established as its role as the purveyor of liberal education, and a role which is a crucial part of the university's contribution to the broader community that pays for it. As John Stuart Mill observed in *On Liberty*, discussion, criticism and debate are not a nicety, but a necessary part of society if it is to constructively address problems, compare alternative solutions, and learn from its mistake. The university is the institution par excellence for this critical role, for a great many reasons—most importantly, because it has in-depth expertise in most areas and because its professors have an autonomy which is provided by tenure and academic freedom.

Looked at from this perspective, it can very plausibly be argued that academics have a positive duty to take up a critical examination of the nature and social impact of restructuring activities in the economy. In this context, it is important to recognize that universities have always been concerned with the issues of the day, and that the tranquil image of the "college" concept—the quiet, remote and communal guild unified in the common love for scholarly conversation and debate—is historically misleading.

Ties to "practical" social, political and economic issues is one of the hallmarks of the modern university. North American universities have had business schools, medical schools, law schools, and other professional schools for more than sixty years. Throughout this period they have flourished. Twenty years ago, Niblett remarked that "the pressure grows on higher education in almost every country to produce graduates useful to a society eager for more and more technology and know-how. This pressure can be seen to have been growing for at least a hundred years" (1974, 2). North American universities have never been a refuge for research and pure scholarship in a way that disallows any concern about careers and political and economic concerns.

A similar preoccupation with timely issues is also apparent if we consider the university's broader role in social and political debate. During the 1950s universities were preoccupied with the political oppression of McCarthyism; in the 1960s there were campus riots in Paris, Columbia, Berkeley, and elsewhere, and the Kent State shooting. The 1970s tended to be more tranquil, but gave rise to the political correctness and gender issues of the 1980s and the aggressive multicultural and postmodernist politics of the 1990s. In light of these historical trends, it is hard to envision the reality of academic life as being quiet, unified, and removed from the issues of the day.

These features of the university are reflected in the fact that universities have themselves been rife with acrimonious political and ideological conflict. It could hardly be otherwise if one accepts the university's role as social critic, which must include criticism of the university as much as other aspects of society. This point can easily be illustrated by listing titles of some of the books most commonly read on campuses over the past thirty years: *Zero Tolerance: Hot Button Politics in Canada's Universities* (1996), *Campus Wars: Multiculturalism and the Politics of Difference* (1995), *The Imperiled Academy* (1993), *Illiberal Education: The Politics of Race and Sex on Campus* (1991), *Tenured Radicals: How Politics Has Corrupted Our Higher Education System* (1990), *Profscam: Professors and the Demise of Higher Education* (1988), *The Closing of the American Mind: How Higher Education Has Failed Democracy and*

Impoverished the Souls of Today's Students (1987), *The Divided Academy: Professors and Politics* (1975), *Death of the American University* (1973), *Confrontation and Counterattack* (1971), *The Academic Revolution* (1968), and so on and so forth.

Looked at from this point of view, the North American university has always been a mix of social, political and economic criticism, "pure" theoretical reflection and vocational training. As Jencks and Reisman write of the latter, "purity of motive and single-mindedness of purpose have never been characteristic of American colleges…the question has always been *how* an institution mixed the academic with the vocational, not *whether* it did so" (1968, 199).

Just because the ideal of the academic community has not been realized in the recent historical past (and is not likely to materialize anytime soon) it does not follow that the ideal is without merit. But it is important to note that Emberley, Bloom and others are lamenting the passage of something that does not seem to have existed, or if so, not for very long. Putting this historical point aside, the deeper issue is whether the consideration of timely social, political and economic issues should occupy an important place in the university. Given our earlier account of the university's goals and mission, this can best be put as the question whether this consideration serves the cause of liberal education.

Here we need remind ourselves that the centrepiece of liberal education is the development of the rational capacities of the mind at some reasonable level of breadth, depth and coherence. Underlying this is an understanding of the principles that support the core subject knowledge in the discipline being learned. We might add that the way in which education must take place cannot be doctrinaire; indeed it should promote free inquiry and the development of intellectual autonomy. Finally, we can say that there must be a commitment to intellectual virtues such as clarity, respect for the facts, relevance, etc. I want to argue that a concern with economic issues like restructuring and its aftermath, and some corresponding commitment to vocational education is consistent with the principles of liberal education.

The first requirement of liberal education, *breadth*, is clearly served by attention to issues like restructuring, just because they are inherently many-sided and interdisciplinary. Whether the issues occur in the context of business, education, health services, etc., a discussion of them presupposes a broad understanding of the nature of the working world and the overarching human context in which it occurs. In this sense, breadth of understanding is of crucial importance.

In order to understand issues that pertain to business, for example, one will frequently need to understand organizational theory, organizational behaviour, business ethics, the social and political contexts of business, and so on. A further key element will often be an understanding of the macro- and the micro-economic environments of business. Probably, the liberal arts provide the ultimate basis of this understanding, which must be rooted in foundational elements of sociology, psychology, philosophy and history.

Those liberal educators who prefer to emphasize breadth rather than depth should, therefore, embrace programs that pay attention to timely social, political, and economic issues, for they consciously require a broad understanding. In comparison, many other university programs give students the opportunity to take courses that result in a very narrow specialization. An honours physics student, for example, can probably opt for course selections that barely go beyond physics, mathematics, and cognate hard sciences. It is difficult to see breadth in this.

This introduces the *depth* criterion. Here it can be said that timely issues presented by economic phenomena like restructuring provide an ideal way to introduce students to an in-depth treatment of the various disciplines and subject areas. Obviously, a focus on these issues is not itself tantamount to an in-depth study of the issues that underlie them. But it can still be said that a full understanding of them requires this kind of study. To fully understand issues in education, for example, one needs a foundational course in philosophy of education which analyses the concepts and principles central to the nature of human learning, knowledge and understanding. Such courses are pursued with the rigour and depth we associate with philosophy departments (and are often taught by philosophy departments). Equally, cognitive psychology in teacher education, and organizational psychology in business education, are necessary prerequisites if we want to analyze the structural elements of human perception, understanding and conduct in depth. And just as psychology is at the core of issues in education, sociology is a major part of issues in social work and economics is a major part of issues in business. Since these social sciences are firmly entrenched in the liberal arts it would be odd to think of them losing their bona fide credentials when they are used as background for the investigation of timely issues.

The *coherence* principle of liberal education is, ironically, better served in the educational preparation which concerns itself with issues of practical import than in its supposed natural home—the arts and science faculties. The reason is that this kind of education needs to integrate the various disciplinary offerings. In the business world, for example, problems do not arise with labels attached identifying them as best dealt with by one academic discipline or another. Instead, they are created out of the complexity of business activities and require those who address them to be able to determine which forms of knowledge most suitably generate the principles that can be applied. Because of this the best education of this sort works hard to develop overall program approaches to curricula which draw together the cognate disciplines in a way that explains how each can make its contribution to understanding complicated situations. This is increasingly the goal of professional education.

By contrast, the arts and sciences are still very much characterized by discipline "silos" in which the departments of, say, history and English are quite separate from one another. Some universities are experimenting with multi-disciplinary programs like environmental studies, but the tendency in most academic institutions is still to maintain the boundaries. Even within the disciplines there is considerable fragmentation, as increasingly course offerings reflect the highly specialized research interests of the professors teaching them rather that an integrated attempt to develop in the student a coherent understanding of the structure of the discipline.

This suggests that addressing issues like restructuring and the new economy supports the three fundamental goals of liberal education—breadth, depth and coherence. What, then, of the other aspects of liberal education? What, for example, should we say about liberal education's commitment to free inquiry and the development of intellectual autonomy? One might in this regard worry that the inevitable attachments to the world of economic activities that come with attention to concrete economic issues like restructuring may result in doctrinaire teaching that promotes "received doctrine" which emanates from various professions, businesses or enterprises; and that this seriously compromises the independence that liberal education requires. The "received doctrine" could take the form of established procedures for performance and codes of conduct which are not open to criticism in the way that an interpretation of a sonnet might be.

Professional schools naturally presume the legitimacy (moral and otherwise) of the work they are preparing students to engage in. A business school, for example, presupposes the acceptability of the market system. In considering the significance of this fact, it is important to remember that professional issues may be considered from the point of view of a number of different disciplines. Business concerns may, for example, be considered in a course that resides in sociology, philosophy, political science or law. Even within a business school, it is important to remember the foundational nature of many business courses. Since they are intended to examine the theoretical underpinnings of the relevant practices, a wide divergence in ideological critiques from students is not only compatible but encouraged. In business ethics classes, professors routinely push students to challenge the economic conservatism of the market economy.

Granted, in functional areas such as finance, it is true that the theoretical constructs usually presuppose as a starting point that in a free-market economy individuals are rational utility maximizers. But it is important to distinguish between accepting the basic assumption of a theory in order to test its internal coherence and explanatory power overall, and accepting the assumption as being itself true or morally legitimate. If a finance professor demands that students commit themselves to the truth or legitimacy of the assumption, rather than requiring that they use it as a hypothetical starting point, then the professor is being doctrinaire, hence illiberal. But there is nothing about business education per se that requires this.

Concern about bias in the treatment of particular issues is to some extent legitimate, but it is easily exaggerated in the context of economic issues and professional education. If one looks at the politicization of the university it should be clear that the risk of doctrinaire teaching and social criticism is as much a concern with the political left so evident in the social sciences as with the conservative right in, for example, the business school. And it is tempting for the former to condemn the latter because of their political orientation. But the challenge can go both ways. What is important to realize is that there is nothing that prevents those in the professional schools from criticizing either the status quo or the direction that the economy is taking. Indeed, professions such as social work which typically advocate for the poor and disadvantaged are likely to do just that.

It is in any case important to remember that every academic field has its orthodoxies: academic journals, for example, require specific styles for footnotes, references and so on, and acceptable kinds of methodological approaches. Doctoral thesis committees have a specified structure in each university, and their members have prescribed responsibilities. Professors and students in both cases can always question the rules. But until the rules are changed, everyone must abide by them. So when graduate students in any field are being trained for the academic world, they must learn their own set of "received doctrines." But just as they can challenge these strictures when admitted to the professorate, so can lawyers, accountants and doctors. In any event, it is only a small part of a student's overall program that is devoted to the prescribed knowledge.

A positive argument in favour of the non-doctrinaire nature of education that focuses on practical issues is that it typically requires considerable use of teaching devices such as case studies and business simulations. Pedagogically, both are a long way from being rigid or doctrinaire. They are very open-ended in terms of what counts as the right answer, since usually the solutions available are numerous. Most solutions have some merit, but certain approaches are better than others in virtue of the desirability of the consequences they bring about. Because of this, students are encouraged to think for themselves, defend their judgments and, in the case of simulations, be prepared to live with the impact of decisions made since they affect the alternative courses of action that will be available for decisions at later stages of the simulation. Courses like this, therefore, tend to promote the autonomous thinking which is a central feature of liberal education.

What, then, of *intellectual virtues* such as clarity, respect for evidence, the willingness to change one's position in light of compelling evidence to the contrary (i.e., academic humility) and tolerance of the opinions of others? They are also crucial to liberal education, especially as Plato construed it. I explained above that degree programs which include an element of issues like restructuring may involve liberal arts courses, professional programs, and courses in functional disciplines. If all components meet the breadth, depth, and coherence tests as we discussed, there appears to be little reason why the intellectual virtues would not be an important educational outcome.

Interestingly, in many applied fields the virtues actually take on an enhanced importance because of their applications to the working world. Accuracy and respect for the facts is extremely important in business, especially where the consequences of being wrong can be severe. Correspondingly, having respect for the opinions of others can enable a business person to make better judgments. A miscalculation by a foreign exchange trader can result in the loss of a great deal of money, and engineering errors in the planning of physical structures such as bridges or aircraft can endanger people. A lack of precision by a doctor or dentist can have, likewise, seriously harmful consequences, and so on. Liberal educators ought, therefore, to embrace education which engages timely concrete issues in order to promote the intellectual virtues.

I think that we can now conclude that liberal education gains rather than loses by engaging practical concerns. Academics should, this suggests, study issues like those discussed in this book. It is interesting to compare these conclusions to the opposing views of Wolff, who writes a generation earlier. He argues that faculty members in professional schools, or those who are otherwise concerned with the economic world, find themselves torn between academe and the working world. He writes, "The inclusion of professional schools and programs within the university [therefore] damages and eventually destroys the unity of the academic community...[In] countless ways, the activities of professors and students of the professional schools reach beyond the university and inevitably loyalties are divided. The professional faculties cannot commit themselves or their energies to the university unconditionally, as professors in the arts and sciences regularly do" (1969, 12–13).

What are we to make of this suggestion that faculty concerned with professional issues will be distracted by their loyalties to their professions, their business connections, and so on? First, it may be said that all academics have divided loyalties and responsibilities. A university professor must serve on departmental and other university committees, take on some community responsibilities, play a role in professional associations, teach, do research, be a parent and spouse or partner, have personal and political commitments, etc. Frequently one distracts from the others and gives rise to the need to prioritize. When a professor has both student term papers to mark and at the same time a deadline for the submission of a conference paper, the need to set priorities arises. Likewise, as an officer of a learned society, there may be many demands when organizing an annual conference that conflict with one's obligation to review a manuscript for a publisher. None of these situations are significantly different from that faced by an accounting professor who is also a member of a professional society.

The suggestion that divided loyalties due to professional and academic commitments are insurmountable in any case overlooks the many divided loyalties that already exist on campus. It is in this regard significant that the image of the "scholarly culture" that invests itself in the aims and methodologies of a liberal education both in the "research" and "college" models of the university rests upon a conception of academic disciplines that sees them as uniform endeavours. Each discipline has internal to it standards of evidence, verification and argumentation, and methods of investigation that are agreed upon by those academics who practise it. And it is the fact of commitment to these rules even across the disciplines that constitutes the unity of academe.

But is this so? When looking at the extreme differences in methodology between the work of theoretical physicists, empirical sociologists and historians, for example, it is hard to see the strict unity. Their rules of evidence, argumentation, and so forth are vastly different. And the reality on university campuses is that they have very little contact with one another. Even within disciplines the methodological differences can be quite disunifying. Political philosophers in the Marxist or Frankfurt School traditions have had great difficulty communicating academically with their counterparts in the analytic mode. Behavioural and Freudian psychologists have fundamental disagreements about method, evidence and proof. And social scientists and humanities professors who support the postmodernist critique of multicultural or gender relations seem to view the role of the academic as being focused on political change rather than seeking objective truth. In light of this, it is difficult to maintain that the disciplines are unified except in a very highly generalized way.

Instead of insisting on a romantic notion of unity within the university, we will do better to recognize the strength in diversity. In the present context, it can be said that there is a symbiotic relationship between the pure and applied disciplines which provides advantages to both. Because applied courses and professional schools serve the needs of a workplace in transition, they can provide a pragmatic anchor for the humanities and social sciences. To complement this, though, the traditional liberal arts departments present a constant challenge to the conservative tendencies of the professional schools. Although I argued above that the professional programs enable the students to appraise critically, and to oppose if they wish, the economic and political assumptions that underpin financial and other theories, there is, still, often a supportive leaning toward the direction that the economic change is taking. This is to be expected because the thrust of a program that prepares students to function well in a particular economic order, or one that is changing in a particular direction, is unlikely at the same time to be encouraging them to act against it. This is not to say that a well-educated person would not be willing to stand against wrong-doings or systematic injustices. It is only that they could reasonably be expected to incline towards support overall. Partly, this is because learning how to function well in the new economy involves acquiring effective strategies. Those strategies presume an acceptance of the conditions that are to be encountered.

On the other hand, professors and students in the humanities and social sciences are not necessarily so disposed to accept new economic trends. They may advocate something very different in their role as social critics. Doing so acts as a check on professional commitments. It forces academics with such commitments to constantly ask themselves about the social and moral acceptability of the world for which students are being prepared. Overall, as a consequence, the applied and pure disciplines provide balance for each other, even if this is at times achieved by tension rather than harmony.

So far I have argued that an effort to address issues like restructuring and its consequences is an important element of university education and in keeping with, rather than opposed to, the goals of liberal education. There remains one issue I have not addressed. It is the notion that liberal education concerns knowledge that has inherent versus instrumental value. This is the most difficult criterion for the kind of education I have been discussing but it seems to me to be the least plausible criterion. It is not clear why all knowledge that is acquired in a university education (in whatever discipline) should be divorced from the utility it might have in a practical sense. In this I agree with Dewey and Whitehead. Professional schools can, for example, blend the inherent and instrumental values of knowledge. The same can be said for other programs which have an applied focus.

It is important in this regard to emphasize that I am not suggesting that *all* university education should have the focus that I have been discussing. I would argue, on the contrary, that part of the university's mandate is to address issues that transcend immediate social, political and economic concerns. I have already argued that an understanding of these issues naturally requires a broader background of the sort that is provided by this kind of study.

I will finish by noting that here we find an answer to the second objection to university education that emphasizes applied issues. Here we might note a function that such education provides even though it is not something that it consciously seeks to do. It is a sheltering effect which protects the non-instrumental aspects of the university curriculum in the face of public demands for careerism and academic relevance. That is, when government policy-makers, the media, and others become fixated, as they are currently, on the idea that universities should do a better job in preparing students for the new economic realities this criticism is not usually aimed at any specific part of the university. Usually it is an expression of frustration with the university as a whole. The public sees an

urgent need for graduates who have different competencies and are looking to the university to improve its programs accordingly. Because the
applied areas of the university, especially the business school, are best
able to respond to this call, they can in some sense draw the fire away
from the disciplines that are both less capable and less disposed to do so
(in part, they can do this by providing the students necessary to sustain
a program—most professional students take 30 to 50 percent of their program directly in the liberal arts, for example). This provides shelter for
disciplines that manifestly should not be addressing economic skill
requirements. It is, quite frankly, abhorrent to think that the study of
poetry or art history ought to serve economic ends or need instrumental
legitimacy in order to survive in academe in the face of funding cuts.

Economic and business restructuring is a reality of the late twentieth
century, and the pace of change is unlikely to abate. Technological
development is accelerating and with it comes the transformation of
work; it eliminates the need for particular functions and creates others.
The old functional jobs are rapidly giving way to new roles and reporting structures. The technology is highly sophisticated, so different levels
of understanding are required not only to utilize it but to manage in the
new environment. This goes well beyond the learning of routinized
skills. It requires an understanding of more complex work environments
and the ability to make judgments within them. Many thousands of
Canadian university graduates enter this work world every year. It would
be wrong to think that each course and program within the university
ought to direct its efforts at preparing students for it. That would tragi-
cally ignore the contribution of the arts and sciences to the development
of a civilized society and the advancement of human knowledge. By the
same token, the education of students who want to prepare themselves
for the new economy should not be denied them by the university.
Professional and applied programs can both meet the test of liberal education and achieve the economic objectives. They deserve a place in the
university and they benefit the university. Should universities and academics (and their books) strive to address the issues presented by the
new economy? The answer, I submit, is yes.

3

The Ethics of Restructuring[1]

Barry Hoffmaster

Few individuals and few institutions will be unscathed by the pervasive "restructuring" of the public and private domains of society. The "downsizing" it encompasses is, for the most part, portrayed in bald economic terms. The need to restructure is attributed to indefensible and unsustainable budget deficits, to the rampant "globalization" of information, capital, currency, and labour, and to the intimidating power of international economic organizations. The effects of restructuring are reported in terms of lay-offs, closures and mergers, bankruptcies, and unemployment rates. Because economics has, for a long time, been severed from ethics, the moral dimensions and impacts of restructuring are scarcely recognized, let alone seriously appraised. It is time to reclaim that lost moral ground and, rather than meekly acceding to what are presented as inexorable economic imperatives, begin asking trenchant questions about what is happening, why it is happening, and what the likely outcomes will be. My modest goal is to provide some background and structure for that kind of moral assessment; my discussion will be rooted in and illustrated by developments in health care, but the lessons can, I hope, be transposed to other fields.

The initial challenge for such an unfamiliar moral inquiry is to sketch its content and its limits. The first step in meeting that challenge is to say something about the nature of morality, but even if I thought I could satisfactorily articulate all the different understandings of morality that exist, I could not do so here. I nevertheless want to repudiate a popular but flawed notion of what morality is, a notion that Rick Salutin calls "the privatization of ethics" (1996, C1).

Notes to this chapter are on pp. 303–304.

There are two aspects of that "privatization." One is the adoption of "buy-and-sell as our moral model," that is, the reduction of ethics to the injunctions and restrictions imposed on market exchanges (on fraud, for example). The other is the narrowing of "the ambit of ethics to a wholly personal plane, while exempting the public and social levels." This "ethical eclipse of the social dimension" occurs in Salutin's own profession when the media scrutinize people in public life but restrict that scrutiny to private aspects of their behaviour. Ethics, as Salutin rightly points out, needs to recover its concern with larger contexts and the state of society as a whole, to move beyond its current preoccupation with individual moral quandaries and character and become genuinely social and public.

When ethics adopts that grander vision, questions can be asked about restructuring and the economy it produces. How, to begin, should the federal and provincial budget deficits, the reduction and eventual elimination of which have precipitated much restructuring and downsizing, be understood? Are they like the outstanding balance on my VISA card, or are they more like the mortgage on my house?[2] The former impinges on my ability to control necessary expenses and enjoy life, and should be eliminated as quickly as possible; the latter is an unavoidable constraint that I strive to reduce prudently but ultimately must accept. I do not sacrifice other important values to the goal of burning my mortgage as soon as I can. Which is a better model for addressing governmental debts?

What, to move to the private sector, are the moral and social responsibilities of corporations and their executives? The chairman and chief executive of Quaker Oats, in trouble since its acquisition of the "new age" beverage business Snapple, recently assured Wall Street analysts that he clearly understands his role as CEO of the company to be a "value builder for shareholders" (Feder 1996, C1). Other corporate executives have gone so far as to apologize publicly for lagging stock prices (Den Tandt 1996, B1). The chief executive of Horsham Corporation, for instance, conceded to shareholders: "We have failed in the most fundamental responsibility that a public company has toward its shareholders and that's really the delivery of value to you" (Waldie 1996, B9).

What has led to such a circumscribed understanding of corporate responsibility? Blaming greedy CEOs is too quick and too glib. Although corporate executives undoubtedly prize and are motivated by the enormous financial compensation they receive, they also respond in rational and predictable ways to social forces that impinge upon them. Defending companies against "the ongoing demonization of corporate

America by some of...[the] most prominent politicians and news organizations," Robert J. Eaton, the chief executive of the Chrysler Corporation, traces those forces to uncomfortable roots:

> Corporations are under pressure from shareholders who are taking an increasingly active role in company business. Rather than selling the stock of companies whose managers they disagree with...the investors pressure the company to change, even ousting a number of chief executives in the process. And standing behind those institutional investors are American workers who have sunk their retirement savings into mutual stock funds and are fighting to be sure they get the best returns possible. Those are some of the same workers who in turn have been laid off as their employers struggle to please investors. (Meredith 1996, C5)

Mr. Eaton presses on: "So if we don't like the kind of pressure these funds put on our companies, we can't point fingers.... 'Them' is us."

The same point, to be sure, applies in this country. Robert Bertram, the senior vice-president of investments for the Ontario Teachers' Pension Plan, which owns twelve billion dollars worth of Canadian company shares, has an equally blinkered view about the function of companies: "Companies are not put together to create jobs. The number one priority is creating shareholder wealth" (Ip 1996, B1). Bertram reports that the 200,000 active and retired teachers in the largest pension plan in the country "want high investment returns so they can get the best possible pensions at the least cost" (Lindgren 1996b, D6), and he believes that boards of directors have a duty to maximize share value for his teachers (Ip 1996, B1). Moreover, in response to the importuning of institutional shareholders, the compensation of senior executives and members of boards of directors can be tied to share price and profit performance (Ip 1996, B1).[3] Given that incentive, management's fixation with maximizing share prices should be no surprise. But is such a fixation even economically defensible? Is the short-term interest of the market consistent with the long-term interest of the economy? And if maximizing shareholder value makes economic sense, is it *morally* defensible? Do corporations not also have obligations to their employees, their customers, and their communities?

The rationale for restructuring, of course, is that it is a necessary evil, that businesses need to become smaller and more efficient simply to survive, let alone prosper, in an increasingly competitive and unforgiving economic environment. Jobs will disappear, but the jobs that remain will, it is claimed, be more secure. Mr. Eaton is of this opinion: "Downsizing and lay-offs are part of the price of becoming more competitive.... The price for not doing it...is much higher in both economic and human terms" (McFarland 1996, B8). Critics dispute that rationale, however. They contend that downsizing does not guarantee that a company will become either more efficient or more profitable;[4] that a demoralized and anxious workforce leads to decreased productivity, though increased shareholder value depends upon increased productivity; and that unemployed workers are unable, and anxious workers are unwilling, to spend the money that would generate profits and stimulate the economy. What corporations need to remember, in short, is that "their profits are deeply integrated in the economic health of our communities" (Hebb and McCracken 1996, B2).

Disagreement about the need for restructuring is as intramural as it is extramural. In a survey conducted by the Canadian Institute of Management, 64 percent of the respondents, mostly middle managers, agreed that companies have a duty to create jobs (*Globe and Mail*, 19/08/96, B3). The respondents were almost equally divided about whether downsizing is still necessary: 48 percent believed it is, while 49 percent said it has gone too far. And although 54 percent of the respondents thought downsizing is essential for Canadian companies to compete internationally, 42 percent felt it is destroying the consumer confidence and individual purchasing power that generate a strong economy.

Amidst this division and uncertainty, people who lose their jobs and their businesses suffer real and certain harms, harms that are particularly grave for older individuals. Other negative consequences attributed to restructuring are more speculative. Wealth, it is reported, is becoming more concentrated in the hands of the rich (Bradsher 1996, 17), and gaps between the incomes of the rich and the poor are widening (Crossette 1996, A3). White-collar crime, it is alleged, is increasing in Canada because unscrupulous employees are trying to pad their bank accounts before they are fired and because downsized police forces no longer have the resources to undertake the expensive investigations required to discover this corruption (Bender 1996, D10).

The recondite nature of the forces that allegedly compel restructuring and the impossibility of comprehending even its short-term impacts make it hard to know whether imposing so many harms on so many people really is justified. When the human stakes are as high as they are here, though, when the interests of so many individuals are being sacrificed so that others can prosper, the question must be pressed. The self-assured, but self-serving, accounts of corporate executives who authorize restructuring, and of the consultants they hire to legitimate and implement it,[5] must be scrutinized. Because such an inquiry cannot be conducted in the abstract, we shall turn to what is happening in health care.

Two pressures, independent in theory, have impelled the restructuring of health care in Canada: the need to cope with substantial reductions in funding on the part of both federal and provincial governments, and the desire to improve the quality of services by eliminating waste and inefficiencies. Reactions to funding cuts include eliminating hospital beds by amalgamating or even closing hospitals, shortening the length of patient stays in hospitals, and providing more services on an outpatient, or ambulatory care, basis. At the same time, efforts to improve the quality of health care services have led to the adoption of comprehensive programs such as Total Quality Management (TQM) or Continuous Quality Improvement (CQI). The Ontario Ministry of Health has advocated these quality improvement initiatives, and the Canadian Council of Health Facilities Accreditation is incorporating such standards into its periodic accreditation reviews of hospitals (Armstrong et al. 1996, 3). Hospital CEOs estimate that 25 to 30 percent of what is done in hospitals is wasteful or inefficient (Hassen 1993, 62). One confidently asserts: "I am damn sure that out of our $260 million budget, there's probably seventy-five to eighty million dollars that should be dropping out of that budget without any compromise to quality of care" (Hassen 1993, 190). Even in prosperous times improving quality by eliminating waste is an eminently sensible, albeit less pressing, goal.

Restructuring need not be in the service of quality improvement, however. The CEO of one Ontario hospital acknowledges that there are some "throughout the province who are downsizing because of the almighty buck, and not with any aspect of quality or for purposes of what they're trying to achieve. It has nothing to do with increasing productivity or becoming more efficient (Hassen 1993, 181)."

The attraction of TQM, according to Philip Hassen, the CEO of St. Joseph's Health Centre in London, Ontario, and one of its most fervent promoters, is not only that it directs restructuring at the goals of achieving "the highest quality of service and patient care" and making "the best use of available health care system resources" (Hassen 1993, 3), but also that it saves money:

> [T]he achievement of quality most often leads to lower costs—a point missed by many businesses and public institutions which, with no clear

goal in mind, are frantically chopping away at their high excess costs through mass layoffs and drastic service or production cuts. They are not viewing the situation from a quality perspective. (14)

But because TQM holds out the prospect of reducing costs, it is dogged, as Hassen acknowledges, by the perception that it is aimed primarily at cost containment (Hassen 1993, 12–13). Along with other advocates of TQM, Hassen is concerned to dispel that impression: "I repeatedly stress to those in health care professions that total quality management is not *primarily* intended as a cost-cutting strategy but rather focuses on quality of care in terms of effectiveness, efficiency, and patient satisfaction" (Hassen 1993, 55, my emphasis). Keeping those two goals separate and distinct is, however, not always easy. Before looking at the problems created by their confusion, what TQM is, and how it functions in hospitals need to be briefly reviewed.

A management focus on quality was instigated within the manufacturing industry in the United States by the introduction of high-quality, low-cost products from Japan during the 1970s (Sahney and Warden, 1996). The considerable loss of market share that resulted prompted large corporations such as Ford Motor Company, Motorola, Xerox, IBM, and 3M to adopt an approach to improving the quality of their products predicated on the ideas of W. Edwards Deming. Deming believes that preventing defects is better than inspecting for defects and that defects can be prevented by improving the processes used to manufacture products. Processes can be improved by recognizing the variability within them and reducing that variability. For Deming, the ultimate touchstone of quality is whether the customer is satisfied with a product.

Advocates of TQM argue that it is as applicable to the processes of health care delivery as it is to the processes of manufacturing. Admitting a patient to hospital or administering medication in hospital is, after all, a process that can be analyzed, redesigned, and tested by the criterion of customer satisfaction. The approach will, to be sure, have to be "customized" to accommodate distinctive features of hospitals, but there is in principle no reason why it cannot be adapted to health care.

In hospitals that have implemented TQM, processes are studied "scientifically" to discover where variations create waste and where inefficiencies exist. Employees are "shadowed" to see, for example, when and where they must repeat a task or how much time they spend idly waiting. Processes and their outcomes are "benchmarked" against those of hospitals regarded as leaders with respect to efficiency and quality.[6] Employees are actively involved in the assessment and redesign of processes because those who do the work know best where the defects are, and are most likely to come up with ideas for improving their work. When more responsibility is given to employees, there is no need for an extensive hierarchy of middle managers and senior executives. Not only does the role of management shift to that of "coaching" employees, but the organization becomes flatter and less bureaucratic. To accommodate the new ways of doing work, traditional departmental structures are jettisoned and replaced by cross-functional, interdisciplinary teams and new management positions with names such as "Profession Leader" and "Discipline Chair." Members of these teams have to be flexible and adaptable, so, in what is known as "multi-skilling," they are trained to perform a variety of tasks.

The goal of this fundamental transformation of how work is done and managed within hospitals is to provide better service to customers. A "customer" is defined as "anyone who receives the product of a health care organization's labour" (Hassen 1993, 44). A hospital's customers can be external or internal. External customers are "people outside the hospital who use its services—patients, their families, universities and community colleges, government, and community physicians" (Hassen 1993, 44). Internal customers are the "people inside hospitals who rely upon each other's services—nurses, laboratory personnel, researchers, clerical workers, kitchen staff, physicians, and so forth" (Hassen 1993, 45). The measure of the quality of a hospital's services is the satisfaction of those customers.

That, briefly, is the theory behind TQM, and the theory is attractive to both hospital executives and workers. Hassen, for example, recognizes that the business terms are foreign and uncongenial to health care workers, but he argues that underneath the "initial strangeness of the language" is a fundamental congruence of values (Hassen 1993, 63). Health care workers are devoted to providing quality care, are used to working together in teams, are committed to evaluating and improving what they do, and are familiar with using scientific methods in that ongoing assessment, so it is not surprising that workers in hospitals in which TQM was introduced were initially enthusiastic about it (Armstrong et al., 6–8). They realized that change was necessary, and they were excited about an approach that promised to take their ideas seriously and give them more responsibility for and control over their work.

What has happened in practice? Although there have been isolated improvements and successes, it is too early for a comprehensive evaluation. Proponents of TQM are quick to emphasize that it is not a "quick fix," that the sweeping transformation it aims to effect requires patience and, in particular, an abiding, enthusiastic commitment on the part of senior management. For it to succeed, the entire culture of an institution has to be changed, and that is an imposing long-term challenge. Appreciating those challenges, two advocates of TQM in a hospital system in the United States concede that "in the majority of the institutions, TQM will fail" (Sahney and Warden 1996, 17).

For some Canadian health care workers, though, TQM has *already* failed.[7] The prospect of more worker control and responsibility never materialized. Employees were not offered a choice about whether TQM should be implemented in their institutions and were not involved in decisions about who gets appointed to key committees. Power remains firmly entrenched in senior management. The middle managers who directly supervise employees were not committed to restructuring because it is their jobs that would disappear from a flatter organizational structure. Training sessions utilized materials that are not appropriate for health care and involved games that employees see as a waste of time. Long, frequent meetings intended to teach the concepts of TQM and change the culture of the institution did not seem productive. "Teamwork" now means that helping fellow employees is obligatory rather than discretionary and is perceived as increasing opportunities for surveillance by other team members. And the increased workloads that resulted from smaller labour forces and the reluctance to replace employees on sick leave have been compounded by the forms and reports that need to be submitted.

An ethical evaluation of health care restructuring is complicated by this gap between theory and practice. These complaints could be the result of botched attempts to implement TQM, in particular to a disregard of all the cautions about how carefully and extensively TQM must be introduced and how long it takes to accomplish its goals. Alternatively, TQM could have been corrupted by allowing the goal of cost containment to overtake the goal of quality improvement. The latter, indeed, is the gist of the workers' complaints: "[M]ost workers understood TQM as mainly a cost cutting measure, one focused on making them work harder" (Armstrong et al. 1996, 19). That was particularly evident to them with respect to multi-skilling. The multi-skilling or cross-training of workers, which in theory "is intended to reduce waste by avoiding any time required to switch from one worker to another," became in practice multi-tasking, "asking people untrained for the job to do the work" (Armstrong et al. 1996, 26). A newspaper report of what is happening in Québec begins, for instance, with the story of a woman who, after handling files for twenty-one years in the archives department of a hospital, got two days of training and is now feeding, bathing, and changing elderly patients on a palliative care floor (Thanh Ha 1996, A9).

Another manifestation of this "down skilling" is the replacement of registered nurses (RNs), who have a college diploma or university degree and study nursing for several years, with registered practical nurses (RPNs), who receive their training in high school or in certificate programs in community colleges.[8] Toronto Hospital, for instance, is replacing RNs in every department, including emergency, intensive care, and operating rooms. The hospital's director of public affairs estimates that one hundred to three hundred RNs will lose their jobs. The RNs who remain, he explains, will supervise the RPNs and "will have more challenging work" (Coutts 1996, A1). Nurses and administrators naturally disagree about the impact of this shift on the quality of patient care (Baumann and Silverman discuss de-professionalization in their contribution to this book). RNs contend that RPNs lack both the training and the judgment seasoned by experience that are necessary to deal with the situations that will confront them.[9] Administrators are confident that RPNs will be able to recognize their limits and work within them. Both views, of course, could be said to be tainted by self-interest.

In addition, TQM's principal goal of improving quality can easily be lost because the innovative approaches it seeks sometimes require that money be spent. One hospital, for example, as part of its move towards increased "patient-centred care" (the rosy description invariably given to health care restructuring) is renovating two operating rooms, creating a new one, and building a nine-bed day surgery unit for surgical outpatients and cardiac catheter patients.[10] These improvements will reduce overcrowding, provide quieter and more friendly surroundings, permit families to visit, and afford patients and their families more privacy. The expected cost is one million dollars. Not all hospitals seem to have that kind of money, though, because employees disenchanted by TQM report that limited resources frequently restrict innovation: "To improve quality you have to spend money.... And they're not willing to do that.... All of this is to save money" (Armstrong et al. 1996, 19).

Inherent in this ambivalence about whether the real goal of health care restructuring is quality improvement or cost containment is a fundamental moral question for all varieties of restructuring: What limits are there to the pursuit of efficiency? My productivity and my efficiency as a university teacher could be increased if I taught larger classes and if I taught more hours per week and more weeks per year. Were that to happen across the University of Western Ontario, we could "process" more and more students per classroom hour and become, in the eyes of the business-minded, more successful.[11] At what point, however, does my effectiveness as a university teacher diminish? When does the quality of the education my students receive begin to suffer? And when are that reduced effectiveness and compromised quality no longer justified by offsetting gains in productivity and efficiency? The central moral issue here is an old one about trade-offs between efficiency and effectiveness, quantity and quality (see, for example, Wright 1996, 36).

Making those trade-offs is difficult for many reasons, but principally because it is hard to decide, in any area, what quality is and who is entitled to determine it. When asked to define "quality" in health care, one CEO committed to TQM replied that it is the "provision of effective services on a timely basis in a fashion that's satisfying to the patients, at a cost that society can afford" (Hassen 1993, 176). Another, looking at quality "more from an ethical point of view," said it is "when we really just give people what they request for a certain outcome and don't continue to perpetuate the need for *ourselves*" (Hassen 1993, 177, original emphasis). Those two proposals disagree about how much say the patient has in determining quality. In the former, it is the manner in which services are provided, not the services themselves, that must meet the test of patient satisfaction. In the latter, patients receive only services intended to produce outcomes they desire.

Framed in this way, the debate about what counts as quality in health care recapitulates the debate about physician paternalism and patient autonomy that has been the centrepiece of contemporary bioethics. Although customer satisfaction is said to be the touchstone of quality for TQM, that doctrine is quickly qualified when TQM meets health care. Even Hassen backs off on this point, defining "quality" as "providing the best possible care through continuously improving hospital services to meet the needs and expectations of patients, the physicians, the hospital staff, and the communities served by the hospital" (Hassen 1993, 15). Quality is a function of satisfying multiple customers, not just patients, and with respect to patients, it is not only their expectations but their needs that count as well. While patients might be the sole arbiters of their expectations they will not be the sole arbiters of their needs. Moreover, there is disagreement about whether quality should be determined by patient expectations. According to one hospital CEO, because patients can have "unrealistic" expectations, health care providers should strive to satisfy only "legitimate customer expectations" (Hassen 1993, 176). But another CEO, apparently more attuned to the spirit of patient autonomy, is not sure that "the public have unrealistic expectations" (ibid.).

Health care workers are also suspicious of defining quality in terms of patient satisfaction. They wonder whether patients are sufficiently knowledgeable about their conditions and the care they require and whether their decision-making capacities are compromised by their illnesses. Taking patient opinions at face value, they point out, leads to a complaint-driven, rather than quality-driven, process that can limit the rights of workers. Moreover, aspects of care that cannot be readily measured or incorporated into a patient satisfaction questionnaire can be regarded as inefficient or wasteful. These workers see serious dangers and limitations in thinking that the quality of patient care can be measured "like the assessment of soap preferences" (Armstrong et al. 1996, 32).

Implicit in the CEOs' two accounts of quality is another difficulty. One of those definitions invokes the notion of "effective" services, and the other appeals to bringing about desired "outcomes." Both presuppose that the outcomes of health care procedures and services have been widely studied and assessed. Although such "outcomes" research is becoming more prevalent, very little has actually been done, particularly in Canada. It is popularly accepted within health care that only 15 to 20 percent of medical practice has ever been proved effective (Hassen 1993, 80).[12] A pertinent exception is a study from Manitoba that looked at whether earlier discharge of patients with four selected conditions was associated with increased hospital admission rates or more frequent physician visits subsequently. The conclusion of this study is that "increased efficiency did not result in more adverse outcomes" (Harrison et al. 1995, 750), but these patients were followed for only thirty days after their discharges.

A principal reason for this unsatisfactory situation is the dearth of resources—conceptual, technical, and economic—for outcomes research. A hospital CEO, for example, observes: "[W]hen resources were adequate for all of our activities, there wasn't the need to measure the outcomes of many of the things we do. Now, when we need to do so, we haven't the tools or appropriate techniques" (Hassen 1993, 179). Perhaps the most commonly used evaluative term in health care is "appropriate." Health care professionals focus their decisions on what care is "appropriate," and efforts to reduce the costs of health care concentrate on eliminating "inappropriate" care. But how are "appropriate" and "inappropriate" to be understood in health care (Lavis and Anderson 1996)? And were satisfactory criteria for "appropriateness" to be devised, what valid and reliable instruments could be constructed to measure it?

Most important of all, how would this research be funded? The hospital CEO who recognizes the challenges for outcomes research continues:

> Now we are beginning to ask the question, "Does the result warrant the resources that went into the process?" However, studies like these are extraordinarily complex, expensive, and time-consuming. If you want to assess the outcome of a common surgical procedure, you probably need a several-year follow-up of a large group of patients in order to see whether in fact the intervention has significantly improved the quality of life. (Hassen 1993, 179)

Where would the money or the people to evaluate all the new procedures and technologies being introduced into health care, let alone all the unproved interventions currently being utilized, be found?

Despite the difficulties facing outcomes research, pressure for it is mounting. Managed care plans in the United States, for example, tout themselves as "No. 1 in customer satisfaction" or "Rated No. 1 in overall member satisfaction." Not impressed by this advertising, large companies, government health programs, and consumer organizations are now pressing the awkward question whether, despite these claims about customer satisfaction and quality care, patients are actually getting better (Freudenheim 1996, A1). Health care plans currently report on what their doctors and nurses do—how many women between fifty-two and sixty-four have mammograms every two years or how many of their diabetes patients have regular eye exams, for instance—and what percentage of their enrollees say they are satisfied. But they do not use the results of lab tests to disclose, for example, whether patients' cholesterol levels are well managed or their blood sugar levels are well controlled. Despite their protests about the unfairness and the cost of collecting and reporting such outcomes measures, these companies could be forced to do so. A health care analyst with a stock brokerage firm observes, in language that pellucidly illustrates the extent to which health care has become a consumer good in the United States: "The challenge for health plans is to re-engineer the business so the product they are selling can be evaluated on a quality basis as opposed to a price basis" (Freudenheim 1996, C2).

The lack of solid evidence about outcomes also raises doubts about some current aspects of hospital restructuring, in particular the replacement of RNs with RPNs. In defence of this substitution, it is said that "as long as RPNs are working within their guidelines—that is, assigned to patients with 'a predictable outcome'—they are entirely capable of doing the job" (Coutts 1996, A8). But how can anyone be confident that outcomes are predictable when the research is not there to support that judgment, and particularly when, as beds are closed, the patients who remain in hospital are more acutely ill? Does an RPN, for instance, possess the training and the experience needed to recognize the subtle changes that indicate that a coronary patient is starting to "go sour"? How much can health care actually be standardized, and to what extent are health care providers generically substitutable?

Another fundamental moral question is whether restructuring health care in terms of a business model is antithetical to the practice and core values of health care. A principal aim of TQM, as we have seen, is eliminating variation from work processes. But is the kind of standardization that results, and that might increase efficiency and productivity in a factory, appropriate for providing care to patients? Health care workers who have experienced TQM see the "formulas" that have been introduced (for example, "formulas prescribing the amount of soap" housekeepers may use) as impairing the quality of their work and as insensitive to "the enormous variations in workload caused by the variations in patients and by the nature of health care work" (Armstrong et al. 1996, 33). Hassen acknowledges that "[p]atients, unlike photocopiers or cars, are human beings with enormous individual differences in their treatment needs and health outcomes" (1993, 14). But how, then, can an approach that is explicitly designed to uncover and eliminate variation be compatible with the provision of health care?

This standardization and the accompanying "scientific" analyses of hospital work also represent a regression with respect to our notion of what health is. Over the years the definition of health has broadened from a narrow understanding of health as simply the absence of disease or illness to a broad, holistic notion of health that recognizes the emotional, psychological, and spiritual dimensions and needs of persons. But quantifying and standardizing health care processes are powerful incentives for and reinforcers of a return to a narrowly biological and reductionistic understanding of health. All the rhetoric about becoming more "patient-centred" is, in this respect, disingenuous if not deceptive.

What would make health care more truly patient-centred—attending to the individual values and emotional, psychological, and spiritual needs of patients—is precisely what fewer and less well trained health care workers have neither the time nor the skills to do. This kind of care would, moreover, escape the quantitative analyses and the standardized work processes of TQM and thus be deemed wasteful and inefficient. Indeed, housekeeping staff under the yoke of TQM report that they no longer have the time or the incentive to converse with patients or get them water, small courtesies that patients undoubtedly regard as contributing to the quality of their care. Many, to their credit, nevertheless give that attention to patients. A "scientific" business approach to health care work is most compatible with regarding patients as cases and collections of organ systems. Designing more efficient processes to manage cases or organ systems leaves out much that is now recognized to be vital to the health and healing of full persons.

What many also find disconcerting about TQM in health care is the language it imports, especially the practice of referring to patients as customers. While proponents of TQM see this as a minor, superficial obstacle, others are worried that the impact will be insidious and invidious. Even advocates of TQM are not, as we have seen, completely faithful here because they shy away from customer satisfaction as the sole test of the quality of health care. Yet if the customer is always right, what else is there?

The more general mistake of TQM proponents is thinking of language in purely technical terms—as a neutral instrument—and ignoring the profound symbolic, metaphorical, and emotional power of language. Language is not simply a tool, but a shaper of ideas and values. Once that power is recognized, the fear of health care workers that transforming patients into customers will substitute a commercial relationship for a caring relationship becomes more credible (Armstrong et al. 1994, 29). The worry about the power of language extends beyond the narrow ambit of the health care provider–patient relationship, however, and encompasses all of health care. One hospital, it is reported, not only looks after clients or customers now, but has converted its departments into "Small Business Units" (Robinson 1996, A18). From that base, it is suggested, it is a short slide to talk about "consumers" of health services and the notion that those "consumers" should pay for what they consume. Converting health care into a commodity—taking away its "special" status[13]—would open the door to more extensive privatization of the health care system. The persuasive power of talk about "customers," "clients," and "consumers" can only soften all of us up for that change.

There are, to conclude, two fundamentally disparate understandings of health care restructuring. One accepts the realities of the new national and international economies and welcomes help from business in maintaining the viability of health care. A hospital CEO says, in this vein:

The driving force to me is the survival of my institution, not in the competitive sense of the US, but in the desire to continue to provide those things we have an obligation to provide. Our funding is decreasing. We have to reduce or eliminate some of the things we currently do, and if we don't make the decisions more intelligently, we'll end up with illogical across-the-board cuts that run the danger of removing some of the things that are good for our patients, as well as some things that aren't. (Hassen 1993, 185–186)[14]

The other view of restructuring in health care is deeply suspicious of economic forces alleged to be ineluctable as well as the business model invoked to deal with them. To these critics the rhetoric of restructuring is a way of smuggling foreign and incompatible fiscal agendas and values into health care. "Decentralizing" health care is, in their view, a code word for dumping patients, and receiving health care "closer to home" really means home alone. Passions are high because the stakes are high.

There is much in health care restructuring that needs to be scrutinized, but to make ethics truly social, that scrutiny must engage fundamental questions of justice. Norman Daniels, in the Preface to his book, *Just Health Care*, remarks that he began working on the topic of justice in the design of a health care system in the mid 1960s, when there was a public perception in the United States that "justice required improved access to health care" (Daniels 1985, x). But subsequently, he reports,

the focus of public discussion in the US began to shift. Constraining rapidly rising health-care costs became the main item on the health-care agenda, and though issues of equity still arise in this context, there is little pretext that the just redesign of a health-care system is a current national objective. (Daniels 1985, xi)

The egalitarianism embedded in the five principles of the *Canada Health Act* is becoming progressively more tenuous because issues of equity have been similarly displaced by the objective of controlling health care costs.

The deep ethical issues in health care restructuring remain issues of equity. At the heart of those issues are the fundamental questions Daniels asks: "What kind of a social good is health care? What are its functions and do these make it different from other commodities?" (Daniels 1985, ix). Is health care a basic need that should be distributed on egalitarian terms? Or is it a commodity, the distribution of which is allowed to be widely inegalitarian? Answers to these bedrock questions will determine what we think of "privatizing" health care by shifting it out of hospitals into homes and thereby imposing the explicit and implicit costs of providing that care on families and friends. These answers, in other words, delimit the social obligation to provide health care and establish how much responsibility for health care individuals and their families and friends may reasonably be expected to assume. They will also determine what we think of the desirability of using business models to manage health care. When health care professionals ask, "Are we health care people in business, or are we business people in health care?" they are asking the right question, but they need to pursue that question to its moral conclusions.

The same lesson applies in other areas. What kinds of social goods are education, food, clothing, shelter, and day care? Answers to those questions will determine whether we strive to reduce inequalities in the distribution of these goods, or whether we allow inequalities in their distribution to proliferate as they are assimilated to the inegalitarian distributions of commodities. They will also determine whether the restructuring that occurs, in these areas as in health care, is driven principally by economic concerns or by concerns about needs, community responsibility, and equity.

It is not surprising that the privatization of ethics is weaning us from a commitment to equity.[15] But unless that commitment remains robust, the privatization of much else is sure to follow.

PART II
The Case Against Restructuring

While no one would deny that we can distinguish between restructuring that is better and worse from an ethical point of view, the extent to which restructuring is changing (and has changed) public and private enterprise raises more fundamental concerns about what some have called "the restructuring craze." One might put these concerns as the general question whether restructuring and the restructuring economy are the product of a genuine economic crisis, or are, in reality, a political agenda motivated by vested interests which seek to radically alter our understanding of society and its obligations to workers, the dispossessed and the least advantaged. Because any informed discussion of restructuring must recognize this fundamental challenge to restructuring, the present section outlines such concerns. Ken Hanly thus argues that restructuring is an unjustified pretext for dismantling the gains that labour and the disadvantaged have made within Western industrial states. Looked at from this point of view, restructuring is a way to dismantle the welfare state and make it "leaner, meaner and inequitable." Echoes of Hanly's critique—and opposing approaches to the ethics of restructuring—are a significant underlying theme in many later chapters of this book.

4

Restructuring the Welfare State: Leaner, Meaner, and Inequitable

Ken Hanly

The term "restructuring" refers to an array of processes including down-sizing, deregulation, privatization, and the reorganization of companies or government services to reduce debt and to increase their competitiveness or efficiency. In this paper I examine two key aspects of economic restructuring within the government rather than the private sector: debt management and privatization. I argue that restructuring erodes welfare and workers' rights and makes further social reforms more difficult. I use the term "social reform" in the older sense to refer to changes in society and the marketplace that advance the welfare of the general public and particularly the less advantaged, although in the present age of Newspeak it often refers to cuts in welfare programs or reductions in the quality of public services.

My analyses are influenced by writers who study social structures of wealth accumulation (see Kotz, McDonough, and Reich 1994) and reg-ulation theory (see Aglietta 1979 and Lipietz 1987). I share the view com-mon to both theories that some key social structures may further the capitalist accumulation of wealth at one time yet block it at another. Economic restructuring is, in my view, an attempt to replace older struc-tures that are now retarding further accumulation with newer structures that will advance it. Among the results of this process are the decline of social reform (Teeple 1995) and the loss of public benefits in such areas as health care, education, employment, recreation, and pensions. Accessibility to services and benefits in all areas are more dependent on income.

We can better understand this account of restructuring by beginning with the era that stretches from the end of the Second World War to the mid-sixties—sometimes called "The Golden Age of Capitalism." It was characterized by a huge growth in state expenditure. In all advanced capitalist countries, welfare programs grew. Elementary and secondary education were free, and in many countries college as well. Except for the United States, most advanced capitalist countries had some type of universal medicare system.

Of course, not all state expenditure was for social programs. The Cold War demanded huge military expenditures that in turn were the lifeblood of many manufacturers. Often the state rescued ailing private enterprises. This process was dubbed "hospitalization." The state took enterprises into the public sector, invested money in them to turn them around, and then sold them back to the private sector. This happened with Jaguar in Great Britain, which is, ironically, often cited as an example of the benefits of privatization (Hardin 1989, 1).

Increases in state expenditures on welfare, the military, and corporations during the Golden Age led to increased state debt and high taxes that were unpopular with both corporations and individuals. These expenditures produced a debt crisis which those opposed to social programs saw not as a problem, but as an opportunity. As Gideon Rosenbluth notes, deficit phobia allows politicians to use the deficit as a convenient excuse for cutting social spending (Rosenbluth 1992, 74), thus destroying or weakening the welfare state institutions of the Golden Age of capitalism. I examine now the role of debt management in economic restructuring.

The Debt Crisis

States use tax revenues from individuals and corporations to pay off debt. As global competition increases, however, capital tends to shift from high-tax to lower-tax countries. This poses a problem for countries wishing to attract and retain capital while raising sufficient revenue to pay off debt. A partial solution is to restructure the tax burden: lower the tax rates on corporations and increase it on individuals. This is precisely what has been taking place (Teeple 1995, 94). Strong opposition to further tax increases on individual incomes forces governments to adopt many new, and often regressive, alternative modes of taxation and revenue collection. In Canada, for example, federal and provincial governments have introduced sales taxes. These are regressive since the poor are likely to pay a greater percentage of their income in sales taxes than the well-off, who typically spend a lesser percentage of their total income on taxable goods. Tax refunds or exemption of basic goods may counteract this regressive aspect of sales taxes. Governments have also used state lotteries and VLTs (video lottery terminals) to generate revenue but this has increased social problems associated with gambling.

Restructured tax systems favour not only corporations but better-off individuals as well. Some critics have suggested that a flat tax should replace the progressive income tax. In the United States, tax cuts for the rich are promoted as encouraging investment and initiative. George Gilder even argues that regressive taxes help the poor (Gilder 1981, 188) by motivating them to do better and increase their income so that they can get into a better tax bracket! Although news commentators and politicians emphasize the need to reduce the deficit, they also often argue for the necessity of lower corporate taxation and tax cuts for individuals to spur investment.

The layperson might be nonplussed that some economists argue that reducing taxes can help reduce the deficit. As Galbraith points out, when new and unpalatable policies are required, economists can always be found to promote them (Galbraith 1992, 78). Enter Arthur Laffer and his Laffer Curve. Laffer starts with two incontrovertible facts: if taxes are zero, government revenues are zero; if all income is taxed away, no incomes will be generated and no tax revenue. In each extreme, government income from taxation is zero. What happens between these two extremes? At first, increases in tax rates mean increases in government revenues, but at a certain optimal stage any increase in tax rates will cause an actual decrease in revenues. Laffer claims that the US tax rate has gone beyond the optimum. Illustrating this hypothesis on a graph is easy, but proving it empirically is more difficult. One would need to experiment: to reduce tax rates and see if government revenues increase as Laffer predicts. Ronald Reagan began this experiment in 1981.

The results did not confirm the theory (Gordon 1987, 456). Some defenders of the theory have claimed that Reagan caused these negative results by cutting some of his business incentives in 1982 and by increasing government spending. This may or may not be the case. Whatever is to be said, the average after tax income of the top 20 percent of income earners in Reagan's America increased from $73,700 in 1981 to $92,000 in 1990 (Galbraith 1992, 105). In Canada, such policies would produce an even greater increase in the after-tax income of higher income earners, given that Canadians pay higher tax rates than Americans.

As the US experience illustrates, changes in tax structure and tax cuts alone will not solve the debt crisis. The tax system became less progressive, the income gap between rich and poor widened, yet government debt grew. Since attempts to increase revenues did not solve the debt problem, cutting spending was suggested as an obvious alternative. Once again the crisis served as an opportunity for reorganization of social structures in a manner that favoured capital accumulation. The rhetoric was predictable. Governments should be downsized and the welfare state diminished if not abolished. Only drastic restructuring of the size and role of government could reduce the debt and, as the politicians put it, save essential social programs. From a capitalist point of view, an added advantage of reductions to unemployment and welfare benefits is that they give incentives for workers to take low-paying jobs with poor working conditions.

But even low-paying jobs require payment of a minimum wage in many jurisdictions. To widen the area for exploitation even further, such standard protections as the minimum wage needed to be weakened or eliminated. Capital could call upon economists to tell us that minimum wages are actually no benefit at all and even produce unemployment for the worst off. In a typical microeconomics textbook, the minimum wage becomes a theoretical problem titled "The Effect of Minimum Wage Laws." The textbook asks students to predict the effects of instituting a minimum wage in a competitive market. The correct answer is that institution of a minimum wage will reduce employment or diminish benefits and that unskilled labour will be most affected, particularly teenagers and most notably black teenagers (Mansfield 1988, 396). But this is an exercise in pure deduction; it does not ask students to confirm the result empirically.

A recent book by David Card and Alan Krueger, *Myth and Measurement*, does look at the empirical data concerning the effects of the minimum wage. Their studies refute rather than confirm the conclusions of the deductive model used in many textbooks, most showing that higher minimum wages have no effect on employment. Some actually show a rise in employment. Rather than harming minorities and teenagers, increases in the minimum wage had the opposite effect (Card and Krueger 1995, 1–4).

The government regulatory system is another favourite target of cost cutters. They argue that regulations and standards have multiplied beyond necessity and that many produce more costs than benefits. Increased government regulation has created a bloated bureaucracy whose interests lie in promotion of more regulations, not in advancing the general welfare. Cuts in the budgets of regulators, cuts in the number of inspectors, deregulation, and self-regulation are the order of the day whenever possible. Though it is true that many government regulations could be simplified and red tape reduced, it is clear a great deal of deregulation primarily serves corporate capital rather than the public interest. Government regulation is often necessary to protect the public from negative consequences caused by corporate pursuit of profit. In many cases, restructuring through deregulation therefore increases risks of harm to the public.

As with restructuring in the tax system, new regulatory policies that aid capital tend to be adopted even if the policies force an increase in government expenditure and contribute to the debt crisis. This shows that the driving force behind economic restructuring is frequently other than that suggested by its defenders. Consider, for example, the passing of Bill C91 in February 1993. This bill both extends the life span of patents to twenty years and eliminates compulsory licensing during the period of patent protection. It applies retroactively to any patent granted after December 20, 1991. Compulsory licensing not only encouraged the development of a generic drug industry in Canada, it produced annual savings of $200 to $420 million (Rachlis and Kushner 1994, 146). To further their interests, multinational drug companies launched a massive and expensive lobbying campaign in support of the bill. Many in the university and medical communities were easily won over in spite of the obvious increases in drug costs that the bill would cause. The retroactive clause saved Merck Frosst $700 million on one drug. Some called the bill the Merck Bill (Rachlis and Kushner 1994, 148).

During the debate on Bill C91, it was made clear that its negative effects would be felt across Canada. Provincial health ministers indicated some costs of the bill to medicare in their jurisdictions. The British Columbia minister claimed that extending patent protection for just two drugs would cost $145 million. Saskatchewan's health minister said the bill would cost that province between three million and ten million dollars per year. The Ontario minister claimed the bill would cost the province one billion dollars over the next decade. Yet groups such as the Canadian Federation of Biological Societies and individual academics lobbied in support of the bill. Why did they not jump on the debt reduction bandwagon and cry out that this bill would add significant costs to our public medicare system? In the end, academics, who should have been promoting the widest spread of knowledge at the lowest cost and for the greatest public benefit, supported extended monopoly property rights for multinational for-profit giants.

Before the debt crisis, universities flourished, and were supported by large government grants in addition to tuition income. Income from corporations was a minor supplemental element. With the debt crisis, and the demand for cutbacks in government spending, the universities were forced either to find new sources of income or cut services back or increase their cost. Universities must now turn to corporations to replace the lost government funding. This changes the educational role of the university (one might compare and contrast the way in which it changes the role of primary and secondary school education, discussed by J.L. Kachur and Derek Briton in this volume). A liberal vision of the university dominated an earlier era. Universities aimed at universal access. They emphasized choice and diversity, but gave a certain priority to the liberal arts, especially when they viewed themselves as havens for scholars (Newson and Buchbinder 1988). This vision could flourish only as long as universities received the funds necessary to implement it.

When the debt crisis hit, universities had to cut programs or find new sources of funding. While corporate funds might replace public funds, the price to be paid was abandoning the liberal agenda and adopting the corporate agenda. This new relationship is articulated in *Partnership for Growth* by Maxwell and Currie (1984), who argue that to solve the financial squeeze, universities should collaborate with key industries. This transformation forces universities to abandon their cherished traditions of academic freedom and institutional autonomy. Academics and universities pipe the corporate tunes because corporations pay the piper and call the tune. Bill C91 is again a case in point. The dean of the Faculty of Health Professions at Dalhousie wrote a letter supporting the bill. When the media attempted to link this letter to a $1.3 million research grant, the dean pointed out that she wrote the letter after the grant had been made, although she admitted that drug companies had sometimes made contracts conditional on support (Rachlis and Kushner 1994, 148). Even in the absence of written agreements, our modern academics are loath to bite the hand that feeds them.

In spite of the blatant contradictions between actual policy and the goal of debt reduction, the overwhelming majority of commentators insist on stressing the debt crisis, "the debt wall," and the need to cut back spending on social programs. In February 1993 Eric Malling hosted a documentary on the deficit that featured, among other things, a baby hippopotamus that was shot because a zoo had no money to raise it. This inspired the title of Linda McQuaig's critique of deficit reduction, *Shooting the Hippo* (1995). The documentary portrays cutting social programs as part of a crusade to save the economy rather than turning the clock to an era of minimal welfare rights. We have been living beyond our means and now must face the consequences (McQuaig 1995, 11).

Repeat the message that there is a debt crisis often enough, and masses of people will come to believe it. As pollster Donna Dasko remarks, the repetition lodges the message in our heads until it becomes "a dull background noise, a kind of invisible and yet inescapable fact of life" (McQuaig 1995, 13). In this environment of deficit phobia, it is impossible to recommend perfectly sane programs such as universal denticare without seeming to be on the radical fringe and not a serious participant in debate on social policy. At the same time, politicians and analysts may seriously suggest that we need to spend billions on new helicopters and increase medical costs by billions to encourage investment by pharmaceutical companies. In the former instance the politicians' own rhetoric about the necessity to reduce debt came back to haunt them: the proposed helicopter purchase produced such an outcry that the deal fell through with the defeat of the Conservative government, but the pharmaceutical lobby was successful. Bill C91 remains untouched under the Liberals.

Eric Malling and others use New Zealand as a prime example of a country forced to adopt neoliberal policies to solve its debt crisis. Malling talks of a debt wall in which New Zealand's credit simply ran out, demanding cuts in social programs and the sale of government assets to restore its credit rating. He claims that this produced a country that is lean, fit and globally competitive. The facts are rather different than Malling claims, as authors such as McQuaig (1995) and Kelsey (1995) have shown.

New Zealand did have a short-term currency crisis, but resolved it when a newly elected government devalued the currency (McQuaig 1995, 13). New Zealand's credit rating has never dropped below Aa3, a low-risk range shared by only twenty-four countries worldwide. So much for its supposed debt wall. The prediction that the changes would stimulate economic growth was, for the most part, also incorrect. Richardson (1996, 14) points out that between 1986 and 1992, the economies of the OECD countries grew 20 percent but the New Zealand economy shrank by 1 percent. McQuaig's figures show the same trend. Between 1985 and 1990 New Zealand's GNP fell by 0.7 percent. This is the worst record of any industrialized country. Over this period, the unemployment rate nearly doubled, yet this is the model held up as a guide for future policy. The GNP began to grow only in 1993, but this growth has now stalled. Strong medicine apparently takes a long time to work, and when its effect wears off, the solution is stronger medicine still.

John McMurtry

The philosopher John McMurtry (1995) uses different imagery, calling the growth of global restructuring the "cancer stage" of capitalism. He likens the benefits of the welfare state to the defences against disease developed by the immune system. As Karl Polanyi has shown in *The Great Transformation* (1944), society has always generated defences against the harmful effects of markets. During the Golden Age of Capitalism these defences were an essential part of the social structures of accumulation. We now have attacks upon these defences and their replacement by neoliberal structures of accumulation. For McMurtry, these attacks, including slashing government spending on social programs, have effects upon the health of the social body much like that of cancer upon the individual physical body. For him, the welfare state was not merely a contingent aspect of a certain stage of capitalist development but essential if the capitalist system was to remain healthy and provide a minimally decent standard of living for all citizens. The cancer is the capitalist elite that appropriates resources for its luxurious lifestyle and for further growth, at the expense of the health of society as a whole.

The defence of workers' rights and the welfare state, on McMurtry's view, are analogous to the immune system's attempt to protect a body against invasion by disease. In the cancerous stage of capitalism the immune response is regarded as the disease, and so the immune system is destroyed, leaving no defence against the growth of capitalism. He is certainly right to suggest that those campaigning for increased welfare and labour rights are often portrayed as the enemy of good government and as special interests opposed to the general good, but he goes too far when he says that they are called terrorists or subversives.

In the course of his discussion, McMurtry makes the important observation that restructuring has meant turning more and more services into commodities. Because these are increasingly available only in a competitive market, and not as a right, continuity of income becomes essential for what he calls vital life sustenance. Restructuring that does away with the welfare state removes this continuity while at the same time increases the gap between rich and poor. He points out (McCurty 1995, 9) that wages in the United States declined overall by 15 percent, and even more, 20 percent, for non-supervisory staff, between 1973 and 1992. In contrast, the real income of the top 1 percent of Americans increased by 60 percent between 1977 and 1992. This top 1 percent now earns more than the bottom 90 percent.

McMurtry uses the results of restructuring in New Zealand as an illustration of the manner in which cancerous capitalism creates an unhealthy community. From 1990 through 1992, New Zealand reduced or eliminated programs for public sector employment, income security, and health care. The New Zealand Department of Statistics recorded a 40 percent increase in poverty, a doubling of youth suicide (making the New Zealand rate the highest in the world), a 50 percent increase in violence against women, and a 40 percent increase in violence against children. At the same time, taxes on the wealthy were cut by half and the government deficit went from twenty-two billion dollars to forty-six billion even though public assets were privatized to the tune of sixteen billion. In Canada the erosion of our social safety net is not as extreme, but it is alarming. Between 1981 and 1991 the poverty rate for working households rose by 30 percent, for unattached individuals 57 percent, and for children by at least 34 percent (McMurtry 1995, 11).

McMurtry claims that society does not recognize or respond effectively to cancerous capitalist growth. According to him, messages contradicting the prevailing message that the neoliberal austerity program is necessary do not register within the community. He exaggerates here. The public does not always accept neoliberal policies with resignation, and sometimes dissenters are heard. McQuaig's book on the deficit became a bestseller. Even the politicians have been forced to talk about jobs as well as the deficit and, on occasion, temper the severity of their cuts. Premier Klein of Alberta, who has used the architect of the New Zealand program (Sir Roger Douglas) as his adviser, chose to pull back when confronted by striking health care workers.

McMurtry's cure is rather utopian, given his own assessment of the power of cancerous capitalism. What we need is regulation! "On the macro level of carcinogenic invasion, effective response now minimally requires global regulatory assertion to subordinate lethal, uncontrolled growth and metastasis" (McMurtry 1995, 22). Unfortunately, McMurtry gives no hint of what social forces could produce this regulation. Given that he holds that opinions contrary to the neoliberal restructuring model do not register on the public mind, how does he think opponents are to generate an effective demand for regulation?

As I see it, McMurtry is suggesting a return to the welfare orientation of the Golden Age augmented by regulations necessary to protect the environment and resources. This overlooks the cause of the attack on welfare structures, which are being destroyed because they no longer aid capital accumulation.

Consider, for example, social programs. They are commonly seen as a prime cause of increased deficits and consequently are priority targets when government cuts spending. Other areas of government spending that contribute considerably to the growth of deficits have not been cut at all, and are even receiving more money. Cuts in welfare programs may contribute to crime and thus cause an increase in expenditures on policing, jails, and crime prevention. Critics of government spending almost never complain about these expenditure increases. A study by statisticians H. Mimoto and P. Cross in 1991 demonstrated clearly that it was not an explosive growth in spending on social programs that caused the present deficit. Unemployment insurance is responsible for only 1 percent of deficit growth from 1975 to 1990. Welfare programs account for 4.5 percent, and pensions 6 percent. Completely ignored by commentators is growth in expenditures to protect persons and property, a category that represents 8 percent of deficit growth. Indeed, this information was left out of the published version of Mimoto's work and was obtained only through the Access to Information Act, which allowed reporters to see earlier drafts (McQuaig 1995, 59).

Privatization

One common mode of debt management is the sale of government enterprises and the privatization of public services. Publicly owned enterprises such as telephone, hydro, and gas utilities, and airlines, railways, airports, and even jails can be put on the auction block to be sold to private interests. The returns can be used to reduce the deficit without raising taxes, a definite political plus. Politicians can thus sell privatization as a painless means of deficit reduction.

Although privatization is related to debt reduction, it is also often justified as increasing competition and efficiency. Before restructuring, public ownership was often used to reduce costs to the private sector that would result from unprofitable infrastructure developments. States owned railways, harbours, airports, canals, road systems, and even various utilities that supplied industry and public alike with power, water, and electricity, often at cheap, subsidized rates. The growth of public debt put the brake on any further increase in public ownership. For advanced capitalist countries, the deficits of central governments grew from 0.2 percent of GDP in 1960–1973 to 2.4 percent in 1974–1979, and then 3.4 percent in 1980–1989. In Canada, the deficit for all levels of government averaged 4.6 percent of GDP in the 1980s (Barber 1992, 101). By the early eighties, many advanced capitalist states were spending more than a third of their gross national expenditure in the public sector while growth in the private sector slowed (Teeple 1995, 90). Public ownership became a fetter on further growth in the developing era of global capitalism.

Privatization is a part of the new social structure of accumulation and is common worldwide. The World Bank and the International Monetary Fund often demand privatization and other neoliberal policies in return for capital needed for economic development. Some countries, such as Haiti, may have privatization more or less thrust upon them, but others, such as New Zealand, Great Britain, and Canada, have adopted it voluntarily. Even so-called communist states, such as China, have encouraged privatization. To understand privatization, we must recognize that it serves a variety of purposes that aid capital accumulation.

First, privatization opens up new areas for capital investment. If the public sector runs campgrounds, extended care homes, hospitals, etc., then capital does not gain the profits these services might generate if they were privately owned. As governments spend less, private companies may offer the services cut by government. Suppliers of inputs still have an outlet for their products while the provision of services now generates profit for the companies offering their services.

Sometimes, privatization is simply the contracting out of services paid for by the government, for example, in home health care in Manitoba. One argument in favour of the policy is that the private sector can give better service at lower cost. This is assumed, not substantiated, despite ample evidence showing that in at least some areas, such as health insurance, a public monopoly is more cost-efficient. Why? In part, because public monopoly insurers can take advantage of economies of scale. As large purchasers, they can demand better prices from healthcare providers than smaller insurers (Rachlis and Kushner 1994, 23).

The prevailing view is that government provision means bloated bureaucracies with huge administrative costs. But, in the case of health insurance, it is the private sector that is less efficient. In the United States, where private insurance predominates, administrative costs are six times higher than in Canada (Woolhandler and Himmelstein 1991). Private companies must also spend large sums to market their products in competition with other insurers, whereas the public insurer need spend only that amount necessary to inform the public about services and regulations.

In the comparison of private and public provision of services, it is often forgotten that a private company needs to make a profit. This, in itself, means that, *ceteris paribus* (as economists like to say), public provision *must* be cheaper, since it only needs to break even. This simple fact has nonetheless been all but expunged from the collective mind.

A further difficulty with private insurance is the problem of creaming. Insurers will wish to cover those who have the fewest health problems and those who can pay high premiums. Insurers will not cover those with severe health problems and those who cannot pay high premiums. In the United States, despite its extensive system of private health insurance, the healthcare costs for this latter group are, therefore, paid by government! Public monopoly insurance covers everyone equally, regardless of income. In a market system, coverage will depend largely upon income.

Countries such as the UK have already developed a two-tier system that features an underfunded public sector with long waiting lists and poorly paid doctors, and a private system with superior care and short waiting lists or none at all, and well-paid doctors. Those better off benefit most from this two-tier system. Public pressure may eventually cause the Canadian government to allow such a system in the provinces if it does not adequately fund our universal, one-tier system.

A second way in which privatization serves the accumulation of capital is by making the state even more dependent on finance capital. Loss of assets may increase the costs of borrowing, and the associated loss of revenue increase the need for borrowing. If privatization involves foreign investors, decisions will be made that advance their profit even though this may not be best for the country that privatizes. Capital flows wherever return is greatest. Reinvestment is not guaranteed in the country that privatized. To retain capital, countries will be forced to create conditions more favourable to investment than other countries competing for capital. This may mean further reduction in corporate taxes, further cuts to social programs, and removal of any remaining barriers to foreign investment. The New Zealand experiment illustrates the necessity for further cuts in social programs and removal of remaining barriers to foreign investment to ensure capital reinvestment once firms are sold to foreign interests.

A third function of privatization is the generation of revenues for particular groups. Just as regulations are the staff of life for a certain group of bureaucrats, so privatization nourishes and enriches a certain group of consultants, stockbrokers, lawyers, and underwriters. According to Hardin (1989, 72), privatizations around the world in 1986 were predicted to generate about four hundred million dollars per year in fees. Consultancy fees tied to the selling of just one firm, British

Telecom, were twenty-five million dollars. And consultancy fees are only one aspect of the expense of restructuring public companies.

Public companies must often be restructured to make them marketable. This, too, can be costly, not only in fees to consultants but in money spent upgrading equipment, paying down debt, or on severance packages associated with downsizing.

A fourth function of privatization is weaning the public from the idea that the state should have an extensive role in providing services. Since the free market is supposed to be superior to government as a producer of goods and services, we should privatize whenever we can. The policy of privatization has become so pervasive and so accepted that virtually no one debates the general principle, only specific cases and the areas that may be privatized. In the United States, privatization has extended even to segments of the prison system, and private policing is becoming a growth service industry.

A fifth function of privatization is the weakening of the trade union movement. When government services are contracted out it is often to nonunion companies that give fewer benefits and pay lower wages. An example is home care services in Manitoba. The largely successful struggle to unionize public sector workers can be defeated by privatization, which governments justify in the name of efficiency.

Allegedly, privatization increases efficiency by lowering wages and benefits for the same work. Supporters of privatization will claim that the public will benefit through lower costs without diminution in the quality of service. But the difference in cost may simply be absorbed by the company as profit, and contracting out can increase the costs of monitoring to ensure quality work. In some cases contracting out to private companies has increased costs and reduced quality to such a degree that the process has been reversed even in these pressing times. Bilik, for example, cites New York and Phoenix as cities that contracted out services in the eighties, only to bring them back in-house in the nineties (Bilik 1992, 339).

Privatization is possible because people view ownership of public property and private property differently. No one would suggest selling one's car as a painless way of paying off a car loan or selling a house as a painless way of solving high mortgage payments. Even more strangely, privatization is often justified as a means by which individuals can gain ownership in a company even though publicly owned companies are already owned collectively by citizens. Governments may go to great trouble and expense to tout the virtues of individual ownership through privatization over collective ownership. The British Columbia

Resources and Investment Corporation (BCRIC), the vehicle for privatization used by Bill Bennett in BC in 1979, is a good case study.

The privatization of BCRIC allowed every eligible man, woman and child in BC to receive five shares in this company. The company was formed from three publicly owned forestry companies and various other publicly owned shares (Hardin 1989, 86). As one would expect, representatives of several securities firms advised Bennett and promoted the scheme. Shares were priced at a discount to their book value, to encourage people to purchase further shares. Critics pointed out that the people owned these corporations before the share issue, but the government responded that the shares represented individual ownership as opposed to big government ownership. People were so alienated from their own government and the idea of collective ownership that this argument had some force for the public. Bennett's great leap forward into people's capitalism quickly bogged down as directors of the company made expensive and questionable acquisitions. Soon shares were trading at the three-dollar level, down from a high of more than nine dollars.

Each person who applied received five shares worth six dollars each. The cost to the government in administration was four dollars per person, and total overhead costs were estimated at forty million dollars (Hardin 1989, 88). In spite of all the claims and hoopla about shareholder democracy, only shareholders with more than one hundred shares had voting rights. This was an enterprise which could not be compared to a cooperative, in which each shareholder gets one vote, or even garden variety corporations, where voting stock gives one vote per share. A promise that no one could own more than 1 percent of stock was broken within three years. Later, the ban on foreign ownership was given up as well.

Privatization is obviously one of the prime new structures of accumulation touted by capital as the cure for debt, supposedly because it makes services cheaper through competition. As we have seen, there are good reasons for thinking that these positive results may not occur, and for thinking that negative consequences are usually overlooked. Considered in the context of debt reduction, privatization does not bode well for the future common good.

Conclusion

I have demonstrated that the new structures created to manage debt, and the policy of privatization, have had quite negative consequences for most citizens. Some policies, such as changes in patent legislation and tax cuts for the well-off, exacerbate debt problems rather than contributing to their solution. While such policies may promote capital accumulation, by deepening the debt crisis they may force further cuts in welfare programs.

It is not an exaggeration to say that under the new structures of accumulation, life in capitalist societies is decreasing in quality for many citizens while capital triumphantly spreads across the globe. I do not share McMurtry's view that decrease in quality of life will force regulation that will bring back an earlier era in which the welfare state finances a substantial social safety net protecting the public from the harms of market capitalism. Minimal environmental regulation and a minimal welfare state may be all that is accepted in the interests of social peace and future development.

Nor do I agree that the present stage of capitalism is cancerous. The technological revolution in communications and other offshoots of advanced capitalism are a potential boon to humanity as a whole and are not analogous to cancer cells destroying the body politic. To stem the tide of neoliberalism, labour and other progressive groups will need to organize on a transnational and global, rather than just a national, scale. Some progress has been made in this regard and has resulted in the incorporation of minimal environmental protection and labour and social rights as part of free trade agreements. But, for now, capital is much stronger than labour at the international level. Nevertheless, as long as cutbacks meet strenuous resistance at the local and national level, capital can press only so far in restructuring. At a certain point, capital will realize that to avoid serious social unrest that may be costly to contain, it must not cut social programs further.

Workers should press for greater rather than less public and cooperative ownership, and for more equitable taxation rather than reduced taxes. Unions could invest their huge pension funds in worker-owned and -run companies, rather than in large private corporations. The public and cooperative sectors must accumulate their own capital. These pools of capital will allow for some production that serves social aims rather than simply maximizing profits.

Nonetheless, within the capitalist system I see no lasting solution to the decline in the overall quality of community life caused by the new social structures of accumulation. The productive forces generated within global capitalism will serve humanity as a whole and equitably only if we socialize the means of production, distribution, and exchange, and increase democratic control over economic decision making. I believe that production should be based upon need, not profit, and that markets should play a small role in the production and distribution of goods and services. I recognize that this all sounds hopelessly out of date in an era when even analytical Marxists are enamoured of neoclassical economics, but then who would have thought that anyone would ever listen to Friedrich Hayek, a founder of neoliberalism, a few decades ago when John Maynard Keynes held sway and Hayek was regarded as a rather clever dinosaur who had strangely survived into the new age of government intervention and the welfare state?

PART III
Responsible and Irresponsible Restructuring

Hanly argues against the standard justifications of the restructuring economy. This is one way to address the ethical issues that it raises. Restructuring is, he suggests, founded on an agenda which illegitimately serves particular interests and is not consistent with our obligations to the disadvantaged or the rights of labour. Other attempts to morally assess restructuring are less radical. Rather than raise doubts about restructuring in general, they distinguish between responsible and irresponsible restructuring. In the process, they elaborate ways to avoid or combat the most ethically objectionable aspects of radical restructuring. The two articles in this section suggest some of the differences that characterize responsible and irresponsible restructuring and ways to promote the former. In "Responsible Restructuring in the Private Sector," Wayne Cascio makes a fundamental distinction between downsizing and responsible restructuring. Paying close attention to the empirical evidence on the effects of restructuring in the private sector, he argues that the latter is preferable from both an ethical and a business point of view. In the article that follows, Todd J. Hostager, David T. Bastien, and Henry H. Miles explain an approach to business they have developed to combat irresponsible restructuring. Like its martial arts analogue, "corporate judo" allows firms to earn a competitive advantage over careless competitors, in this case by exploiting the weaknesses they themselves create by ill-considered restructuring initiatives. This approach to business provides an important free-market mechanism which can combat such restructurers, and so penalize that restructuring which is most objectionable from an ethical point of view.

5

Responsible Restructuring in the Private Sector

Wayne F. Cascio

How safe is my job? For many people, this is the issue of today. This is true whether one's job is in the private or the public sector, in business, health or education. Restructuring and downsizing affect all areas and the economy. In this paper, I will nevertheless focus on issues raised by the restructuring of business, for this is what I have studied. It should be clear that many of the lessons we can learn from this exercise can be applied to other sectors of the economy, including the public sector.

The importance of a better understanding of downsizing and restructuring in business is highlighted by general economic trends, which make it increasingly clear that corporate cutbacks were not an oddity of the 1980s and are likely to persist. Involuntary lay-offs are never pleasant, and responsible management policies which potentially involve them must consider their impacts on those who leave, on those who stay, on the local community, and on the company in question.

Termination is a traumatic experience. Egos are shattered, and employees who remain may be bitter and angry. Family problems may occur because of the added emotional and financial strain. Outplacement programs that help laid-off employees deal with the psychological stages of career transition (anger, grief, depression, family stress), assess individual strengths and weaknesses, and develop support networks which can be beneficial. Within broader communities, lay-offs have had significant impacts on local economies and social service agencies.

For those who remain, it is important to take steps to ensure that they retain the highest level of loyalty, trust, teamwork, motivation, and productivity possible. This doesn't just happen and unless there is a good deal of face-to-face, candid, open communication between senior management and "survivors," it probably won't.

The downside of downsizing has been well documented (see Leana 1996; for a specific case, see Collins in this volume). Downsizing may carry some very high costs—psychological, social, and financial. Executives should, therefore, consider carefully whether such costs are justified by the presumed benefits of any downsizing of their workforce. Let us begin this account of responsible restructuring by putting down-sizing in perspective.

Downsizing is the planned elimination of positions or jobs. It has had, and will continue to have, profound effects on many organizations, managers at all levels, employees, labour markets, customers, and share-holders. In the United States, more than nine million permanent lay-offs have been announced since 1987. Downsizing continues as a result of fundamental, structural changes in economies and markets, in the nature of international competition, in deregulation (e.g., with respect to health care reform), and in domestic competition (e.g., from low-cost airlines or small, high-technology firms). Firms downsize in order to make the best possible use of their resources: human, capital, and physical. Although they may do this in a number of ways—by reducing the num-ber of employees, by investing in new technology, by changing the way work is done, and so on—cutting headcount has been an especially popular strategy. Why? What is the lure of downsizing?

The "menu" of potential strategies to become more efficient and more productive is a long one, but a reduction in headcount is includ-ed on almost every executive's list. There are really only two ways for companies to become more profitable: either by increasing revenues or cutting costs. Because most observers would agree that future costs are more predictable than future revenues, and because human resources represent costs, to become more profitable it seems logical to reduce those costs by decreasing a corporation's number of employees. The theory may be logical, but in practice it is very problematic.

Recently, finance professor James Morris, marketing professor Clifford Young and I collaborated on a large-scale research project to examine the long-term financial consequences of downsizing. We examined the employment levels and financial performance of the five hundred largest firms traded on the New York Stock Exchange (Standard & Poor's 500) over a fifteen-year period (1980–1994). We compared downsizers to sta-ble-employment firms in the same industry that did not downsize. We found that, at the end of the year of downsizing and in the subsequent two years, downsizers were never better off in terms of productivity, expenses, profitability, or total return on common stock (Cascio, Young, and Morris 1996). Stock prices do tend to spike upwards on the day the downsizing is announced, but over time such gains do not persist.

Despite such evidence, many of the same executives who tout people as "our greatest assets" nevertheless see those assets as ripe opportunities for cutting costs. At Scott Paper Company, chief executive officer Albert Dunlap cut 11,200 jobs before selling the company to Kimberly Clark. He walked away with one hundred million dollars (Petzinger 1996). At American Telephone and Telegraph, on the day that CEO Robert Allen announced forty thousand lay-offs his own AT&T stock rose two million dollars in value. AT&T, once known warmly as Ma Bell, has become vilified as an icon of American corporate greed. The public flailing has been broad-based, from the Secretary of Labor, to *Newsweek*, to politicians (Keller 1996). Are there exceptions to this behaviour? To see that there are, we need to distinguish two different philosophies, downsizing and restructuring.

Downsizing asks, what is the irreducible core number of people we need to run our business?

Restructuring asks, how can we change the way we do business so that we can use the people we have most effectively?

I believe that a change in orientation from downsizing to restructuring can pay handsome dividends over the long term. To illustrate this point I offer the following four examples, which present some restructuring strategies that executives have developed to cut costs without cutting people. They, and others like them, are described more fully in the *Guide to Responsible Restructuring*, published by the US Department of Labor in 1995.

Example 1: De-layering Without Downsizing Employees

Ford Motor Co. is a world leader in the automotive industry, selling vehicles in more than 200 markets, and employing more than 322,000 people in plants, laboratories, and offices around the world. Although sales topped $128 billion in 1994, and profits were up 110 percent over 1993, Ford realized it had an emerging problem: product development. It simply couldn't design new cars and trucks as quickly as competitors like Toyota. Concerned about Ford's ability to compete in the twenty-first century, Chairman and CEO Alex Trotman launched a bold restructuring effort designed to change the company's business processes and organizational structure to function more efficiently on a global basis. Increasingly, Trotman believed, the evolution from regional to worldwide processes and systems in product development, manufacturing, supply, and sales activities will be based on the use of high-technology, data, and communications systems (Trotman 1994, Sedgwick 1994, Ford Motor Co. 1994, *Business Week*, 6/03/95, 101).

Still, there is that nagging question: Why now? Ed Hagenlocker, president of Ford Automotive Operations, described the company's rationale in an August, 1994 speech:

> We want to do it when times are good...not in a crisis mode when times are bad. We want to do it at a pace that we determine, where we can evaluate and make the decisions when we want. We want to be able to communicate our actions throughout the company and have the understanding and buy-in of our employees. We don't want to be communicating change during times of economic uncertainty. And we are going about it very deliberately and methodically. (Hagenlocker 1994, 4)

The company's restructuring, dubbed "Ford 2000," was accomplished without the threat of recession or corporate raiders, and without mass lay-offs, divestitures, or wrenching disruptions (Suris 1994). Here are some of the changes as of January 1, 1995:

- The company combined Ford Automotive Operations, North American Automotive Operations, and Automotive Components Group into a single unit.
- The company established five Vehicle Program Centers, each with worldwide responsibility for the design, development, and engineering of the vehicles assigned to it. Europe's product team is responsible for designing small cars, while the other four product teams located in Dearborn, Michigan are responsible for mid-sized cars, luxury cars, personal trucks, and commercial trucks.
- As part of its matrix organization structure, Ford formed "core" groups that specialize in manufacturing, engineering, and marketing. The core groups loan specialists to each vehicle team on a project or "as needed" basis.
- Ford's white-collar automotive workforce of some eighty thousand has been reshuffled into half as many organization-chart boxes as before;
- more than three hundred senior and middle managers have accepted early retirement offers to leave; and
- nearly all of Ford's four thousand-plus high-level managers are learning new responsibilities.

What's the payoff from all of this? According to Chairman and CEO Trotman, Ford expects to save two to three billion dollars per year by the end of the decade. "That assures a better return for stockholders, a more certain future for Ford employees, and a broader array of high-quality vehicles in more parts of the world for our customers" (Ford Motor Co. 1994, 3).

Ford's experience provides four key lessons for other firms struggling to reinvent themselves for the twenty-first century:

- *Get the whole company involved.* After spending months studying other restructurings, CEO Alex Trotman concluded that a common mistake is that restructuring often is ordered by top management, but implemented by subordinates who understand the objectives poorly. Although much of Ford's reorganization planning was conducted by 150 executives working at headquarters, the company included hundreds of others in the process. The principle is simple: *Get the people who will have to live with changes involved in making changes.* (Suris 1994)

- *Reorganize in the open.* Ford's internal public relations machine rivals anything the company has ever used to launch a new-car model. It published a weekly faxed newspaper ("The Grapevine"), ran an electronic bulletin board, broadcast a weekly in-house TV show, and convened four meetings attended by nearly two thousand employees to keep them up to date on developments. Said one group vice-president: "The communication has been consistent, constant, and outstanding." (Suris 1994)

- *Punch the fast-forward button.* Because the CEO believed that it was important to move quickly, and not allow time for barriers resulting from uncertainty to arise, he set an eight-month schedule for revamping an organization that took ninety years to build. The idea has been to put all the decision makers in one place and force them to hash out decisions on the spot, rather than waste months passing around memos and binders of data in the old Ford fashion. Managers of the task force were expected to reassign their other duties and concentrate solely on the reorganization.

- *Expect confusion and manage it.* Ford acknowledged that hundreds of careers are disrupted as organization charts are ripped up, job titles are redefined, and reporting relationships are altered. To ease the fears, team members made presentations, fielded questions, and learned how to present early-retirement offers to emphasize that nobody was being forced out. Despite all these efforts, Ford executives know that the model won't be complete the day it is rolled out. But their careful planning and execution show how the process ought to work.

Example 2: Providing Employment Security Through Redeployment

Redeployment, that is, providing other opportunities within a corporation for employees affected by restructuring, is an option for some large corporations, which can either grow the business into new areas or build on existing product lines or services. Intel, the company that invented the microchip (and whose average product life cycle is just 2.5 years) has, for example, avoided major lay-offs through a strong in-house redeployment policy. Every employee receives a brochure entitled "Owning Your Own Employability," and is afforded tools and resources to take advantage of the redeployment option. A redeployment event occurs when there is a business downturn or lack of a need for a particular skill. It does not replace performance management, as Intel's Marile Robinson, corporate manager of redeployment, points out: "It's not meant to shift around people with poor skills, poor performers, or those with behavioural problems" (Stuller 1993, 40). To qualify, a full-time employee must have two consecutive years of performance reviews that "meet requirements."

Should an employee become eligible for redeployment, he or she is given options, tools, and resources. The company has five employee development centres offering self-assessment tools, career counselling, educational opportunities, and job listings within Intel. Job skills have been redefined to encourage people to find new places within the company, and temporary assignments (as many as two assignments for a total of twelve months) and up to eight thousand dollars of training are provided to prepare them for new positions. Funds are also available for relocation. The entire process is managed through a system that provides centralized tracking and reporting of all redeployment activity.

The ranks of Intel employees are filled with those who have made successful transitions from shop floor to sales and public-relations positions, or from obsolete technology divisions to high-margin technology centres within the corporation. If none of this works, the company pays for outplacement assistance for affected employees. Redeployment is a continuing challenge at Intel because the company's competitive strategy is to stay ahead of its rivals by making its products obsolete.

Between 1989 and 1991, Intel closed plants employing two thousand people, and redeployed approximately 80 percent of the affected workers. From 1991 to 1994, redeployment events impacted 3,409 employees. The company placed 90 percent of them internally, and in 1994 there was zero litigation as a result of plant closures (Robinson 1995).

As part of a major restructuring, New Orleans–based Chevron USA offered all affected employees the opportunity to participate in a redeployment process that featured retraining and a chance for placement at Chevron subsidiaries. The company's cost-reduction measures affected a broad spectrum of employees: geologists, engineers, technicians, pilots, secretaries, information systems specialists, offshore oil platform workers, and others (Vitiello 1994). One aspect of the training focused on developing computer-based competencies. Chevron hired Manpower, Inc., a provider of temporary help and employment services, to conduct on-site classes in four software programs: WordPerfect, Windows, Lotus, and dBase III Plus. Over a six-week period, more than two hundred computer training sessions were conducted at Chevron's career centre. Most trainees took all four courses, and approximately 85 percent of them found jobs subsequently. Other company-sponsored programs include outplacement services (interviewing, resume writing, networking), a 75 percent reimbursement of the cost of tuition and books for employees who wished to attend local universities, and a Chevron-sponsored program that helps professionals in the sciences earn their teaching certificates at an accelerated pace. While it was not possible to redeploy all affected workers within Chevron, even as the company reduced its workforce by several thousand employees in 1992, it redeployed about nine hundred of them, thereby saving more than twenty-five million dollars in severance costs alone (Stuller 1993). The company's overall approach reflects a genuine concern with helping employees to maintain employment security (i.e., marketable skills), and is a fine example of responsible restructuring.

Minnesota Mining and Manufacturing Co. can serve as a final example of a large company that actively promotes redeployment of surplus workers. When business lags at one of its forty-nine divisions, excess workers are found similar work at another division. Over the past decade, 3M has reassigned about 3,500 workers this way, failing to place only a "handful," according to Richard Lidstad, vice-president of human resources. "Our employees are corporate assets, not assets of a given business. It's like production machinery. In a downturn, you don't just throw it out" (*Business Week*, 7/12/92, 101). How has 3M done? In 1994 sales and profits were both up over 1993 levels, and the company earned a 19.6 percent return on common equity (*Business Week*, 6/03/95, 109).

Lynn Williams, the international president of the United Steelworkers of America, has captured the very essence of the employment concerns that make redeployment such a productive option.

Whether they belong to a union or not, whether white collar, blue collar, or pink collar, "we cannot expect American workers to contribute all their good ideas and all the things they understand about the workplace...if the result of doing so is that they get laid off as a result of [productivity] improvements" (Williams 1993, 8). Redeployment policies like those adopted at Intel, Chevron, and 3M address the issue of employment security head-on and assuage the concerns of workers.

Example 3: Providing Employment Security Through Voluntary Leaves of Absence

Voluntary leave of absence (LOA) plans, with or without pay, can be win–win strategies for both employers and workers. Such plans help employers to retain the loyalty, commitment, and competencies of a trained workforce, while at the same time allowing workers to keep their jobs. Reflexite of Avon, Connecticut, is an example of a company that has developed a creative LOA plan. It produces retro-reflective materials that reflect light back to its source. To produce such materials, it uses a patented method of moulding thousands of microscopic prisms onto every square inch of a plastic sheet. Examples of products that use retro-reflective materials are street signs, barricades, fire fighting equipment, life preservers, and reflective clothing. Reflexite is an employee-owned company, with 42 percent of company stock held by the ESOP (Employee Stock Ownership Plan) and an additional 25 percent held by over ninety other employees, who purchased company stock outside of the ESOP.

Though Reflexite was not losing customers or market share, the company faced a 40 percent decline in sales in 1991, a result of the economic recession. In the face of these economic pressures, it went to great lengths to avoid employee lay-offs. Cecil Ursprung, chief executive officer, defied the advice of his managers to lay employees off, and instead instituted a two-part plan to cut costs. First, everyone took a cut in pay. Top management took a 10 percent cut, middle managers a 7 percent cut, lower-level managers a 5 percent cut, and all other employees took a 5 percent cut in the form of one day off per month without pay when the plant was closed.

Second, Reflexite developed a voluntary LOA plan in cooperation with the State of Connecticut. Under the plan, employees could take voluntary, unpaid leave for from anywhere between two weeks and five months, while maintaining full benefits and receiving unemployment compensation from the state. Under an agreement with the local unemployment office, the company took responsibility for filing all necessary forms for participating employees. In addition, all participating employees maintained their seniority and owners' bonus rights, and had a guaranteed date when they could return to the company.

About ninety employees participated in the voluntary leave-of-absence program, saving the company over four hundred thousand dollars in payroll costs. The combination of the voluntary leave program and the salary cuts produced a 17 percent budget savings. Other company expenses in manufacturing and administration were cut back dramatically, and a planned facility expansion was postponed. Finally, all employees at the employee-owned company received information on exactly how much money these measures saved. Through these efforts, Reflexite avoided the lay-off of even a single employee. Business rebounded after the recession, and the corporation has been profitable every year since 1991. In 1992, sales hit thirty million dollars. In 1995, Reflexite was a fifty-million-dollar company (Edgar 1995).

One important feature of Reflexite's operations is its willingness to go to considerable lengths to disclose operating and strategic business information to its employees. One example is its Business Downturn Grid, a four-stage plan outlining actions to be taken by the company during periods of slow business. It attempts to provide full disclosure of each stage and the symptoms that will trigger a particular course of action.

Here is an example.

At Stage II, the following actions will be taken:

- Revise selling, general, and administrative expenditures
- Revise sales forecast
- Solicit ideas to cut costs, improve productivity and efficiency from employee owners
- Cut overtime
- Cut discretionary spending
- Redeploy the sales force
- Increase cold calls
- Accelerate new product introductions

The expected results?

- Revenue and expenses will be adjusted to meet the new business plan
- Preserve all jobs and the expected future of the company's stock

Lay-offs occur at the fourth and final stage, and are a last resort to save the company. To date, Reflexite's creative approach to managing its employees has made this step unnecessary. In recognition of the value that Reflexite places on employee involvement, *all* of the company's employee-owners were presented with *Inc*. magazine's Entrepreneur of the Year award in 1992.

Example 4: Training and Education For Survivors, While Downsizing Without Involuntary Lay-offs

NYNEX Corporation, the regional telephone company serving New York and New England, negotiated a new contract with the Communications Workers of America (CWA) nearly two years before the old one was to expire. The new contract was negotiated in response to the company's need to eliminate eight thousand of the company's thirty-five thousand hourly positions (about 23 percent) as part of an overall cutback of 16,500 jobs.

To a large extent, such massive downsizing became necessary as a result of changes in four areas: *process re-engineering* (the goal of which is to eliminate activities that do not add value to the company), *technology* (only half as many employees are required when working with digital switching using fibre-optic cable), *computers* (today's powerful PCs can match traditional mainframes), and *customers* (who now have a choice of providers as a result of deregulation) (Dowdall and Bahr 1994).

The overall intent of the new agreement is to allow the company to become "lean" without being "mean." That is, the company will eliminate jobs without involuntary lay-offs, transfers, or downgrades (barring external events of a significant size, such as the loss of a major customer or a defined level of market share). Under the agreement, NYNEX will take the following steps in order to make involuntary downsizing unnecessary (Dowdall and Bahr 1994):

1. Offer early retirement incentives to pension-eligible employees (in a specific area) that allow extra credit for age and years of service, supplemental pension benefits until age sixty-two, and retention of full health-care coverage. These "sweeteners" will boost pension payouts by 20 percent to 25 percent.
2. If Step One proves insufficient, contiguous or adjacent areas will receive the same offer.
3. If this proves insufficient, the early retirement offer will be broadened to include an entire work group in an area.
4. Ask employees (regardless of their eligibility for a pension) in the affected area to accept a voluntary severance arrangement.

5. Offer voluntary severance to all employees in the work group.
6. Institute job sharing as a way of preserving jobs.
7. Have all work that had been contracted out performed in-house.
8. Close out temporary employees.

For the remaining NYNEX workers, the new contract established a two-year associate degree in applied science, under a cooperative agreement with the State University of New York. Employees who elect to participate will work for four days a week, go to school on the fifth day, and will receive five days' pay while they are enrolled in class. Under this agreement, completion of the degree will require approximately four years. Upon completion of their degrees, new graduates will receive a "super tech" wage differential above the base wage rates specified in the contract. By effectively creating a four-day work week for much of its workforce, NYNEX also will slow the pace of job cuts, retaining enough extra people to cover the 20 percent reduction in the work week.

CWA members who have been with NYNEX at least five years and who want to go on to earn a four-year college degree can take a two-year educational leave of absence. The leave is unpaid, but employees retain all benefits and seniority, and will have a guaranteed job when they return. NYNEX will pay as much as ten thousand dollars a year in educational assistance.

In an industry constantly redefining itself, the long-term goal of company and CWA negotiators is to act in the best interests of both parties. A prime example of this is the effort to upgrade workers' educational levels while providing them with employment security. Why would NYNEX agree to such an expensive program? "Because we can never have enough technically educable people; they provide versatility.... We see the employee as a resource—we'll grow everything in-house" (Dowdall and Bahr 1994).

Conclusion

After the first atomic reaction in 1942, Albert Einstein remarked, "Everything has changed, except our way of thinking and thus we drift toward...disaster" (quoted from Williams 1993, 2). The firms described in these four examples have changed their way of thinking. For those who share their commitments, and want to move from commitment into action, the following can serve as guidelines for responsible restructuring. In essence, they make the point that restructuring is responsible to the extent that it acknowledges the concerns, expectations, and inputs of all stakeholders who will be affected by it.

1. Articulate a vision of what you want your organization to achieve.
2. Establish a corporate culture that views people as assets to be developed rather than as costs to be cut.
3. Be clear about your short- and long-range objectives, e.g., to cut costs (short-range) and to improve customer service and shareholder value through more effective use of assets (long-range).
4. Establish an alternative menu of options for reaching the short- and long-range objectives.
5. Ensure that the people who will have to live with the changes are involved in making them; provide opportunities for input at all levels.
6. Communicate, communicate, communicate! Share as much information as possible about prospective changes with those who will be affected by them.
7. Recognize that employees are unlikely to contribute creative, ingenious ways to cut costs if they think their own employment security will be jeopardized as a result.
8. If cutting costs by cutting people is inevitable, establish a set of priorities for doing so (e.g., outside contractors and temporaries go first) and stick to it. Show by word and deed that full-time, value-adding employees will be the last to go.
9. If employees must be laid off, provide as much advance notice as possible, treat them with dignity and respect, and provide assistance (financial, counselling) to help them find new jobs.
10. Consider redeploying surplus workers, retraining them to make better use of existing human assets and to promote employment security and self-reliance.
11. Give surviving employees a reason to stay. Explain what new opportunities will be available to them.
12. View restructuring as part of a process of continual improvement—with sub-goals and measurable check points over time—rather than as a one-time event.

The companies described earlier, and the restructuring strategies they used, represent considered choices among alternative courses of action. The interests of all parties were clarified, and the risks and gains were evaluated openly and mutually. These kinds of actions define ethical choices (Mirvis and Seashore 1979).

The traditional view of the firm says that corporations have many constituencies: the stockholders or shareowners, the customers, the employees, and the community (or communities) in which they do business.

These groups are "stakeholders"—people who have a stake in the firm. Chief executive officers such as Albert Dunlap, formerly of Scott Paper Company, deride this view as "total rubbish. It's the shareholders who own the company" (Leana 1996, 16). However true this may be, it is the employees and suppliers who make the company function, and it is the communities they reside in which support the firm by providing the infrastructure that allows it to operate (e.g., roads, bridges, railways, schools, hospitals, police and fire protection). Isn't it therefore reasonable to consider the interests of these parties in any decision to downsize?

One of the unfortunate myths about downsizing is that it occurs in desperate situations, where the very survival of the firm is at stake. In fact, the data indicate that for many companies, downsizing is a *first* resort. Right Associates, an outplacement firm headquartered in Philadelphia, reports that before downsizing, only 6 percent of companies tried to reduce costs by cutting pay, 9 percent tried unpaid holidays, 9 percent tried reduced work weeks, and 14 percent tried job sharing (Right Associates 1992). A survey by the American Management Association suggests that 81 percent of those firms that downsized in 1994 were profitable in that year (American Management Association 1994).

Responsible restructuring requires that firms consider carefully the interests of all stakeholders, not just stockholders, before laying workers off. The data on the financial performance of downsizing companies do not support the long-term benefits of this strategy. Is there a lesson here? Indeed there is, for the firms that showed the best results in the fifteen-year study of the S&P 500 described earlier were those that were increasing assets and *adding* employees. Growing the business is a much more viable long-term strategy than simply cutting workers. In short, a firm can't save its way into prosperity. The real key is new products, new services and new markets.

6

Corporate Judo

*Todd J. Hostager, David T. Bastien, and
Henry H. Miles*

> Layoffs are intended to reduce costs and promote an efficient, lean, and
> mean organization. However, what tends to result is a sad and angry
> organization, populated by depressed survivors. The basic bind is that
> the process of reducing staff to achieve increased efficiency and pro-
> ductivity often creates conditions that lead to the opposite result—an
> organization that is risk averse and less productive. (Noer 1993, 6)

Ask any employee in a recently restructured company and they will tell
you what David Noer is talking about. Recent studies support the view
from the front line: restructuring often damages organizations and their
customer relations, resulting in lower productivity, morale, market share,
and revenues (see Cascio 1993, De Meuse et al. 1994, Downs 1995, Noer
1993, and Stambaug 1992; on mergers and acquisitions see Bastien 1987,
Boyle and Jaynes 1972, Marks and Mirvis 1985, and Zweig et al. 1995).
The view from the boardroom and Wall Street is a different matter. Many
executives and investors still see restructuring as an effective way to cut
costs, enhance performance, improve the bottom line, and better serve
the interests of stockholders (see Jones 1996, Dunlap 1996, and Pickens
1988). Which view is correct? Is restructuring good or bad?

The truth of the matter is not so simple or so clear cut. Restructurings
come in many different forms, including downsizings, mergers, acquisitions, divestitures, turnarounds, hostile takeovers, friendly takeovers,
leveraged buyouts, and employee stock ownership plans.[16] Some restructurings are voluntary and some are involuntary. Some are driven by the
selfish motives of raiders and empire-builders and some are designed to

---

Notes to this chapter are on p. 304.

defend firms against these attacks. Some are driven by a concern for quarterly profits and some are necessary to insure the very survival of the firm.

Different restructurings vary in their impacts on employees, customers, communities, and other stakeholders. While no form of change is painless, some restructurings inflict less stakeholder damage than others (see Cascio 1995, Hitt et al. 1994, Hendricks 1992, and Lieber 1995). As we enter the increasingly turbulent, complex, and interdependent world of the twenty-first century, one of our key challenges is to identify the most effective ways to deter restructuring which is harmful.

How do we discourage change that damages stakeholders? Current responses to this challenge fall into one of two categories: education, and government intervention. Cascio 1995, Hitt et al. 1994 and other advocates of rightsizing and responsible restructuring see education as a key to minimizing stakeholder damage. According to this view, part of the problem stems from a fundamental ignorance of (1) why restructurings should be done and (2) how to properly implement them. The solution is to study the principles and practices that underlie the least harmful and most beneficial instances of restructuring. Those who believe that governments should intervene suggest laws regulating plant closures, advanced notice and severance packages, and that governments play a role in labour–management negotiations, and employee and public buyouts.

But are education and government intervention the only weapons in the war against harmful restructuring driven by ignorance and/or unchecked greed? Our research suggests otherwise. Ironically, a powerful new weapon has emerged from the market itself. This weapon— *corporate judo*—has a number of unique features that make it effective as a selective deterrent against harmful restructuring.

We begin the present paper by describing the process through which we discovered and developed corporate judo. We then provide an overview of the corporate judo framework. We describe the underlying philosophy of judo, generic waves of opportunities to "judo" a restructured firm, and the role that competitive intelligence plays in judo. We then identify four generic approaches to restructuring: the "What, me worry?" approach, education, government intervention, and corporate judo. We compare the relative merits of these responses as methods for discouraging harmful restructuring practices. Among other things, we show that corporate judo and corporate raiding are opposites, and that judo can be used to punish harmful attacks by raiders and empire-builders. We conclude by noting some ways of combining corporate judo with education and government action.

The Discovery and Development of Corporate Judo

The story of corporate judo is a mixture of empirical observation, practical insight, and theory. It all began during a lunchtime conversation about the market for consulting in merger and acquisition (M&A) implementation. We wondered why so many executives believed that they could manage a merger on their own, without the benefit of learning from the past mistakes and successes of others.[17] One of us had recently completed a study of the damage that a merged firm unleashed upon itself and the resulting exodus of employees and customers to competing firms. The light bulb of practical insight flashed at this point—if the executives in charge of merged or acquired firms don't want to learn about the problems and pitfalls of their restructuring, why not sell that information to their *competitors*?

This makes good sense, for detailed knowledge of the fallout from the restructuring of one firm can help competing firms gain valuable customers and talented employees at its expense. This is the essence of corporate judo. Like its analogue in the martial arts, it derives its power from an opponent's own actions, exploiting the forces they unleash and the weaknesses they expose during the heat of competition (see Domini 1977, Seabourne and Herndon 1983, and Sun Tzu 1963). But corporate judo is more than just another tactic on the competitive battlefield. We believed that the threat of "getting nailed by a competitor" which it poses might create a compelling incentive for executives to seriously consider (1) whether or not a restructuring is warranted in the first place, and (2) how to plan and implement a restructuring so that benefits are maximized and the damage minimized.

Armed with these basic insights, we tackled the task of developing a systematic approach to corporate judo. We looked for relevant research findings, useful theoretical concepts, and examples of judo in practice. The most difficult part of the task was finding real-world examples. In one case, we learned that a community bank had doubled or tripled its rate of growth in net income, loans, and deposits by exploiting the fallout at a recently acquired rival bank. Dave Knopick, the president of the bank, acknowledged that he had stumbled onto the idea of corporate judo and that a systematic approach would have helped the bank more thoroughly exploit it (see Bastien et al. 1996).

Telephone interviews yielded several additional examples of corporate judo in the financial services sector. Through these contacts, we learned that it was difficult to confirm cases of judo-in-use precisely because it is an effective tactic and corporations may not wish to share it with others, especially their competitors, and especially as identifying its use may draw attention to one's firm and result in retaliation by opponents now or in the future. On the other hand, we found that judo was being practised without a thorough understanding of the full range of available opportunities and tactics. In view of this, our next step was to incorporate relevant theory, research, and practice into a systematic corporate judo framework.

Overview of the Corporate Judo Framework

We wanted to develop a corporate judo framework for two reasons: (1) to help firms exploit the competitive opportunities that opponents present when they over-restructure, and (2) to put corporate raiders, executives and investors on notice that they might suffer retaliation if they engage in harmful restructuring practices. The framework we developed includes a statement of the basic judo philosophy, a review of the opportunities presented by restructuring, a list of tactics for exploiting these opportunities, and a discussion of the power behind the approach.

The Corporate Judo Philosophy

Judo is "an art of weaponless self-defence developed in China and Japan that uses throws, holds, and blows, and derives added power from the attacker's own weight and strength." (*American Heritage Dictionary*)

This definition of the martial art called judo points to three key components of the corporate judo approach. First and foremost, judo is *a defensive reaction to moves initiated by an attacker*. Viewed in this context, all forms of restructuring—downsizings, mergers, acquisitions, takeovers, etc.—are offensive moves that aim to improve a firm's performance and, thereby, its position vis-à-vis their competitors. It is only natural that these competitors look for ways to defend their own positions: any weaknesses exposed by an attacker during a restructuring are, in the name of self-defence, fair game.

The second component is *a focus on the opportunities that lie beneath the surface of an attack*. Like a well-trained martial artist, practitioners of the art of corporate judo pay close attention to their opponent's moves, looking for signs of weakness and for opportunities to gain leverage by using the force and momentum of the attacker's own moves. In the case of a restructuring, this means that competing firms should study the situation for evidence of obvious and not-so-obvious weaknesses. For example, a restructured firm's new streamlined and consolidated order processing system may actually cause more harm than good in the short term. Savvy judo practitioners will probe to find and exploit these types of hidden opportunities.

The third component of corporate judo is *an interactive view of competition that disciplines the self and the opponent.* Like traditional judo, corporate judo relies on the ability to see actions and their consequences in a truly interactive context. The strength or weakness of one party's action depends on how the other party perceives it and responds to it. If one firm implements a merger and a competitor perceives this action in the stereotypical way, the merger will be viewed as a strength and a threat. If, in contrast, the competitor closely studies its opponent, it may find a way to see the merger as a weakness and an opportunity which allows a very different set of responses.

Through judo, we learn to carefully study an opponent's actions for hidden weaknesses and the corresponding opportunities. On another level, skill in scrutinizing opponents can help us to see how our opponents might scrutinize our own actions. In this way, judo refines our ability to think and act in a strategic manner, using a move–countermove mentality.

Judo disciplines *the self* by forcing us to consider how other parties may perceive our actions and what they may do in response. Judo disciplines *the opponent* whenever competitors are aware that we are scrutinizing their actions and are looking to take advantage of hidden weaknesses and opportunities. In a competitive context, the result is pressure to minimize the weaknesses and the opportunities that you expose to your opponents. Judo discipline thus impacts what actions you and your opponents take.

Generic Opportunities to "Judo" a Restructured Firm

Corporate judo is possible whenever an opponent disrupts its own flow of goods and services by engaging in a restructuring effort. The key for judo practitioners is to learn as much as possible about the nature and timing of this disruption and the opportunities it presents to their own firm. Two sources are especially helpful in this regard: (1) *social scientific research*, which provides generic insights into change-based disruption, and (2) *competitive intelligence*, which yields situation-specific information about the exact pattern of disruption caused by an opponent's action and the location and timing of each window of judo opportunity. In the remainder of this section we will focus on the generic insights afforded by existing social scientific research.

We adopt a generic *stakeholder "shock wave" model* that represents the cascading waves of damage which often result from a restructuring. At the core of this model is the belief that a firm and its actions should not be viewed in a vacuum; a firm and its actions should be consciously and explicitly located within the broader context of its relationships with customers, suppliers, communities, and investors. To do otherwise implies poor ethics and poor business (see Bastien 1994).

The "First Wave" of Judo Opportunities

The decision to restructure lies at the centre of the storm that it creates. *News* of an impending restructuring sends the first wave of uncertainty rippling outward through the organization to customers, suppliers, local communities, and investors. Among other things, news of a restructuring signals the end of the psychological contract of unwritten agreements between the firm and its stakeholders (see Cascio 1987, Rousseau 1995, Rousseau 1996, Rousseau and Tijoriwala 1996, and Drinkwalter in this volume). This initial stakeholder shock wave presents competitors with the first window of opportunity to profit from the damage that a restructured firm has inflicted upon itself and its stakeholders.

Rumours often provide the first news of a restructuring. News travels fast within the firm, the local business community, the industry, and the investment community. The *official announcement* of a restructuring adds momentum to the propagating stakeholder shock wave. While the announcement may reduce some areas of uncertainty—who will receive a pink slip, which facilities will close, etc.—it typically generates additional uncertainties and increased fear and anxiety (see Bastien 1987, Brockner et al. 1987, and Noer 1993). Soon-to-be-ex-employees worry about their futures. Retained employees wonder how secure their job really is. Uncertainty, fear, and anxiety detract from performance and productivity, further feeding the wave of stakeholder damage.

The mere news of a restructuring can have a great impact because it calls into question the fundamental nature of a firm's relationships with its employees, customers, suppliers, communities and investors. Employees wonder if they will still have a job and, if so, how long they can count on it before the next round of pink slips is issued. Customers wonder if they will continue to receive goods and services in the manner to which they have become accustomed, including price, quality, quantity, delivery, and service. Suppliers wonder if they will continue to be able to count on the same volume of orders and ability to pay in a timely fashion. Communities wonder if the restructuring will lead to pink slips or shutdowns, resulting in a smaller tax base, a greater strain on social services, and a damaged sense of pride in the community and its local economy. Investors may wonder if they should pay attention to the dismal track record of returns on restructuring and sell their interests, or take a gamble and hold or even buy.

The damage would be bad enough even if it were restricted to *stakeholder uncertainty*. But this is not the case. Research shows that stakeholders will divert substantial time, energy, and resources from their regular activities to reduce their uncertainty. One study found that employees spent up to 20 percent of their time seeking and discussing information that would help them to make sense of the situation (Bastien et al. 1995). Employees also spend time looking for other jobs. These activities divert precious resources away from the conduct of daily business, leading to delays, errors, etc. Turnover and absenteeism escalate, further eroding the ability of the firm to deliver its goods and services in a timely, acceptable manner. Customer dissatisfaction mounts, making customers consider a switch to an alternative vendor (Bastien 1994).

The generic "first wave" opportunities for knowledgeable competitors are clear: Pay close attention to an opponent's employees and customers when it announces a restructuring. Soliciting dissatisfied employees and customers can be a quick and easy route to new talent and an increase in profits.

The "Second Wave" of Judo Opportunities

A second stakeholder shock wave is set in motion when the opponent begins to *implement* the restructuring. Change begets additional uncertainty as remaining employees wonder if they are next in line for a pink slip. Change also means overload as employees scramble to accomplish their regular tasks and the work of departed colleagues. Valuable time and effort is also diverted to doing the "job" of implementing changes dictated by the restructuring. New tasks, procedures, and systems impose significant learning requirements, leading to further declines in performance and productivity. The result is costly for the employees and the restructured organization—increased stress, illness, absenteeism, turnover, inefficiency, and errors (see Bastien 1987, Leana and Feldman 1992, Mirvis and Marks 1992, and Noer 1993).

To make matters worse, the added work, costs, and uncertainties quickly spill over the firm's boundary, damaging relationships with customers, suppliers, and communities. Customers suffer from the uncertainty, mistakes, delays, and decreased quality that often accompany a restructuring (Bastien 1994). Dissatisfied customers mean fewer sales and greater uncertainty in demand. Suppliers become dissatisfied, in turn, when they receive smaller and less predictable orders from the restructured firm. The bottom line for communities is no different—the cascade of disrupted work and dissatisfied employees, customers, and suppliers spills over into the broader community-at-large, leading to an eroded tax base, a drain in government services, damaged civic pride, etc. (Downs 1995, Leana and Feldman 1992).

Like the first wave, the second wave provides savvy competitors with significant opportunities to gain talented employees and increased profits at the expense of a self-disrupted opponent. Unlike the first wave, the broad scope of second-wave stakeholder damage means that competitors can also take advantage of the harm that suppliers, communities, and investors have suffered at the hand of an opponent's restructuring. The same "switching" phenomenon that occurs with employees and customers may also occur with suppliers, communities, and investors. Competitors might be able to gain new suppliers and investors when they begin to profit from an opponent's restructuring effort. Furthermore, communities may be willing to shift their support from firms that are restructuring to firms that are not restructuring. As a result, competitors that demonstrate their opposition to harmful restructuring practices may receive packages that include property tax relief and incentives for new and expanded facilities.

The "Third Wave" of Judo Opportunities

The first two waves originated at the centre of it all—the decision to restructure. First came the rumour, then the announcement, then the implementation. A third wave may originate from competing firms. Competitors that exploit an opponent's self-disruption by soliciting unhappy employees and customers send another shock wave back toward the centre. Losing employees and customers to competitors means larger workloads and fewer resources which, in turn, results in further cutbacks and other cost-saving measures that damage the firm's ability to deliver quality products and services in a timely and affordable manner. This creates a "ripple effect" of waves and counter-waves fuelled by escalating causal effects that provides new opportunities for competitors (see Maruyama 1963, Masuch 1985, and Weick 1979). And so on, and so on....

Waves and Counter-waves of Stakeholder Damage

One benefit of the shock-wave model is that it can be used to track the spread of stakeholder damage across time. Knowing which stakeholders become dissatisfied at what times has obvious value for competitors who wish to take full advantage of a restructured opponent. The model can also be used to track inwardly, propagating counter-waves of stakeholder damage. This phenomenon occurs whenever a stakeholder responds to the damage they have received by returning the harm to the offending firm. The most obvious example is when employees leave to find another job at a competing firm. Another example is customers switching to a competing vendor. In either case, when stakeholders exit the field, they remove themselves from the damage and set a third wave of damage back toward the restructured firm.

In response to the loss of revenue and market share, executives in charge of the restructured firm may decide to lay additional employees off as a cost-cutting measure which, in turn, may lead to further task overload, declines in productivity, errors, decreased quality, etc. The response by executives thus initiates another outwardly propagating wave of stakeholder damage which invariably leads to increased customer dissatisfaction and which, in turn, leads to an additional loss of revenue and market share. The shock-wave model graphically demonstrates the futility of responding to damage with damage.

Firms that fail to locate themselves and their actions within the broad context of stakeholder relations will find it harder to see how damage set in motion by restructuring can come back to haunt them. The stakeholder shock-wave model can help them see these effects. As such, it is a graphic reminder of the need to locate the firm and its actions within the broad context of its consequences. Despite these benefits, competitors who wish to practise corporate judo must go beyond the shock-wave model by using competitive intelligence to fill in the details of their specific situation. By so doing, they will be able to most precisely and effectively take advantage of the damage that a restructured opponent has inflicted upon itself and its stakeholders.

The Role of Competitive Intelligence in Corporate Judo

When viewed from the perspective of corporate judo, successive waves of stakeholder damage present a restructured firm's *competitors* with opportunities to make significant gains in talent, sales, and profits, and to substantially improve its standing with suppliers, communities, and investors. The key to effective corporate judo is to augment the generic information provided by social science with situation-specific information obtained through competitive intelligence. For example, the shock-wave model identifies generic signs of weakness and probable sequences of events as the processes of self-disruption propagate throughout a restructuring firm and its web of stakeholders. Competitive intelligence is the next necessary step in order to determine exactly what is happening, and how and where and when and why, in your specific situation.

Competitive intelligence is a growing field of practice and inquiry (see Sutton 1988, Vella and McGonagle 1987). In the restructuring context, good competitive intelligence is important because it helps firms to see the complete range of available opportunities and to determine precisely how and where and when to "judo" a restructured opponent. Competitive intelligence is available from a variety of different sources, including (1) *public sources* such as government documents and articles in regional, national, and international newspapers and periodicals, and (2) *field sources* such as dissatisfied employees and customers, the sales and service representatives of the restructurer, suppliers to the restructurer, networking via professional and trade associations, and advertising agencies (see Porter 1980, Coombs and Moorhead 1992, McGonagle and Vella 1990). Good competitive intelligence helps competitors effectively target their moves to "judo" a restructured opponent.

Corporate Judo as a Response to Harmful Restructuring

Opportunities to "judo" a recently restructured opponent are real and substantial. By executing a few basic moves, Dave Knopick was able to attract enough dissatisfied employees and customers away from an opponent that he more than doubled his own bank's growth in net income, loans, and deposits (Bastein et al. 1996). The ability to make such gains by rescuing dissatisfied stakeholders from the throes of uncertainty, task overload, poor performance and error characterizes the corporate judo response to restructuring. In this section we will explore some additional benefits that occur when it becomes a tactical response and a deterrent to harmful restructuring. We begin by examining three alternatives to corporate judo.

What, Me Worry?

Alfred E. Neuman's infamous question best captures the spirit and practice of the status quo—business as usual. Despite the mountain of evidence to the contrary, executives and investors still embrace restructuring as a means to quick and easy profits (see Jones 1996, Dunlap 1996, Pickens 1988). Albert Dunlap, Robert Eaton, and others wonder what all the fuss is about; after all, they are performing a valuable service to stockholders and society by saving firms from their downfall. According to this "mad" view, we shouldn't worry when thousands lose their jobs, since *tens* of thousands of jobs were saved in the process. In a nutshell, the default response is that no response to harmful restructuring is needed, since the harm would be far greater if we disallowed or severely limited existing restructuring practices.

The main problem with the "What, me worry?" response is its assumption that the *invisible hand* of the free market is sufficient as a moral arbiter and a safeguard against unwarranted, harmful restructuring. If the market allows it to be done, it must be proper, at least according to the moral metric of capitalistic ideology as realized in the free market system. But this view mistakenly equates the *morality of actions* with *mechanisms* that allow them to occur. But allowing an action to occur does not automatically sanction it or attest to its moral status.

If the invisible hand of the free market provides no guarantee against harmful restructuring practices what, then, can we do in order to deter such practices? Cascio, Hitt, and others have suggested that we learn how to minimize damage and maximize benefits by studying the best practices of rightsizing and responsible restructuring. Hanly, Reich, and others suggest that we go beyond education by involving the government as a means of regulating against harmful restructuring practices. We have developed a third alternative that does not rely on appeals to learned self-restraint or intervention by a governmental agency: corporate judo. In the remainder of this section, we will examine the comparative strengths and weaknesses of education, government intervention and corporate judo as responses to harmful restructuring practices.

Education

Education is the heart of the rightsizing and responsible restructuring movement. According to this approach, we can discourage the harm and encourage the benefits by studying how restructuring should and should not be done. Systematic, scientific studies of best and worst cases in restructuring have begun to yield fruit in this regard (see Bruton et al. 1996, Cameron et al. 1991, Cascio 1993 and 1995, and Hitt et al. 1994). Education does have several clear benefits as a response to restructuring. It provides specific information about proper and improper restructuring practices (*prescriptions* and *proscriptions*). Education is consistent with the free market *ideology*, hence it does not suffer from the same criticisms as government intervention. Moreover, education can be an *efficient* or cost-effective response when delivered in the form of articles and books.

Despite these benefits, education suffers from two major weaknesses that prevent it from being sufficient as a "stand-alone" response to restructuring. First of all, learning how to right-size or to responsibly restructure can help us to become increasingly moral in *how we plan and execute a decision to do a restructuring*. Current education is designed to help us formulate and implement restructurings that yield minimal stakeholder damage and maximal stakeholder benefits. But it does not teach us how to determine *whether or not a restructuring is warranted in the first place*.

Education in its present form is at best a partial deterrent to harmful restructuring, a response that addresses harm that results from poor planning and execution. But even the best planned and executed restructurings may be ill-advised from the very beginning. Restructurings undertaken primarily for selfish, short-term financial gain may damage the firm beyond repair and fatally harm its ability to compete in the free market. Ironically, the education movement may actually help to keep corporate raiders and empire-builders in business. The bottom line is that while the education response is selective in discriminating between good and bad ways to plan and execute restructurings, it is *not* selective in discriminating between good and bad restructuring decisions.

A second weakness of the education response is that it overestimates the impact of rational appeals in the print medium on executive decision-making and planning. The crux of this critique is contained in one crucial question: What really motivates or *compels* executives to "do the right thing" with regard to restructuring decisions, plans, and implementations? Do rational appeals, including explicit prescriptions and proscriptions, make an appreciable impact on executive decisions and organizational practices? A valid answer to this question is not possible without looking at the historical record. For example, decades of published research on the do's and don'ts of mergers and acquisitions have failed to make a demonstrable dent in the number of M&As undertaken and the rates of success and failure (see Herman and Lowenstein 1988, Hogarty 1970, Zweig et al. 1995).

What do executives really pay attention to? Their peers, pocketbooks, stockholders, and competitors. One of the key benefits of corporate judo is that it hits executives where it counts in each of these regards. Judo is a compelling deterrent to harmful restructuring because it poses a serious threat to the gains executives have promised themselves and their stockholders. The source of this threat—competing firms directed by peer executives—carries more weight than rational appeals by academics in the print medium to "do the right thing."

In summary, education is at best a partial response to harmful restructuring. The real strengths of education lie in its ability to provide us with detailed prescriptions and proscriptions in a manner that is efficient and consistent with free market ideology. Education in its present form falls short of the mark in helping us to discriminate between good and bad restructuring decisions and in its ability to compel executives to make, plan, and execute restructuring decisions that yield minimal damage and maximal benefits across stakeholders. Table 1 summarizes these points and provides an explicit comparison of education, government intervention, and corporate judo as responses to harmful restructuring. This table summarizes the substantive points that underlie our remaining discussions of government intervention and corporate judo.

Government Intervention

While one government is currently involved in the business of writing prescriptions for responsible restructuring (Cascio 1995), the main thrust of proposed government interventions is *proscriptive* in nature. Government interventionists feel that the writing is already on the wall: to date, education and free market mechanisms have failed to make a demonstrable impact on the number of restructurings, the rate of failed restructurings, and the stakeholder fallout that often results from restructuring (Herman and Lowenstein 1988, Zweig et al. 1995). According to this view, the next logical step is to allow the government to intervene on the behalf of aggrieved stakeholders by enacting policies, rules, and regulations that curtail and, where possible, prevent the damage. US Secretary of Labor Reich, for instance, has recently broached the issue of tax incentives for firms that restructure in a responsible manner.[18]

The problem is that the weaknesses of this approach are substantial and that some of its alleged strengths are more apparent than real.

Table 1

A Comparison of Three Responses to Harmful Restructuring

RESPONSE	PROPONENTS	Six Generic Criteria for Comparing Responses to Restructuring					
		Prescriptive?	Proscriptive?	Selective?	Efficient?	Free Market Ideology?	Compelling?
Education	Cascio (1995) Hitt et al. (1994)	Yes	Yes	Yes & No	Yes	Yes	No
Government Intervention	Hanly (1992) Reich (1996)	Yes	Yes	No	No	No	No
Corporate Judo	Bastien, Hostager and Miles (1996)	No	Yes	Yes	Yes	Yes	Yes

Government intervention is notoriously inefficient and costly. Policing corporate behaviour and enforcing new laws requires additional time, effort, personnel, and resources, all of which are scarce commodities in an era of budget cutbacks and retrenchment. A more pressing issue underlies the concern for cost and efficiency, however: government intervention is not the most compelling way to change the decisions and actions of executives in corporate America. The response by private industry to new rules and regulations has often been one of grudging acceptance with "behind-the-scenes" activity to find ways to minimize the costs associated with compliance.

On a deeper level, however, government intervention suffers from the fact that it runs counter to the free market ideology that undergirds so many of our decisions and actions. Government interventionists mistakenly assume that we have identified and exhausted all viable free market responses to restructuring. To be sure, the track record shows that *corporate raiding* is not a terribly effective and selective means of disciplining executive decisions, plans, and actions. Recent case evidence, however, suggests that corporate judo is a viable free market response to harmful restructuring driven by selfish gain at the expense of employees, customers, and other stakeholders (Bastien et al. 1996).

Corporate Judo

Dave Knopick and others have stumbled onto a sorely needed check-and-balance against harmful restructuring. Corporate judo is entirely consistent with the ideology of the free market and the competitive premise that only the fittest will survive. For example, if corporate raiders are indeed sincere in the claim that they serve a necessary purpose by culling the weak from the herd and trimming the fat down to lean and mean competitive muscle, why not give the raiders (and the empire-builders, for that matter) a dose of their own medicine? Why not through corporate judo, to use the damage they have unleashed through their self-interested restructuring efforts against them? All the regulations and rational appeals in the world will not stop a smart, self-interested executive who is acting in the professed interest of stockholders.

A key challenge, then, is to find a way to motivate executives to make restructuring decisions and plans that reflect the best interests of *all* stakeholders, including employees, customers, suppliers, communities, and investors. Corporate judo does this in a compelling and convincing manner. Judo is not an abstract rational appeal by academics in an educational mode. Judo is not a series of government sanctions on corporate behaviour. Judo is something much more immediate and forceful—it is a real, emerging free market phenomenon that poses a direct threat to the profits that self-interested raiders, empire-builders, executives, and investors have come to expect when they do a restructuring. What better incentive to "do the right thing" than knowing that peer executives can direct their own firms to "rescue" your dissatisfied employees and customers if you open windows of opportunity by doing an ill-advised or ill-planned restructuring?

Although judo may sound like raiding—and both *are* forms of market discipline on corporate behaviour—judo is in fact the polar opposite. Unlike corporate raiding, which derives its power from the *value* that a firm has accumulated over the years, corporate judo derives its power from the *destruction of value* that often results from restructuring (see Campbell et al. 1995, M.E. Porter 1987).

Judo thrives in direct proportion to the amount of damage and disruption that an opponent unleashes upon itself and its stakeholders. Higher levels of stakeholder damage (uncertainty, dissatisfaction, etc.) mean more opportunities for knowledgable competitors to "judo" the restructured opponent. Moving in the other direction, the power of judo diminishes in direct proportion to decreases in stakeholder damage. Indeed, a key advantage of corporate judo is that the amount of stakeholder damage places a natural upper limit on the force of the judo response; corporate judo is the only free market response that punishes a harmful restructuring in direct proportion to the harm it unleashes.

More importantly, however, a damage-based approach like judo enables us to avoid the thorny, complex, time-consuming and often impossible matters of (1) trying to discern the real intentions behind a restructuring and (2) trying to predict the eventual success or failure of a current restructuring effort. Competitors, educators, researchers, consultants, and government employees could expend significant amounts of time, effort, and resources attempting to determine the real intentions—good or bad—behind a restructuring. They could do the same for outcomes, as well, trying to determine whether or not the restructuring will ultimately succeed or fail.

Corporate judo provides us with a far more efficient and tractable alternative: focus on the damage and forget about intentions and possible outcomes. If the intentions behind a restructuring are indeed good, then executives need to carry through on these intentions by ensuring that the restructuring is properly planned and implemented, with minimal damage to stakeholders. Knowing that competitors can dash one's good intentions is a compelling incentive to take the proper steps to ensure that the firm is heading into the change with more than just good intentions. To do otherwise is not only objectionable on moral grounds—unnecessary harm incurred by employees, customers, and other stakeholders—it is equally objectionable on economic grounds as bad business. What the firm needs is good intentions *and* a thorough plan based on input from all stakeholders.

While we would like to know the outcome of a restructuring in advance, this is neither practically nor theoretically possible in most cases. At best, we can use the existing literatures to make educated guesses as to which restructurings are more and less likely to succeed. Corporate judo suggests that we instead devote our time and energies to take advantage of the damage that results from restructuring, the corporate equivalent of *punishing behaviour instead of trying to ascribe intentionality and read minds.* We prefer to work with what is observable and actionable. Indeed, research has shown that "good postmerger integration rarely makes a really bad deal work, but bad execution almost always wrecks one that might have had a shot" (Zweig et al. 1995, 124). Corporate judo is a powerful incentive for executives to do a good job in choosing, planning, and executing restructurings. To do otherwise is to ruin your shot at success and increase your chances of getting "nailed" by a savvy competitor who will be only too happy to come in and "rescue" your dissatisfied employees and customers.

But no approach is without its limitations. The primary weakness of corporate judo lies in the area of prescriptions and proscriptions for *restructurers*—it does not, and does not intend to furnish explicit, systematic advice on the do's and don'ts of restructuring. Restructurers can, however, still glean some valuable advice regarding the types of damage that they should avoid at what times. The stakeholder shock-wave model may, for example, help restructurers to plan and implement change in a way that yields minimal stakeholder damage.

Conclusion

Corporate judo is a newly emerging free market phenomenon that has several important advantages over education and government intervention as a response to harmful restructuring. Corporate judo is an efficient, selective, and proportionate response, and it offers a compelling incentive to executives to (1) seriously consider whether a restructuring is really warranted, once the potential for damage has been fully explored and (2) plan and implement the restructuring in a responsible manner, with minimal stakeholder damage. We look forward to a day in which the *practice* of corporate judo becomes obsolete while the *idea* of corporate judo remains in force as a deterrent to harmful restructuring—a day in which all restructuring is done for the right reasons and with minimum damage and maximum benefits to stakeholders. Until that day, we must continue to spread the word about judo. This means, of course, that a marriage of corporate judo and education responses could be mutually beneficial.

We envision a series of seminars, workshops, books, and videos aimed at promoting the idea and practice of corporate judo. Indeed, the inaugural corporate judo workshop has already been held at the University of Wisconsin–Eau Claire. Partnerships with government are not out of the question. Government-sponsored town meetings, consortiums, seminars, workshops, pamphlets, books, etc., may also help to educate the general public. The growing number of corporate judo cases suggests that this is an idea whose time has come. Our job is to describe the phenomenon, develop it as a usable practice, and spread the word.

PART IV
Methods of Restructuring

Wayne Cascio's article has already made the important point that we can distinguish between different kinds of restructuring and their ethical implications. One might extend this basic insight to an account of different methods of restructuring, for they raise different ethical issues. Even in cases where this is not the case, a close look at a particular form of restructuring can shed a great deal of light on the issues raised by restructuring in general. In view of such considerations, the four articles in this section discuss four different forms of restructuring: cause-related marketing (CRM), amalgamation (merger), regionalization, and employee ownership.

Cause-related marketing means the corporate sponsorship of not-for-profit organizations in return for marketing rights and privileges. It provides an important new avenue for the funding of such organizations at a time when public funds are increasingly difficult to obtain. But it creates many important ethical issues in conjunction with the opportunities it provides; they are discussed by Peggy Cunningham and Pamela Cushing in the first article in this section. In the article that follows, Leo Groarke investigates the ethical issues that are raised by amalgamation (merger) when it is adopted as a restructuring strategy. He reviews the benefits and the pitfalls of amalgamation with special reference to the controversy that surrounded the amalgamation of the six municipalities that now make up metropolitan Toronto. He argues that one of the prime issues raised by restructuring and especially amalgamation is conflict of interest, and that a professional obligation to avoid conflicts of interest implies that large-scale restructuring decisions should not be made by the normal decision makers in restructuring institutions.

Michael Yeo, John R. Williams, and Wayne Hooper examine the ethical issues raised by regionalization in health care and social services. The basis of their analysis is a detailed study of the formation of the Queens Region Board in Prince Edward Island which highlights the way in which ethical values may properly inform the kinds of decisions which the process of regionalization requires—decisions which often raise ethical issues which are not raised (or at least not raised so clearly) by the structure of social services before regionalization.

In the last article included in this section, Vincent Di Norcia examines the ethical issues which are raised by corporate restructuring. Like Cascio, he argues that there are ways to restructure which are ethically preferable. In particular, he advocates employee ownership as a form of corporate ownership that can better address the pressures that create the need for restructuring and the ethical challenges it presents.

7

Cause-Related Marketing: A Restructuring Alternative?

Peggy Cunningham and Pamela J. Cushing

The superintendent of a medium-sized school board located in eastern Ontario is trying to balance the budget for the upcoming school year in the face of a 30 percent reduction in government funding. As the trade-offs about cutting staff, programs, or maintenance race through her head, a fax arrives from a local sporting goods chain outlining a proposal to help the school board out of its dilemma. In return for every pair of shoes, item of warm-up clothing, and T-shirt bought by students or faculty during the period September through December, the retailer promises to donate 2 percent of the purchase price of the goods as well as a lump sum payment of five thousand dollars. The board can allocate these funds to the athletic programs of their choice. In return for this sponsorship, the retailer wants to place advertisements in locker rooms of every school in the district, and to be endorsed as the "board approved" supplier of athletic equipment. Given the pressing fiscal circumstances the Board is facing, the superintendent wonders if she should accept this offer.

As government restructuring makes public funding more difficult to obtain, many not-for-profit organizations are considering partnerships like the fictional one outlined above. While these partnerships present an alternative avenue to generate much-needed funds, they can also be described as an ethical minefield. Since such partnerships are a relatively new phenomenon, neither business nor their non-profit partners have much experience in developing or managing these associations. When partnerships are formed on an ad hoc basis, managers give little consideration to potential pitfalls and the fiscal pressures caused by restructuring may lead to ethical compromises. The drive for survival can result in the misguided thinking that the ends justify the means.

There are other concerns. Only popular programs or attractive causes may attract corporate funding, and the stakeholders of both the non-
profit and the corporation may view these associations as inappropriate.
Many educators and parents, for example, don't think business has any
place in the school, and some corporate shareholders don't think supporting causes is an appropriate use of business funds. Even in the best-
case scenario, these alliances bring together partners with distinctly different goals and agendas. The goals of the more powerful partner may
be stressed to the detriment of those of the weaker member of the
alliance, and the partners may have totally different perspectives on
what constitutes ethical behaviour or what contributes to social welfare.

The ethical issues associated with the fictional case described at the
outset may represent only the tip of the iceberg. This paper is written,
therefore, with two purposes in mind. The first is to explore the ethical
questions associated with business and not-for-profit partnerships
brought about by restructuring. The second is to present information that
will help non-profit organizations understand the nature of corporate
sponsorship so that many of the potential ethical pitfalls can be avoided.

As a result of competitive and economic pressures, corporations
themselves are restructuring and looking for concrete returns from their
donations. Many can no longer regard their sponsorships as pure philanthropy; they are increasingly treating donations as an investment. In other
words, "no strings attached" support is often a thing of the past and considerable corporate funding for non-profits is funnelled through the firm's
marketing department. Businesses align themselves with not-for-profit
organizations in order to break through the clutter of traditional advertising, to enhance their ability to reach specific audiences, and to attempt
to add distinctiveness and value to their offerings. The result is a practice labelled *cause-related marketing* (CRM), a form of marketing relationship that involves the affiliation of corporate "for-profit" marketing
activities with the fund-raising requirements of "not-for-profit" organizations, a process which involves the co-alignment of marketing strategy
and corporate philanthropy (Varadarajan and Menon 1988).

Examples of CRM are common in the area of health care and medical research. The Juvenile Diabetes Foundation of Canada's association
with Bell Mobility's charity golf tournament, the Celebrity Classic, is one
example. Both partners benefit, since the Diabetes Foundation received
$240,000 in additional funding over a three-year period while Bell
Mobility enhanced its ability to target potential cellular telephone users,
a large number of whom are golfers. Another corporation which uses

CRM is Avon. It enlists its extensive network of sales representatives to sell pins for breast cancer research in conjunction with its traditional product line. To date, the program has raised twenty-five million dollars for breast cancer research. A third example is Molson Breweries, which has an ongoing program which donates a percentage of its sales of designated brands during specific time periods to support AIDS research. Four million dollars have been raised to date.

Outside the health sector, educators are also beginning to see the benefits of CRM. The Toronto Board of Education recently entered into a partnership with Pepsi. The firm promised to donate $1.14 million in return for exclusive distributorship rights in Toronto schools. At the University of British Columbia, "Coke is it," and benefits from the partnership are expected to generate annual returns of one hundred thousand dollars per year for the university. Such associations may also generate benefits beyond dollar support. In the United States, the KFC Corporation works with high school students, allowing them to run their own Kentucky Fried Chicken restaurant to enhance their classroom studies in the fields of management, marketing and entrepreneurship. The information services division of Westinghouse provides Burlington, Ontario, students with work experience and awards an annual Co-op Student of the Year award (Pollock 1995). Corporations have also sponsored the creation of P.E. TV, which is aired weekly to enhance the teaching of Physical Education. Although the twelve-minute videos are commercial free, corporate logos for companies such as Reebok appear at the beginning of the programming.

While such evidence indicates that many of these associations are undeniably beneficial, they are also often fraught with controversy. There is no question that CRM is ripe for ethical examination. Sometimes it is argued that such practices undermine traditional philanthropy, that partnerships with business exploit causes and their constituents, that CRM programs turn the needy into commodities, and that they subvert charitable missions of not-for-profit organizations for commercial purposes (see Cunningham forthcoming). In spite of such concerns, little has been done to systematically explore the ethical issues inherent in CRM or to develop ethical standards that can be used to explore, assess, and understand these concerns.

The Evolution of Cause-Related Marketing

The name "cause-related marketing" was coined in 1983, when American Express copyrighted the term in connection with its Statue of Liberty restoration campaign. The first academic study of the concept, Varadarajan and Menon's *Journal of Marketing* paper, was published in 1988.

CRM can be understood as a response to the era of change which has accompanied the restructuring of corporations, institutions, and governments. It reflects a change in the paradigms of not-for-profit organizations, consumers, and corporate managers. Instead of relying on traditional funding sources (personal and corporate philanthropy, and government grants), not-for-profit organizations have adopted and adapted many of the marketing techniques that were once the sole domain of for-profit organizations. Corporations have a heightened awareness that consumers are increasingly considering issues of corporate social responsibility when making purchase decisions. In an era of mature, highly competitive, homogeneous product-markets, business managers are finding it increasingly difficult to differentiate their products and develop sustainable sources of competitive advantage. They are turning to affiliations with not-for-profits to demonstrate their social concerns while leveraging their marketing platforms.

These tandem forces have fostered the formation of strategic, mutually beneficial alignments between corporations and social causes. Marketing practitioners believe that these alignments have many benefits. Among other things, they have led to pioneering advantages, have driven sales, have broken through the clutter of fragmented media, have added value to their products and services, have improved corporate image among a variety of constituents, have increased corporate and product visibility, have motivated employees, and have made tax savings possible. Directors of non-profits see these associations as equally advantageous because they provide a means of expanding the funding base, increasing cash flow and donations, better serving clientele, and acquiring marketing expertise and fiscal management skills. Sponsorships also present an opportunity to speak to a wider audience, which includes people working within the sponsoring corporation.

Barnes (1991) surveyed executives of marketing departments and charities and found 83 percent of business people and 86 percent of the non-profit managers felt both partners benefited from the use of CRM, and that 90 percent of the respondents believed that it was profitable. The increasing importance of CRM is reflected in its phenomenal growth. One billion dollars was allocated to CRM programs in 1993 alone, an increase of 24 percent over 1992 expenditures (Smith and Stodghill 1994). Despite this growth, there remains little empirical research on the topic.

Clarifying the Domain

Since many of the ethical criticisms lobbed at CRM have resulted from a faulty understanding of the goals and the definition of the practice, it is essential to understand how CRM differs from both philanthropy and social marketing. Many writers have used terms such as "strategic philanthropy," "strategic giving," "mission marketing," "social marketing," and "cause-related marketing" interchangeably (Duncan 1995, Smith 1994). But CRM should *not* be confused with philanthropy since the programs are not altruistic in nature. A specific return is expected from a CRM program. In contrast, a donation or philanthropic gift is given without an expectation of return. While the for-profit partner in a CRM relationship may have the intention of doing good while pursuing profit, the primary purpose for undertaking a CRM campaign is the accomplishment of business objectives. Johnson & Johnson's Shelter Aid program was, for example, designed to promote its Personal Products division. While the cause campaign undeniably addressed an important social issue, its primary purpose was promotion that would increase product sales.

Similarly, CRM should *not* be confused with social marketing, since the primary purpose of the two types of marketing is distinctly different. The primary purpose of a social marketing campaign is an increase in social welfare arising from a change in attitudes, beliefs, or behaviour, as in campaigns to encourage people to quit smoking or practise safe sex (Andreasen 1994). The primary purpose of CRM, by contrast, is the achievement of some economic benefit for the sponsoring firm (e.g., positioning a product or driving sales). Inducing social change is an important, but secondary purpose of these programs. The following definition makes the marketing objectives associated with CRM clear:

> Cause-related marketing is the process of formulating and implementing marketing activities that are characterized by an offer from the firm to contribute a specified amount to a designated cause when customers engage in revenue-providing exchanges that satisfy organizational and individual objectives. (Varadarajan and Menon 1988, 60)

CRM programs can be either strategic or tactical. Strategic efforts are those that are tied into the accomplishment of the long-term objectives and positioning strategy of the non-profit and its corporate partner. An example is the Body Shop's Cultural Survival program. The Body Shop uses the social cause as a focal point in positioning certain products in the minds of their target consumers. Tactical programs are shorter in duration and often have the objective of driving short-term product sales. Many CRM programs that promise to make donations based on the number of coupons redeemed during a specific period are representative of these tactical programs.

While some CRM associations have resulted in significant benefits for all parties, others have failed. Research in the business-to-*business* alliance field indicates that 60 percent of these ventures fail. While almost no research exists which examines business and *not-for-profit* alliances, failure rates may be even higher in profit/non-profit alliances given that the goals, cultures, management styles, and operating domains of for-profit and not-for-profit partners are even less alike.

Many industry practitioners describe the relationships between business and not-for-profit organizations in terms of a love affair. While some move from infatuation to courtship to devotion and marriage, others flounder. Infatuation may turn into disrespect, the partners may cheat on each other, and promiscuity rather than monogamy may reign. While the dissolution of these relationships may be the result of multiple factors, a failure to consider the perspectives of the numerous stakeholder groups involved in any CRM program, and a parallel failure to consider the ethical issues associated with these partnerships can contribute to acrimony and "divorce."

Ethics in Relationship Marketing: An Essential Ingredient for CRM Success

The joining of a business with a not-for-profit to form an alliance implies that both parties will benefit from the partnership. *Alliances* are defined in Merrian-Webster's Collegiate Dictionary, tenth ed. as, "Association[s] to further the common interests of the members." This definition speaks of three critical aspects of the coming together of a business organization with a not-for-profit entity: the presence of at least one mutual goal, the ability of each partner to contribute something of value to the association, and the creation of mutual benefits. While the partners may have certain distinct objectives, they must share some common ground and co-operatively work toward achieving a common purpose and a win–win outcome for both partners. Table 1 illustrates the mutual benefits that can be associated with a CRM program.

The second criterion, that each partner must bring something of value into the association, is often overlooked by the non-profit partner. Rather than approaching prospective partners "hat in hand," non-profits

Table 1
Benefits of Cause-Related Marketing Programs

Firm	Non-Profit
• Increases sales and profits • Differentiates itself from competitors • Improves its image, visibility, and reputation • Learns about key issues associated with an important social issue, and how to energize employees • Increases the power of its advertising • Enhances employee motivation	• Expands funding base • Enhances its credibility and reputation • Increases its visibility • Learns new skills (marketing, information processing and data base management) • Provides access to new audiences • Generates favourable publicity • Enhances ability to accomplish mission

have many assets that they can contribute. The first is their ability to attract a specific audience. Causes attract specific target audiences by their very nature. In other words, they are relevant to narrow, well-defined groups. Second, non-profit managers understand the complexities of the social issue and can educate their business partner on these issues. They know the other organizations working to resolve the issue and they can provide a bridge to these organizations. Finally, non-profits have considerable experience working with volunteer workers. Learning how to motivate people without having to compensate them is an asset many corporations highly value.

An examination of the definitions of CRM and alliances also helps ascertain whether CRM meets, or can meet, with standards of ethical behaviour. Such an examination requires both a deontological and a teleological perspective (Hunt and Vitell 1991). Deontology is a principle-based approach to morality which focuses on the intentions associated with a particular behaviour (Ferrell and Fraedrich 1991); the word is derived from the Greek for obligation or duty. On this view, individuals or organizations ought to perform right actions, not because they produce good results, but because it is their moral duty to do so—because it is their duty to practise care, justice, non-exploitation, and so on. Deontology is an especially important benchmark, since its focus is on relationships and the obligations borne by the parties within the association. The second perspective, teleology, is named from the Greek word "telos" meaning goal or end. This approach to morality suggests that all actions must be judged exclusively by their consequences or outcomes.

An act is considered morally right if it produces a desirable result—for example, the maximization of social welfare while minimizing harm to any party or constituency.

Combining the two perspectives derived from moral philosophy, we can define *ethical CRM partnerships* as those in which the partners enter the association with the *intention* of creating *beneficial outcomes* that are *greater* than those that could be achieved by either party operating independently, while being cognizant of the duties of care, justice, non-exploitation, and benefice.

At the centre of any CRM is the relationship between a for-profit firm and a non-profit entity. The relationship marketing literature suggests that one factor is essential to successful relationships or alliances: trust (Morgan and Hunt 1994). It depends on the presence of shared values, and the absence of opportunistic behaviour (i.e., the absence of self-interest–seeking behaviour accompanied by guile). From these central variables flow other relationship-enhancing characteristics: communication, defined as constructive dialogue and timely information exchange; mutual commitment, in that the relationship is seen as important enough that maximum effort will be exerted to maintain it; cooperation to achieve goals; and the overcoming of conflicts in a constructive, relationship-strengthening manner. When these factors characterize a relationship, they work to counterbalance other adverse factors that tend to undermine the relationship—for example, conflict and competitive pressures (Bucklin and Sengupta 1993).

Trust cannot be fostered without ethical behaviour on the part of both partners in the relationship. The importance of ethics and integrity in marketing relationships is noted by Moorman, Deshpandé, and Zaltman, who state that, "perceived integrity is an...unwillingness to sacrifice ethical standards to achieve individual or organizational objectives" (1993, 84). In the case of business/not-for-profit alliances, ethics and trust are especially important given the relative power of the two parties involved often differs enormously. Many CRM programs involve the association of a David and Goliath. The not-for-profit often has fewer resources, a smaller constituency, and less direct access to regulators or the press than its behemoth business partner. It is not surprising that fears of exploitation of causes by businesses run rampant. However, the not-for-profit is not the only party in a vulnerable position. The corporation must share its strategic plans with its not-for-profit partner if they are to work together. If the association with a cause fails, the corporation's reputation and image may be tarnished, and it may lose credibility in the eyes of a key audience. Without ethical behaviour, trust, and integrity, the mutual vulnerability of the partners cannot be managed successfully.

Ethical Issues Throughout the Relationship Life Cycle

As the "love affair" metaphor used earlier in this paper suggests, relationships progress through stages. The building of trust and commitment evolves over time. Trust can be fostered and many ethical issues avoided if each stage of the relationship is managed wisely and ethically. It is proposed that for-profit–not-for-profit relationships evolve through four stages: initiation, negotiation, implementation, and redesign/termination. Distinct ethical issues may arise at each of these four stages. Table 2 outlines the key steps in partnership formation and the ethical issues common to these stages.

I. Initiation—Envisioning the Possibilities

The initiation of a relationship must be approached judiciously so that ethical criticisms can be avoided or better understood. Relationships between business and non-profits can be triggered by either party. While corporations are frequently approached by charities seeking funding, corporate sponsors may also seek out a not-for-profit ally. Before any relationship is initiated, both parties should clearly articulate their mission, goals, and the benefits or positive consequences that can arise from the partnership. Regardless of which organization initiates the discussion, both parties need to be aware of the potential at this stage for glossing over true intentions, needs, and organizational objectives. Neither party should "massage" their data or downplay their motives for entering into the alliance. Open and honest communication is essential in order to establish the trust demonstrated to be critical to joint venture success.

While it is unquestionable that the two parties will have different primary goals, it is imperative that they share some common ground: that of furthering or improving social welfare. The clarification of goals will forestall the criticism that charitable organizations are changing their objectives or their mandate to meet the needs of sponsoring corporations (Gurin 1987).

The outcome arising from the relationship should be greater than that which could have been accomplished by either party alone. When both parties add value to the association and create a whole greater than the two independent parts, the synergy will forestall many criticisms—for

Table 2
Key Tasks in CRM Development and Ethical Issue Mitigation

Stage	Key Tasks	Actions to Mitigate Ethical Concerns
Initiation	• establish mission and objectives for partnership • establish selection criteria for partner	• establish how partnership will facilitate achievement of objectives • clarify values and ethical principles to guide association • consult with all stakeholders
Negotiation	• establish terms of agreement including total resources committed, allocation of resources, and time frame of program • clarify value each partner brings to alliance • stipulate outcomes, accountability, and measurement criteria	• avoid jargon; stress clear, open and honest communication • establish rules of association: willingness to learn from each other; mutual respect • assure stakeholder buy-in
Implementation	• assign management team and commit resources • monitor progress and take timely remedial action • share decision-making authority and discuss conflicts in a non-adversarial fashion	• assign competent and committed managers • avoid conflicts of interest • fulfil promises • use referent and legitimate power versus coercive power
Revision	• evaluate outcomes from perspective of both partners • assess appropriateness of measures • provide feedback • negotiate revisions • provide maximum lead time if partnership is to be terminated	• be sure that measures of success are not distorting mission and objectives • facilitate open and honest feedback from partners and constituents • revise to enhance effectiveness

example, the suggestions that the not for-profit has sold its soul to business, or that the corporate sponsor is manipulating or exploiting the cause.

No matter which party makes the first move, both should do their homework and learn about each other. Potential business sponsors must understand what the non-profit is trying to accomplish and what social institutions are working to resolve the social issue. Critics of CRM often accuse corporations of meddling in issues they don't understand. Both potential partners should think carefully about criteria for selecting a suitable partner in order to avoid ethical problems. Corporate sponsors are particularly interested in not-for-profits whose stakeholders match the target market for the firm's products or whose cause draws attention from their target group, and those that can be leveraged on a national or international basis.

Since the proposed association involves a transfer of symbols and attitudes, caution should be used. Much attention has been paid to the image benefits business firms accrue from being associated with "good" causes. Far less concern has been paid to the contention that corporate symbols are also transferred to the non-profit. While the non-profit can benefit from increased legitimacy and credibility as a result of being associated with a major corporation, it can also be branded by the transfer of less savoury images. One frequently heard criticism is that causes accept funding from "undesirable" sources (from "sin" industries such as tobacco and spirit companies, for example, or from chemical companies with poor environmental records, or import firms with questionable employment practices—see Gurin 1987). The screening of potential sponsors can be facilitated by a service like EthicScan, which ranks firms by industry according to their performance on a wide variety of ethical criteria.

Before a marriage is conceived, non-profits must consult their stakeholders and beneficiaries to ensure that they view the union in a positive light. Non-profits should not see their constituents as a means to an end. If they do, they may be accused of acting in a paternalistic manner and deciding what is "good" for their constituents, or they may be accused of exploiting their constituents (Gurin 1987). The non-profit must not fall into the ethical trap of thinking that the ends justify the means. The author heard one non-profit manager justify a union with an ethically questionable corporate sponsor with the statement, "as long as we get the money...."

One of the most widely accepted models of ethical decision making in marketing (Hunt and Vitell 1991) stresses the importance of considering the consequences for different stakeholders when making decisions with ethical implications. This requires that one judge the probability of these consequences occurring and the relative importance of the stakeholders groups. Since alliances between for-profits and non-profits involve so many stakeholders, this can be an extremely demanding task. Consider one case mentioned earlier: the Pepsi sponsorship of the Toronto Board of Education. Stakeholders include board members, teachers, school administrators, students, parents, other school boards competing for sponsorship funds, corporate marketing and donations staff, corporate customers and suppliers, the corporation's competitors, reporters and media representatives, government regulators, and community members as well as social critics. Understanding and ordering the interests of stakeholders will help avoid future ethical conflicts as well as the temptation to exploit stakeholders.

Other accusations of exploitation and invasion of privacy have occurred when not-for-profits make their membership lists available to businesses for direct marketing campaigns without the permission of these constituents. CRM programs are inherently controversial. With an increasingly vigilant press and certain members of the public convinced for-profit/not-for-profit associations are inherently unethical, managers planning CRM campaigns must be prepared to defend their decision to enter into such a partnership. The Arthritis Foundation, for example, believes that it was advance planning in this regard that prevented ethical criticisms of their program from escalating into a public-relations nightmare. They aligned themselves with a manufacturer of a generic pain reliever. By clearly establishing how the partnership better enabled them to accomplish their mission through the ability to put information about arthritis in the packages of the product, they could demonstrate the benefits of the program were greater than what the foundation could have achieved on its own.

2. Negotiation—Writing the Rules

During the negotiation stage, the partners work out the terms of their relationship. Since partners are often from different worlds, a lack of a common language can lead to misunderstandings. Both partners must be learning organizations that take the time to understand the mandate of their partner while striving to communicate in terms the other can understand so that intentions are clear and obligations understood. Such understandings prevent later accusations that promises were broken or misleading.

This is a stage in which it is crucial that partners avoid opportunism. Those who reject CRM have noted opportunistic practices by both parties to the relationship. Causes have been accused of misrepresenting themselves to businesses by, for example, over-stating their ability to solve a social problem or the size of a target audience they can involve with a firm's products. Business firms have been damned for promising support that never materializes, and for unfairly limiting the size of the donation or the time frame over which the cause campaign runs.

Clearly articulating who is and is not a part of the relationship is also important if partners are to avoid ethical infractions on both sides. Establishing who will act as the prime sponsor and their level of commitment versus those who will play secondary roles can be difficult. Corporations usually demand that competitors be excluded from any particular campaign. This often causes concerns on the part of non-profits, since it may limit the donation base or sponsorship for the non-profit, giving rise to the criticism that social welfare is being compromised. Causes must be careful to abide by the intent of the partnership agreement and avoid behaviour which might not violate specific rules when approaching a partner's competitors. Arranging sponsorship with a competitor for a similar sponsorship drive, especially one aimed at the same target audience, is ethically questionable.

The responsibilities of each party must be carefully articulated. Fulfilling duties and responsibilities lie at the heart of ethical partnerships. When negotiating responsibilities, both parties must be aware of how they use their individual power and the types of power they use to resolve conflicts. Power imbalances enhance the potential for conflict, and the potential that the powerful partner will exploit the weaker member. To diminish this dependency, the weaker partner may attempt to enter additional agreements with the partner's competitors as an offsetting measure, in the process diminishing the position of the partner in the eyes of its constituents, and failing to employ all the resources promised in the sponsorship agreement (Bucklin and Sengupta 1993). Many of these actions can lead to charges of unethical behaviour. To overcome these problems, each partner must treat the other with respect and value the inherent worth of their partner's organization. While the use of referent power may be an ethical means of resolving conflict (e.g., "my expertise in this area gives me more say in resolution of this issue"), the use of coercion should be frowned upon (i.e., "I will withdraw my support unless...").

3. Implementation—Walking the Talk

The implementation of the relationship strategy is critical to the future success of a partnership. Implementation means translating plans into actions. From an ethical point of view, the process of achieving the ends is just as important as the ends themselves. The ability to successfully implement a strategy often depends on (1) the ability of the managers assigned to managing the project from both the sponsoring corporation and from the non-profit, and (2) the resources devoted to making the relationship a success. When either partner fails to assign adequate management talent or resources to the project, the result is often accusations that one party has failed to pull its load or has broken its promises (Bucklin and Sengupta 1993). Conflict can also arise because control of the project must be shared between the two partners. The question of who controls a particular stage is, therefore, of paramount importance. The ability to share control and meld the core competencies of both parties at this stage can help avoid ethical pitfalls. For example, while the corporation may be the expert in terms of marketing and cost control, the non-profit may better understand how to deliver a concrete benefit to the needy or how to bring about the solution of a social problem.

The marketing-mix elements (product, promotion, price and distribution) used to bring the sponsorship to life often prove to be a minefield. The type of product that must be purchased in order to initiate a donation to the cause has raised ethical questions. The promise to support a cause if a consumer visits a specific distribution location where they are exposed to a high pressure sales pitch raises similar concerns. The price the consumer must pay for a cause-associated good should not be above that of competitive offerings or accusations of exploitation will be the result.

Questions of how advertising materials are used to promote the relationship are particularly troublesome. Stereotyping the needy or dehumanizing them in any way raises legitimate criticism. Using advertising "hype" that suggests simplistic solutions to complex social issues also raises ethical concerns. Promises such as "for one dollar you can end world hunger" are highly misleading and objectionable. Avoiding misleading claims about the benefit of the cause association is also of critical importance. CRM campaigns which disguise the fact that there is a ceiling to the amount the corporation will donate, or the time period over which the program will run, have been condemned. Finally, corporations must be careful to balance the resources they devote to promoting the cause association with the amount that is actually provided to support the cause (Gurin 1987).

4. Revision/Termination—Reality Check

No matter how carefully a relationship is initiated and designed, feedback from constituents of both partners will result in demands for revision and redesign of the partnership. The same care used to develop the original goals for the partnership must be exercised when they are modified. While a willingness to be flexible and adaptable to the needs of the other partner is important in any long-term association, the founding mission of the association must not be forgotten. As partnerships evolve, the focus may, however, shift to maintenance issues rather than highlighting the original mission of the relationship.

Knowing when to end an association may prove to be one of the thorniest issues of all. As conditions in the environment of both the non-profit and the corporation continue to evolve, one or both partners may desire to withdraw from the association. If one party has become overly dependent on the other for support, ethical concerns about abandonment may be raised. It is important, therefore, to give ample notice when a party has decided to end a relationship. Having agreed upon points at which to reevaluate the partnership and make continue/drop decisions helps both parties understand that the relationship is always subject to revision.

Conclusion

Cause-related marketing campaigns can be highly successful and effective forms of marketing for both non-profit and for-profit organizations. In times characterized by the economic realities of restructuring and the new economy and the limited funds they make available for not-for-profit goals, they provide a much-needed alternative source of revenue for many worthy causes. This being said, CRM must be approached with caution, for we have seen that it raises a myriad of ethical issues that must be dealt with carefully. This caution being noted, an understanding of the ethical issues that are embedded in these associations can help to bring about the trust, cooperation, and commitment that make such partnerships work.

8

Realism, Restructuring, and Amalgamation: What Can We Learn from the Mega-mess in Toronto?

Leo Groarke

One of the most popular forms of restructuring is amalgamation (or "merger"). It joins two organizations or institutions in an effort to create new efficiencies and strengths. In practice it often has disastrous consequences which stem from the bitter internal conflict that may arise as those in the affected institutions struggle to ensure that their interests are protected in the major structural changes that inevitably ensue. In this paper I want to address three questions in this context: (1) What are the obligations of decision makers in the context of restructuring? (2) What concerns do these obligations raise in the context of amalgamation? and (3) What kind of theoretical perspective can help us better understand restructuring, and amalgamation in particular?

In attempting to answer these three questions I shall frequently discuss the Ontario government's amalgamation of the six municipalities that make up Metropolitan Toronto—an amalgamation which was the subject of intense media coverage and heated political debate. Though I offer some conclusions about the Toronto case, and criticize some of the actions taken by both municipal leaders (who opposed amalgamation) and the provincial government (which directed it), the Toronto case is not my principal concern. It serves only as an illustration which can, I hope, help me elaborate one way of understanding both the dynamics of restructuring and the ethical responsibilities that it imposes on those who run restructuring institutions, especially in the context of amalgamation.

Note to this chapter is on p. 304.

Throughout my discussion I will adopt a "realist" theoretical per-spective. It is founded on the conviction that many (and perhaps most) human actions are best understood as attempts to further economic interests. Though I hope to demonstrate that such a perspective can shed light on restructuring and amalgamation in particular, a philosoph-ical defence of realism is beyond the scope of the present paper. In its place, it must suffice to say that realism is a familiar theoretical per-spective in political, philosophical, and ethical analysis. It is especially notable that it plays a prominent role in the thought of thinkers like Hobbes, Marx, and Nietzsche, and in "political realism" (the view that nation states act in ways that further their own self interest). I do not propose realism because I hold that economic interests rather than moral principles *should* govern human action, but because it is important to recognize the role that vested interest frequently plays in political and moral debate, and because a recognition of such interests is an impor-tant prelude to ethical assessment, even when policies and actions are justified and defended on moral grounds (see Groarke 1989).

In debates about restructuring, realism implicitly informs the views of commentators who portray it as a smoke screen for fundamental eco-nomic changes which serve vested interests and the political agendas they give rise to. In the present book, such views are an important theme in essays by Hanly, Baumann and Silverman, Reed, and Kachur and Briton. I believe that such analyses are important, but also that they sometimes overlook the possibility that *opposition* to restructuring may be rooted in vested interest and the political agendas it gives rise to. I want to illustrate this point in the context of amalgamation, but it is important to recognize that one might use it to explain opposition to restructuring in many other cases.

One means of restructuring in health care is, for example, deprofes-sionalization. It cuts costs by assigning tasks which have been tradition-ally performed by one profession to another. The most radical forms of deprofessionalization would see many of the functions now performed by general practitioners assigned to midwives and nurse practitioners, who could function as much less costly front-line medical consultants. Such changes have sometimes been proposed—on medical as well as economic grounds—but have been opposed by doctors and doctors' groups on the grounds that they would seriously decrease the quality of health care. Others have taken issue with the latter claim. In the present context, the important point is that one might easily interpret doctors' opposition to deprofessionalization of this sort in a realist way, as an attempt to defend their economic interests in the face of other professions which threaten to usurp them. This analysis may be mistaken, but realism demands that we treat it seriously in attempting to understand the dynamics of deprofessionalization and the restructuring that it implies (it goes without saying that it also demands that we recognize the role that the vested interests of midwives and nurse practitioners may play in such restructuring).

Looked at from the point of view of realism, opposition to restructuring functions as a means of defending a prevailing status quo. Such opposition serves the economic interests of those who benefit from this status quo and we must, therefore, take seriously the possibility that it may be predicated on these interests. Professions, institutions, and individuals naturally emphasize their own interests and perspective, and the bias this implies may easily be implicit and unconscious. In such cases, such bias needs to be uncovered by determining whose interests are served by particular measures, and by asking whether they have exerted undue influence on policy decisions (something which will not, in every instance, be the case).

The significance of realism for restructuring can be illustrated in the context of amalgamation. Its proponents typically suggest four ways in which it can minimize the negative aspects of restructuring and thus benefit institutions and their stakeholders. These "benefits of amalgamation" might be summarized as follows:

- amalgamation eliminates duplication;
- amalgamation allows economies of scale;
- amalgamation promotes administrative efficiency by downsizing management;
- amalgamation provides an opportunity to constructively change the operations of an institution.

An example which illustrates the potential benefits of amalgamation is the Thunder Bay Regional Hospital, which was formed by amalgamating three local hospitals. Its most notable accomplishment is the savings it made possible by dramatically reducing the number of administrative and management positions in the hospital.

> The end result...has been a reduction in senior and middle management for the new corporation from 78 to 38 positions, with an accompanying saving in salaries and benefits of approximately $2.2 million. Since this is a permanent reduction in management costs, the new corporation will

> continue to save this $2.2 million every year. The $2.5 million cost of
> severance packages for this reduction, on the other hand, was borne
> only once and was absorbed by the accumulated surpluses. (Levac
> 1996, 31)

It is important to recognize that savings of this sort allow an amalgamated institution to minimize the "front line" job losses which would
otherwise accompany restructuring. In the case of a hospital, this means
that more administrators will go, but that fewer nurses, therapists, and
support staff will lose their jobs. Because the administrative positions
which are eliminated are much more costly than front-line jobs, amalgamation can in this way minimize the number of job losses associated
with restructuring. This is an important point to which I shall return.

Other ways in which amalgamation seeks to increase efficiency
extend beyond administrative structure. Educational institutions which
serve the same or a similar market will, for example, perform many of
the same tasks, often in competition with each other. Two universities in
the same city will spend large sums of money attempting to attract students through advertising, community and secondary school liaison, and
promotional events. The same universities are likely to fund competing
intervarsity athletic teams, to house libraries with overlapping collections
of books and journals (even when they are seldom used), to support
independent public relations departments, and so on. In all these cases,
amalgamation can, if it is accomplished well, create a new institution
that can significantly reduce costs by eliminating duplication.

The potential benefits of amalgamation do not, of course, mean that
it is always appropriate or successful. Good amalgamation requires that
two institutions fit together well (culturally as well as operationally) and
the process of amalgamation is a complex and difficult undertaking.
A superficial amalgamation may actually compound rather than reduce
duplication (by preserving old bureaucracies and merely adding inter-
mediaries), and may bring inefficiencies rather than efficiencies of scale.
The potential benefits of amalgamation are nonetheless real, and one
might reasonably expect a history of amalgamation to be a positive
account of the gains and benefits which it has allowed. Instead, a look
at real amalgamations suggests a propensity to produce internal difficulties and ill will. The history of corporate mergers and acquisitions is,
in particular, characterized by battles between amalgamation partners,
by "hostile" takeovers, by vehement public criticism and debate, and by
bitter conflicts between competing managers, and between managers

and shareholders (see Jensen 1993, Newton 1993, and the many references in the Hostager et al. contribution to this volume).

Looked at from a realist perspective, the conflict that characterizes many attempts at amalgamation comes as no surprise, for amalgamation creates and exacerbates internal strife between different vested interests which may undermine any gains that it theoretically makes possible. The same problems often arise in other kinds of restructuring, for they inevitably create winners and losers who lose their livelihood and their careers in the worst scenario. Given these high stakes, the process of restructuring often creates a situation in which potential losers will do their utmost to ensure that the negative fallout of restructuring is borne by someone else. In the case of amalgamation, the problems this "jockeying for position" creates are exacerbated, for the potential losers include high-level decision makers who have a great deal of power and influence which they can wield in an attempt to thwart amalgamation plans. Even if they do not intentionally do so, it is difficult for them to make decisions about amalgamation which are not affected by conscious or unconscious attempts to protect their own self-interest.

These dynamics—and the standard arguments for and against amalgamation—are well illustrated by the incidents that surround the Ontario government's merging of the six municipalities that make up Metropolitan Toronto (Toronto, Etobicoke, North York, Scarborough, East York, and York). Noting that they are serviced by seven road departments, seven parks departments, seven planning departments, and six fire departments (each with its own administration, training, and communications), Municipal Affairs Minister Al Leach first proposed amalgamation on the grounds that it would leave behind "overlap and duplication, escalating costs, confused priorities and conflicting mandates" (DeMara and Walker 1997, A7). Looked at from this point of view, amalgamation can be seen as a logical expansion of the Metro Toronto Council, which already governs Metro-wide transit, policing, ambulances, and social services. The advantages of such expansion are detailed in a study by the accounting firm KPMG (commissioned by the provincial government), which concluded that it would allow $685 million savings in the first three years, and three hundred million dollars each year afterward. It is significant that these savings were, in part, to be achieved by reducing the number of municipal government leaders from seven to one, and the number of municipal councillors from 106 to forty-five.

The critics of Toronto amalgamation rejected it on a variety of grounds. Many claimed it threatened local communities, which would lose their unique identities as they were swallowed up in a Toronto "megacity." Frequently it was said that the amalgamation process was rushed and anti-democratic. The latter criticism singled out the role of an unelected government transition team which was appointed to oversee the transition to the new city. Opponents of amalgamation enlisted the support of a number of experts who argue that smaller cities are more innovative and responsive to human needs (DeMara and Walker 1997, A7). In particular, they argued that wages and services in an amalgamated city inevitably rise to the highest level found in the pre-amalgamation partners, raising rather than lowering the costs of providing services (it is ironic that no one pointed out that this implies that labour had, in some cases, something to *gain* from amalgamation plans). The provincial government replied that such concerns would not, in this instance, override the benefits of amalgamation.

The vehemence of opposition to amalgamation was manifest in a series of manoeuvres designed to thwart the provincial government's merger plans. After noisy protests, denunciations, and a great deal of media coverage, mayors and municipal councils in the six affected municipalities organized referenda asking voters if they supported the megacity proposal. On March 3, voters in all six municipalities overwhelmingly rejected it (*Toronto Star* 1997b, A1). In the wake of the results, the provincial government dropped controversial plans to download welfare funding to the new amalgamated city, but continued with its planned amalgamation.

In an attempt to stop or at least stall the provincial legislation which would establish the new Toronto, provincial opposition parties introduced more than thirteen thousand amendments to the amalgamation bill. For nine days, the legislative assembly met around the clock. Tempers flared on both sides, but the overriding mood was one of colossal boredom. The only excitement came from government attempts to speed up the process, from opposition attempts to slow it down, and from an NDP amendment that accidentally slipped through, giving the residents of a tiny Etobicoke street—Cafon Court—the power to call further hearings on provincial plans. Their moment of fame faded when the government decided to avoid the issue by scrapping the relevant sections of the bill.

When the provincial opposition's stall-by-endless-amendment tactics—like the earlier municipal referenda—failed to stop amalgamation, five of the six affected municipalities launched a court challenge, arguing that the provincial government's actions violated the Canadian

Charter of Rights (DeMara and Moloney 1997, A8). North York did not contribute to legal costs on the grounds that there was no chance of winning (DeMara and Wright 1997, A7). On July 24, Justice Stephen Borins dismissed the case. Though this essentially ended the amalgamation battle, its reverberations were not over. In the months that followed, some bitter municipal councils (in a move in some ways reminiscent of corporate attempts to sell "crown jewels" before a merger) "raided" reserve accounts in order to ensure that they were spent before they could be transferred to the new amalgamated city (*Toronto Star* 1997c, A14). And in the fall of 1997, labour threatened a province-wide strike to protest Bill 136—provincial legislation designed to ease the process of amalgamation in Toronto and elsewhere in the province.

Taken as a case study, Toronto poses some important questions about restructuring and amalgamation. In particular, one might ask how one should understand such vehement opposition to amalgamation. Those who led this opposition clearly saw their battle as a battle for democratic principles. John Sewell, a former mayor of Toronto, helped spearhead protests by forming a group called Citizens for Local Democracy. The other major leaders were politicians in the affected municipalities, who took the success of their referenda as proof of renewed democracy in Toronto. Many Toronto journalists agreed. According to Michelle Landsberg, "Something powerful is stirring in the citizenry" and "I have never before seen such a ferment of civic activism and protest" (Landsberg 1997, A2). The day after the referenda, John Barber of the *Globe and Mail* hailed them in an interview on CBC Radio, calling them "something exciting" which contained the "first glimmer of direct democracy." In anticipation of the provincial government's impending decision to proceed with amalgamation anyway, Dalton McGuinty, the leader of the provincial opposition, accused the government of "an affront to the people of Toronto" which showed "a complete and wanton disregard for the fundamental principles of democracy" (Girard 1997, A7).

These sentiments notwithstanding, events in Toronto are open to a very different reading. Looked at from a realist point of view, it seems no coincidence that mayors and councillors threatened with the loss of their jobs were found at the forefront of the anti-amalgamation movement. It would be naïve to ignore the possibility that their vested interests played a central role in their decision to launch a bitter fight against provincial plans, especially as the affected mayors were in favour of restructuring and denounced it only when it became clear that it was their jobs which were in jeopardy. As an editorial in the *Toronto Star* put it, "the mayors, who themselves recommended one level of local government in Metro and an end to duplication, resorted to prophecies of doom and gloom once it became clear that the level of government facing the axe would be their own" (1997a, B2).

It is difficult to believe that a concern for democratic fair play was the driving force behind opposition to amalgamation given that the principles this implies were continually violated by anti-amalgamation forces in the municipal referenda. Democratic principles require that one scrupulously ensure that the democratic process be neutral and unbiased, and encourage the informed debate that makes democracy work. It is hard to reconcile this with what happened in Toronto given that:

- Municipal councils distributed anti- (but not pro-) amalgamation literature with referendum ballots.
- Municipal politicians spent millions of dollars of public money, not only to launch referenda and a debatable court challenge, but to openly support the anti-amalgamation campaign. In North York, city staff were given paid leave to organize anti-amalgamation activities. In Toronto, each councillor was given an anti-amalgamation slush fund to support anti-amalgamation activities in their own ward.
- The tone of the campaign against amalgamation was one of heavy-handed intimidation. Despite his opposition to provincial plans, North York mayor Mel Lastman lamented an undemocratic mood which made people committed to amalgamation afraid to attend public meetings "for fear of the abuse they might face" and because they would not be "able to express themselves without worrying about fending off catcalls, jeering and insults" (Levy 1997, A4). Phoning in to register for the referendum in Mr. Lastman's own municipality nonetheless required that one dial "2-VOTE-NO" (if one persisted and tried to vote "Yes" a voice, said to be that of the mayor, asked, "Are you *sure?*").
- The referenda were characterized by ballot irregularities. The balloting process did not ensure ballot secrecy (though many people felt intimidated) and a week before the vote Canada Post reported that huge numbers of ballots were being returned because they were improperly addressed. People complained of "ballots being delivered to dead people, ballots being delivered to people who no longer live there, ballots being delivered to people who don't seem to exist" (Van Rijn 1997, A4). Hundreds of ballots piled up in apartment lobbies where they could easily be picked up and used illegitimately. *Toronto Star* columnist David Lewis Stein, who was given ten North York ballots and could have voted ten times in a city in which he doesn't live, wrote, "I am told that some anti-amalgamation enthusiasts in North

York have been gathering up unused ballots in apartment houses and phoning in No votes. I couldn't discover yesterday whether this was true, but I did find out it would have been easy enough for someone to do." (Stein 1997, A8; cf. *Toronto Star* 1997a, B2).

Michael Marzolini, the president of the polling company Polara, well summed up these problems when he suggested that the mayors and councillors who argued that the results of the referenda should determine the future of Toronto should ask themselves if they would be willing to run for re-election in a similar kind of vote (Rusk 1997, A3).

Not surprisingly given this background, the challenges to amalgamation were characterized by a widespread lack of informed debate. More frequently, opposition meant noisy confrontation, confused issues and hyperbole (like John Sewell's repeated claim that the proposed amalgamation transition team would *steal* reserve funds from the City of Toronto and send them to the provincial treasury). Instead of being clear about the amalgamation issue, the opposition continually conflated it with a variety of other issues and a general disenchantment with the Harris government's performance on other matters. Especially common was a failure to separate the question whether Toronto should be amalgamated and the question whether the government should download new taxes to the city. A North York leaflet read, "Amalgamation and downloading are two separate issues.... Both issues combined give me a very compelling reason to vote 'No' [in the amalgamation referendum]" (Stein 1997, A8). North York Councillor Howard Moscoe declared that Premier Mike Harris "had better pay attention" to the results of the referenda, because "I think this is more of a vote against the Harris government than it is against amalgamation" (Lakey 1997, A9), and Christie Blatchford of the *Toronto Sun* spoke of the accurate information that allowed citizens to see the issues clearly but went on to claim that "Al Leach saw it coming…when he said about 10 days ago that the debate wasn't about amalgamation anymore."

The extent to which such confusion may have affected the results of Toronto voting was evident in a *Toronto Star* poll two days before the referenda. It found that the majority of voters opposed amalgamation only because they associated it with property tax increases (significantly, the majority of respondents agreed that Toronto municipal government should be streamlined—Spears 1997, A1). As the *Star* put it, the megacity referendum had turned "into something larger: a mid-term protest vote against the Mike Harris government" (*Toronto Star* 1997a, B2).

The many issues raised by the way in which the anti-amalgamation campaign was conducted provided the proponents of amalgamation with ready ammunition in a counterattack against its credibility. As Andrew Coyne put it:

> After weeks of unrelenting front-page coverage, in which the entire urban area was said to face imminent destruction, to be condemned to spiralling taxes, crime and poverty by a provincial government variously described as totalitarian, the enemy of the people and worse, with the help of postal, telephone, and mail voting, not to mention limitless potential for determined opponents of the proposal to fill in multiple ballots, enraged local citizens rushed to the polls to save their cities, pushing voter turnout across Metropolitan Toronto to…26 percent…. They've had a grand time, feeding the media's addiction to emotional displays…. The "democracy" that opponents of the [amalgamation] bill hanker for appears to include shouting down your opponents, issuing a torrent of alarmist assertions, and vague threats….
>
> Maybe the province should have put it to a vote itself. But the cities were not actually forced to stuff anti-amalgamation propaganda in the same envelopes as the ballots, or provide funding only to groups for the No, or phrase the question using the loaded term "megacity." (Coyne 1997, A27; cf. Wanagas 1997)

Looked at from a broader point of view, it is regrettable that many of the most important issues raised by the Toronto amalgamation were lost in the bitterness, politicking, and confusion that surrounded it.

Considered from a realist point of view, the Toronto case well illustrates the nature of amalgamation, and an important aspect of restructuring. One cannot attribute all the opposition to the Toronto plan to vested interest, but the evidence does support the suggestion that opposition was at least fuelled by municipalities and municipal officials whose status and interests were threatened. Like most people who stand to lose something of paramount importance to them, they seemed willing to thwart amalgamation with tactics that were at best questionable and at worst patently unfair. When the CEO of the Bank of Montreal warns of the dangers that will ensue if banks are regulated, we all invoke a healthy scepticism. When city officials say that the sky will fall if amalgamation and restructuring eliminate their own positions, we should do the same.

And something more can be said in this regard. Professionals have an obligation to avoid conflicts of interest and it is in view of this that one might easily argue that Toronto municipal officials (both politicians and non-elected officials) violated an important ethical constraint which should have governed their conduct. This will be clearer if we consider a standard case of conflict of interest. It hardly need be said that it would not be appropriate for me to oversee a hiring competition in a public institution (or a publicly owned corporation) in circumstances in which my spouse is a candidate for the position. Because I have a great deal to gain by hiring her and there would, in such a case, be reasonable grounds for doubting whether I can act impartially. As an officer of the institution, I have a duty to avoid the consequent conflict of interest, even if I believe that I can act without bias, for bias may be subtle and unconscious, and because the process in which I am engaged must be unbiased and be *seen* to be unbiased.

It has not been widely recognized that this basic account of conflict of interest raises thorny questions in the context of restructuring and amalgamation (in dealing with mergers, for example, Werhane 1993 and Newton 1993 do not take these questions seriously). This is because those who are frequently called upon to make restructuring decisions— i.e., normal decision makers in restructuring institutions—have a great deal to gain or lose from the adoption of particular restructuring plans. Especially in the context of amalgamation, for one of the principal ways in which it attempts to cut costs is by eliminating the positions of many of these decision makers. When they personally have so much to lose, it is difficult to see how they can act impartially. Indeed, it is arguable that this conflict of interest is much more blatant than the one in the standard example I have already outlined, for this is a case where a decision maker's own livelihood and career is on the line.

The conflict of interest that characterizes decision making in the context of amalgamation and restructuring is compounded by an aspect of restructuring which was ignored in the course of the Toronto debate. Given that massive restructuring undertaken to very significantly reduce costs (as in Toronto) will inevitably produce some losers, a choice between different restructuring options is a choice which determines who these losers will be. Because decision makers themselves are potential losers, their decision for or against particular options is a decision whether they *or other employees* will be most adversely affected by restructuring. This is especially true in the case of amalgamation, for it minimizes lower-end job losses by eliminating higher-end positions. This means that decision makers choosing for or against amalgamation are choosing the extent to which they or lower-end employees will suffer the costs of restructuring. It is difficult to see how the conflict of interest this implies can be made consistent with their professional obligation to treat lower-end employees fairly and equitably.

Putting aside ethical concerns, conflicts of interest of this sort help explain why normal methods of decision making are frequently not productive in the context of amalgamation and restructuring more generally. As Barry Hoffmaster has put it, "You can't ask people to sit around a table and decide by consensus whose legs will be cut off."[19] Instead, such decision making produces just what one finds in many amalgamations, i.e., employees' desperate attempts to use any and all means to avoid disastrous consequences for themselves and their closest colleagues. If ought implies can, and these dynamics mean that reasonable restructuring decisions can't be made in this way, then this is yet another reason why a concern for ethical considerations leads to the conclusion that restructuring should employ extra ordinary means of decision making.

Some of the problems this implies are reflected in the conclusions of Gaston Levac, the CEO of the Thunder Bay Regional Hospital. Contrasting its successful amalgamation with the strife, ill will and political manoeuvring which characterized attempted hospital amalgamation in Sudbury, he points to a Sudbury decision to restrict membership on the restructuring committee to representatives of the hospitals. "If your entire scope of responsibility is as the representative of an institution, that's what you promote and that's what you defend" (Coutts 1995, A8). In marked contrast, Thunder Bay was not hamstrung by institutional allegiances and was able to successfully achieve amalgamation because it put people from outside the hospital community on the reorganization committee—"people who could see the big picture without particular loyalties." In the present context, the important point is that loyalties become more entrenched and more difficult when they coincide with vested interest.

The conclusion that a duty to avoid conflicts of interest implies that normal decision makers should not be the ones to choose between amalgamation and other restructuring options obviously leaves us with the question "Who *should* choose?" I shall not try to answer this question in any detailed manner, especially as different arrangements may be appropriate in different kinds of cases. This said, some general remarks are called for.

To begin with, it is important to distinguish a decision for or against restructuring, and a decision for or against particular restructuring options. Consider again the Toronto case. Here it is plausible to claim that a reasonable decision to restructure had been made, for the provincial government could fairly claim that it was duly elected on a platform (the so-called Common Sense Revolution) that made no bones about its commitment to massive restructuring. Whether or not one likes this commitment, this democratic mandate is a reasonable basis for a decision to restructure municipal government in Toronto. All the more so given that Toronto municipal governments agreed that the status quo was not an option, and that municipal affairs would have to be streamlined to significantly reduce costs.

But the decision to restructure is distinct from the decision *how* one will restructure. Once one commits oneself to restructuring, there will be different options which are possible. In Toronto, one might have restructured by retaining the present municipal governments and eliminating Metro Council (a strategy favoured by the municipalities which opposed amalgamation). One might have decided to leave municipal government as it is and achieve substantial savings through cutbacks in service or through other internal changes. It is in deciding between these options that it will be necessary to carefully consider the internal operations of an institution, and it is in this process that conflicts of interest are most likely to arise. I have already suggested that concerns about conflicts of interest favour the conclusion that such decisions should not be made in the normal way, but by decision makers who operate at arm's length from the normal workings of an institution. The "restructuring boards" that this implies must be composed of individuals who have both credibility and no direct vested interest in the outcome of their decisions. Such boards have a responsibility to listen to the concerns of all stakeholders who will be affected by restructuring—including, of course, those who oppose amalgamation as an option. To some extent this has been the model adopted in restructuring Ontario health care, for provincial restructuring has been orchestrated by a Health Services Restructuring Commission, which receives input from all stakeholders and then makes decisions on the closing, amalgamation and restructuring of hospitals in the province.

It must in this regard be said that matters are more complex in the case of Metro Toronto, for this is a case where one is restructuring a democratically elected government and one might therefore argue that this restructuring has an obligation to respect the exercise of this democratic right. It is here that there may be an important grain of truth in the arguments of those who opposed the provincial government's amalgamation plans. It must suffice to say that the questions of jurisdiction that this raises are complex ones that would require more discussion than is possible here. In lieu of such discussion, the important point is that municipal leaders are not appropriate decision makers even if one accepts that the making of restructuring decisions must include a democratic element. Their conflicts of interest remain, and it is therefore more appropriate to include a democratic element in decision making in some other way. Most obviously, this could be accomplished by having a restructuring board clearly demarcate restructuring options and by having various electorates choose between them (or, alternatively, by allowing some democratic process to determine or at least influence board membership). Obviously, the details of such decision making would have to be worked out. The important point is that these details need not alter the conclusion that independent restructuring boards should make restructuring decisions.

It may be replied that the proposed restructuring boards make the restructuring process a more complex undertaking. To some extent this may be true, though its more scrupulous concern for fair decision making is likely to reduce the kind of politicking that make so many restructurings so difficult (it would be naïve to suppose that it can be entirely eliminated). Beyond this, it must be said that restructuring on the scale we have been discussing implies massive changes that have enormous human costs, and that this imposes a strong obligation to restructure properly, with due respect for the ethical concerns that restructuring raises. If one is not willing to introduce a restructuring process that fulfills this obligation by invoking an arm's length decision-making process, then one has no business undertaking a process which will have the enormous consequences which restructuring typically implies.

The analysis I have proposed suggests that officials in the six municipalities affected by Toronto amalgamation failed to recognize and avoid significant conflicts of interests that characterize restructuring situations. I have argued that a duty to avoid these conflicts of interest implies, in the case of large-scale restructuring, that restructuring decisions should not be made by an institution's normal decision makers. Arm's length restructuring "boards" can provide a general framework for such decisions, though I would emphasize that much remains to be said about their composition and their operation. Much that is relevant will apply only to particular contexts. Finally, and most importantly, I hope to have demonstrated that realism has something to offer as a theoretical perspective in the context of restructuring.

9

Ethics and Regional Health Boards[20]

Michael Yeo, John R. Williams, and Wayne Hooper

Restructuring is occurring in virtually every sector of society. In this paper, our topic is restructuring by "regionalization" in the health sector. Our particular focus is the experience of one regional health board and its approach to the ethical issues it faced as a consequence of restructuring. At the most general level, restructuring means revisiting how some organization or system has been organized with a view to structuring it differently in light of new objectives and constraints. In this broad sense, regionalization can be understood as one kind of restructuring.

In one respect, health care has always been regionalized in Canada. In the division of powers specified in the *British North America Act* (1867), health care was assigned to the provinces. Although the federal government became heavily involved in the financing of health care after World War II, and particularly with the establishment of a national health insurance plan (medicare) in the 1960s, the delivery of health care has always been a provincial (and more recently, a territorial) responsibility. When we speak about regionalization in this paper, we refer to the restructuring of health care delivery *within* provinces and territories.

In this restricted sense, the idea of regionalization in health care can be traced as far back as 1920. Recently, it appeared on the policy agenda in several federal reports in the 1960s, and was subsequently advocated in a number of provincial reports in the early 1970s. By 1974, the idea of regionalization was pervasive enough that the federal government felt the need to publish a survey of regionalization developments (Department of National Health and Welfare 1974).

Notes to this chapter are on pp. 304–305.

But strong support for regionalization in reports and position papers is one thing; policy and political changes to implement it are another. Although regional health authorities now exist in most Canadian provinces, the move from regionalization in idea to regionalization in practice only began in earnest in the 1990s. This coincides approximately with the broader movement toward restructuring that developed in the late 1980s and early 1990s. It seems reasonable to suppose that common factors and determinants brought each of these movements into prominence at this time.

Any account of regionalization demands a definition of the term. One definition glibly describes it as "the centralization or decentralization of something" (Sutherland and Fulton 1992). This is accurate as far as it goes, but hardly advances our understanding of the idea. Another account suggests that "[r]egionalization of health care generally can be described as the transfer of power and authority from one group (e.g., government) to a newly established or a pre-existing organization with jurisdiction over specified units or responsibilities" (CMA 1993, 10). This is more helpful, but does not address a number of important issues. Exactly what power and authority get transferred? From whom, and to whom, do they get transferred? How is the regional body constituted, and on what grounds does it make decisions?

Answers to these questions vary from province to province, and to some extent between regional bodies within a single province, but several common features inform virtually all regionalization initiatives. In the first place, one finds common themes in the rationale for regionalization as this is elaborated in reports, mission statements, and other official documents. One recurrent and prominent rationale is to bring decision making "closer to home." Regionalization is thus valued as a way of allowing communities and those most affected greater input into and control over decision making. In theory, at least, it increases accountability and ensures greater sensitivity to local needs and values by connecting decision makers (i.e., the regional boards) to those affected by their decisions.

When the rationale for regionalization is conceived in these terms it is primarily regionalization as decentralization that is intended. But regionalization may also be a centralizing movement. The creation of a common board for a number of hospitals and agencies in a community where each previously had its own board—a common regionalization scenario—may move decision making not closer but further away from home.

In such cases, a common rationale for regionalization is to integrate and coordinate services and programs (a common theme in restructuring). Bringing diverse programs and services under a single authority facilitates greater information sharing and coordination of goals and objectives among them. The expectation is that this will result both in better care and in more efficient delivery systems.

Of course, the reasons extolling regionalization may not coincide with the causes that have propelled regionalization to the top of the health care policy agenda. Whatever the rationale proclaimed, there can be no doubt that financial concerns have been a major driving force behind regionalization across Canada. It is no accident that regionalization (which is not a new idea) has come into vogue at a time when every Canadian province is grappling with reduced funding for health care and greater demands on public money.

Ethics at the Level of the Regional Authority

At the most general level of health policy, the fundamental ethical issue is whether regionalization is a good or desirable policy option. The answer to this question will depend on how regionalization measures up in light of the values or ends to be promoted. There may be some contention about what those values are, but most will identify "meeting health needs," "choice," "fairness or equity," and "fiscal responsibility" as important. How these and other values should be weighed and balanced when in conflict is more controversial.

In assessing regionalization in value terms, the weight given to economic and political considerations matters a great deal. Regionalization can be a smoke screen obscuring or obfuscating the unpleasant realities of fiscal restraint. It can also be a way of displacing the negative feelings restraint engenders by shifting the responsibility for unpopular decisions from one group (the federal or provincial government) onto another (i.e., regional boards). Fiscal prudence is an important public policy value, but it is not the only value that must be brought to bear on an ethical evaluation of regionalization.

However, our concern in this paper is not the ethics of regionalization as such, but rather the ethical issues that arise once regionalization has been adopted as a policy option. In many jurisdictions, the decision to regionalize has been taken, for good or ill, and complex ethical issues have emerged in the context of restructuring. The loci for these issues are the newly constituted regional health authorities or boards. The mandate of these new boards, especially in an environment of shrinking resources and increasing demands, poses profound ethical issues involving cherished but contentious values such as autonomy, accountability, and justice in resource allocation. These values concern both the fairness of the procedures used for decision making (the extent to which they involve stakeholders, etc.) and the substantive issues which must be grappled with.

The need for ethical expertise in policy formation and application has been recognized for some time now at the macro (federal and provincial) and micro (individual patient) levels. Many national governments have established ethics committees and commissions to provide advice on thorny ethical issues, such as the new reproductive technologies, procurement of organs for transplantation, and euthanasia. At the micro level, most educational programs for health professionals provide training in ethical decision making to prepare future practitioners to recognize and deal with ethical problems in their encounters with patients, clients, and populations. All research establishments and many health care institutions have ethics committees to educate their constituents about the ethical aspects of research and therapy. The one large group of health care decision makers for whom such training opportunities are lacking is the body of appointed and elected members of regional and institutional boards.

How then should regional boards manage the ethical issues with which they are confronted? In this paper we will explore this question in light of the experience of the Queens Region Board[21] in Prince Edward Island, with which all three authors[22] have had direct involvement. We begin by describing the Queens Region Board and putting its ethical challenges in social and historical context. We proceed from there to outline how it went about the task of managing the ethical issues with which it was faced. In the final part of the paper we extrapolate from the Queens Region Board experience to questions, issues, and potential solutions relevant to other regional boards.

The Queens Region Board

Prince Edward Island embraced regionalization with a vengeance in the early 1990s. In response to the report of the PEI Health Task Force (1992), the minister of Health and Social Services established a Health Transition Team to recommend a plan for implementation of the Task Force's recommendations. The Health Transition Team (1993) recommended a restructured system of health and community services with four levels of authority: a regional system of governance that would integrate, coordinate, and deliver services at the local level; a Health and Community Services Agency that would provide overall responsibility for leadership, coordination, and management of health services; a provincial Health Policy Council that would monitor how well the system was doing at improving health and advise the minister regarding the overall direction of the health system; and the Department of Health and Social Services of the provincial government.

The government responded by establishing five regional boards on the Island. Board members—made up of interested community members, many of whom had a limited knowledge of the systems for which they were now responsible—were appointed by the minister of Health and Social Services during the summer of 1993. Staff were hired shortly afterwards.

The Queens Region Board has the largest catchment on the island. It provides services to approximately sixty-five thousand Islanders, and many secondary and tertiary services for the whole province. Its scope encompasses not only acute health care services, but also long-term care, home care, mental health, dental, pharmacare, and other social services, such as welfare, housing, and corrections. The establishment of the Board represents a remarkable departure from the preceding structures in the province—semi-autonomous hospital, addictions, and housing boards as well as Provincial Department of Health Divisions—which had much narrower mandates.

Early in its mandate, the Board spent a great deal of time orienting itself to the nature and scope of services for which it was now responsible. Staff from the various services made numerous presentations to the Board members, who varied considerably in their knowledge of the system and its parts. It became evident to the Board very early on that the level of complexity they were dealing with was tremendous. The more they learned about the new reality, the more complex things appeared.

The health reform philosophy adopted by the province had moved the focus of the governing body away from institutions to the individuals and populations to be served. In the new system, increased emphasis was placed upon how individuals interacted with the system as a whole, not just its parts. The intent of this new approach was to address such complex problems as those posed by the addictions client who was also involved with mental health and welfare services, the mental health patient at the psychiatric hospital also being served by the ambulatory service at the acute hospital and community mental health clinics, and the indigent population which, although small, had contact at various times with almost all parts of the Region.

Thousands of staff and a budget in excess of one hundred million dollars quickly brought the Board to the realization that it would be impossible to become sufficiently "expert" in all of these areas to make informed decisions at the day-to-day level. Establishing a governance model was therefore identified as a priority for the Board, which hired an expert in board leadership theory to help with this task. The model chosen distinguishes sharply between ends or aims, which are the pre-rogative of the Board, and the means to achieve these ends or aims, which are the prerogative of the staff (Queens Region Health and Community Services 1994).

This policy governance model was designed to allow the Board to concentrate its efforts on *what* the organization should accomplish and to ensure that it did so in a way that allowed management, within the limits of the set policy, to determine *how* that would be done. Under traditional management/board models, the CEO typically provides endless financial reports and analyses to the Board, detailing expenses, variances, transfers ad nauseam, and spending many precious hours of Board time explaining the past. Under this new model, the policy "Don't spend more than you have without Board approval!" left the CEO and the management team to manage *how* that would be done within the confines of the Board's policies.

Having decided on a governance model and philosophy, the Board began to develop and implement a strategic planning process. This included five components: a vision, mission, and values statement; regional priorities; planning around client/patient/population needs; the identification of specific goals and objectives for meeting the needs for service and program areas; and the development of an implementation plan. In keeping with its commitment to accountability, the Board published a brochure outlining the strategic planning process (Queens Region Health and Community Services 1995) and commissioned a consultation process to help it determine the needs and priorities of the community (Queens Region 1995).

As it advanced along the way of strategic planning, issues became more and more complex. The community needs assessment identified a broad range of issues and concerns. These included maintaining existing services and supports, additional help for catastrophic physical, emotional or financial events, and interestingly, the need to look beyond the symptoms to the root causes of a variety of problems: unemployment, pesticide use, low use of bicycle helmets, to name a few. Many identified needs were being met; others were not. In addition, gaping inconsistencies in the direction and focus of different programs became evident. For example, a young man turned up at the regional office seeking assistance with the purchase of medicine he had been prescribed, which cost several thousand dollars per year. Unfortunately, he had to be told that the system was unable to help him until he had exhausted his own resources, thereby qualifying for welfare. This contrasted with the universal program in place to assist people with diabetes, regardless of their means, to purchase insulin.

Such issues were exacerbated by the economic constraints on the system. Dramatic changes were taking place in a system that had been accustomed to growing at rates well above inflation for decades. The province's current financial situation was very serious. There had been no increase in funding for several years. Reductions had been made in a number of areas, and more were expected.

As it developed its draft vision, mission, and values statement, the Board began to consider how to establish priorities for allocating its increasingly scarce resources. There was very little room to move. In addition to the pressures from existing programs, there were also demands to find resources that would give life to a number of health reform objectives, including such things as community health centres and increased health promotion and disease prevention. In general, there were increasing demands for resources but less total resources to work with. Given that not all needs within the Region could be met, which needs (and whose needs) should receive priority? How could the interests of the various stakeholders be balanced? What were the Board's ultimate goals?

The Board realized that these were not just management issues but also ethical issues. To be sure, they were not new. However, in the past, with the continued growth in available resources and the institutional "stove pipe" approach to service delivery, these issues had not been made explicit and addressed in a principled way. Vested-interest groups, squeaky wheels, back-room politics, and expediency had often driven such decisions. In the new climate of increased accountability and demands for greater transparency, decision making along these lines was not an option.

Having recognized the centrality of ethics to its task, the Board decided this was a prime area in which it needed education and advice, and arranged a full-day ethics workshop to help it with these issues.

Two ethicists were contracted, and after extensive discussions with the CEO, agreement was reached about goals and methods for the workshop.

The workshop was divided into four main parts, each focusing on a different task, issue or problem. The two morning sessions were devoted to educating the Board about ethics and resource allocation and to an attempt to establish the main values of importance to the Board and the community. The values enumerated can be summarized as follows.

Justice (fairness, equality): Ensure that individuals, families, and communities receive a fair share of resources, recognizing that some have greater needs than others. Equality is a main element of justice. It requires that equal needs be given equal consideration, and that unequal needs be given an unequal allocation of resources.

Maximizing Benefits: Achieve as much good or benefit as possible with the resources available. Options should be compared in terms of how much benefit each yields per unit or resources or per dollar ("bang for the buck").

Beneficence: Promote the good of others and at the very least avoid doing others harm. Historically this is interpreted as doing good for those who are especially needy. There is, so to speak, a "preferential option" for the sick, the poor, and the needy.

Autonomy: Promote self-determination and allow individuals, families, and communities as much choice as possible in decision making.

Self-Reliance: Nurture and strengthen the sometime latent powers that reside in individuals, families, and communities, and avoid fostering dependencies. Self-reliance—whether that of individuals, families or entire communities—means realizing one's powers and drawing from such resources as one has available to set and accomplish one's goals.

The afternoon sessions of the ethics workshop took the form of facilitated discussion and deliberation about the Board's policy-development tasks, especially the formulation of end statements establishing allocation priorities. During the final session, Board members proposed various end statements reflecting the dominant values identified earlier in the day. Following the workshop, the ethicists reworked these statements and proposed several options for organizing and setting priorities among them. The Board was to choose among these options at its subsequent meetings.

In their report, the ethicists also organized various ethical issues that arose from the workshop under themes like the following:

a) *Balance between prevention/health promotion and meeting immediate needs*: There was Board consensus that more emphasis should be placed on addressing broad determinants of health within the region. However, some members were very apprehensive about moving in this direction to the extent that doing so would mean redirecting resources away from the sickness care system, which was already under strain.

b) *Gap between expert and community view*: Initial consultation had turned up some evidence of a gap between the views of "experts" and the public with respect to values and priorities, or between what experts might think the public needs and what the public wants, or even what it can afford. The Board thought that this gap could be narrowed considerably through thoughtful public education, with particular care taken to communicate the logic of opportunity costs.

c) *Community involvement/consultation*: The Board was committed to the principle that it must be guided in its work by the values and principles of the community or ownership. The Board understood that such consultation as had been done to date was not sufficient to gage the values of the community with any great degree of confidence, and that it needed to explore other ways of determining the community's values.

d) *Evolution or revolution*: The Board understood that it did not have a mandate from the public to make sweeping changes, and therefore initially should proceed in an evolutionary way, constantly tracking and monitoring the values of the public.

The workshop and the report that followed helped the Board understand more clearly its priority-setting task and the ethical principles relevant to this task. Even so, the Board felt that it needed to focus its commitments yet more sharply. In particular, the Board wanted to explore the feasibility of organizing the values and principles it had identified into some kind of decision framework or procedure that could be used to guide its deliberations. The Board therefore decided to hold a second ethics workshop to address its needs.

The second workshop took place several months after the first one. It was devoted to issues concerning the choice of a framework, such as how directive the framework should be, what values it should incorporate, and whether and how these values should be prioritized. Four sample frameworks ranging along a continuum from minimally to maximally directive were presented and discussed. These included a generic framework (Table 1) and others that gave prominence to a particular value or theoretical approach to ethical decision making. This enabled the Board to gain a good sense of the strengths and limitations of different frameworks and of the issues involved in developing and choosing a framework.

Table I
A Non-directive Framework for Ethical Decision Making

(R-E-S-P-E-C-T)
1. Recognize moral dimension of task or problem.
2. Enumerate guiding and evaluative principles and policies.
3. Specify stakeholders and their principles.
4. Plot various action alternatives.
5. Evaluate alternatives in light of principles, policies, and stakeholders.
6. Consult or involve stakeholders as appropriate.
7. Take decision that, all things considered, is best.

In the afternoon session, the Board divided into two facilitated discussion groups. These groups tested one of the frameworks (centred on the value of achieving as much benefit as possible given resource limitations) with reference to several representative cases. This exercise helped the Board clarify the things they thought it important to include in a framework, and what things they wanted to avoid. On the basis of this discussion, staff were directed to draft a framework incorporating the main points upon which the Board agreed at the meeting (Table 2). This was approved by the Board at a subsequent meeting.

The next steps now seemed clear. Some type of public dialogue on the framework was needed. The particular methodology used for this dialogue would need to be carefully considered: focus groups with selected community leaders, surveys based on case studies, or public meetings? There needed to be similar discussions with staff. Public apprehension about the future of the system, staff frustration, exhaustion with changes that had been made, and turnover at both the Board and staff level would further complicate an already difficult task.

Analysis

For the most part, the ethical issues with which regional boards must contend are not new. How should the competing needs, interests, wants, and values of various stakeholders to a decision be balanced? Who ought to have input into such decisions, and how much influence should they have over the decision? Construed in these broad terms, policy-making in health care and social services has always been a matter of setting priorities and balancing competing interests, rights, and goods.

Table 2
The Queens Region Decision Framework

1. Describe the need for the decision or the problem to be solved. What is the problem we are trying to address or why do we need to make a choice?
2. Gather data as necessary to understand the problem. What general information do we need to understand the problem? What are the main issues to be considered in making the decision? Describe the values to be considered and outline any potential conflicts between values.
3. Identify relevant stakeholders, how they may be affected, and consult with them.
4. Develop alternatives and impacts. What are the alternatives to be considered? Project the consequences and opportunity costs of each alternative, both short and long term. Identify the value conflicts inherent in the various alternatives.
5. Apply criteria for decision making and evaluate alternatives or options.
    (1) Apply the value of achieving as much benefit or good as possible for the community with the resources available. Benefit or good could be measured objectively in years of life gained and quality-of-life years maintained or improved. Information on these indicators may fall under one of three categories: there is clear and definitive information about the benefits, good or harm; there is unclear or conflicting information; there is no evidence. Clearly documented information is required for further review in the next steps.
    (2) Review the alternatives in light of existing policies, laws, principles of primary health care, and increased community involvement. How do our options fit with that direction?
    (3) Evaluate the relative costs, actual verified short-, medium- and long-term savings and compare to each other. Include the opportunity costs, e.g., the cost of doing this and not doing that.
    (4) Evaluate the options in light of relevant values, projecting how each alternative will impinge on values.
    (5) Choose the option that on balance provides the most benefit (good) to the most people for the best cost unless it:
        a) Impinges inappropriately upon the autonomy of individuals or groups of individuals within the community.
        b) Impinges inappropriately upon the access to service or support of individuals or groups of individuals within the community.
        c) Impinges inappropriately upon emergency service or support (threat to life — financial, physical, psychological).
        d) Impinges inappropriately on self-reliance of individuals or communities.
6. Make decision. Based on the information and decisions from your most-benefit-or-good and health-reform analysis, and considering that, on balance, key values as defined have not been violated, the best decision is....
7. Educate, inform, and evaluate decision.

But several factors complicate the task and challenge of ethical decision making at the level of regional authority. In the first place, regional boards are coming into existence under very dire economic conditions. The acute economic constraints within which they operate necessitate hard choices. In Prince Edward Island, as in other provinces, decision makers were able to avoid hard choices in the past because new money was continually coming into the system. Those days are gone.

In the second place, regional boards will be subject to much greater scrutiny than their antecedents. In part, this is due to economic constraints. It will be necessary for boards to say "no" more frequently to those individuals, groups, and agencies vying for resources under conditions of increasing scarcity. Those affected—particularly those unsuccessful in their petitions—will monitor and review board decisions very closely.

Moreover, the governance philosophy that informs most regionalization initiatives across the country mandates that boards be open to public scrutiny. This philosophy places a premium on accountability, explicitness, and transparency in decision making. Whereas in the past decision making took place out of public view, under regionalization decision makers must proceed in the knowledge that their decisions will be more carefully studied. They will be held to higher standards of justification.

Finally, most boards (as in PEI) include individuals with a broad range of talents and perspectives. Some of these people will have no experience in the health care field. Even those who do will normally be limited in their experience and expertise to but one or a few parts of the field. It is unlikely that any board members will have experience managing ethical issues so diverse, interdisciplinary, and interprofessional.

One option for managing ethical issues at the regional level would be not to explicitly address issues in any systematic way but rather to deal with them on an ad hoc basis as they arise. For the most part, that is how ethical issues were managed before regional boards were implemented. This does not mean that decision making in the previous system took place upon no grounds whatsoever. To be sure, it is difficult to determine what rules or principles guided decision making in the past, since there was no requirement to be explicit about these things. Nonetheless, "insiders" can identify a number of operative realpolitik principles, including the "that's how we've always done it" principle, the principle of "the squeaky wheel," and the "who you know" principle.

Decision making along these lines is not a live option for regional boards. The ethical issues they must face are so acute it is not possible to keep them buried or out of sight. The issues will be brought forward in the communities of concern. If public expectations regarding account- ability, explicitness, and transparency are to be met, a publicly defensi- ble means of managing these issues will be required. As soon as the realpolitik principles identified above have been brought to light it is apparent that they will not survive scrutiny, which is to say that they can flourish only in a climate of non-disclosure.

A *guiding principles* approach involves the board in deciding upon a set of guiding principles and applying these principles or otherwise bringing them to bear upon decisions at hand. As unassailable as this approach may be in idea, in practice it poses a number of difficulties. One difficulty has to do with identifying the principles that are to count. The Queens Region Board looked to several sources for this, including a comprehensive regional needs assessment and an ethics workshop that used a variety of examples and scenarios to elicit the values of Board members.

The legitimacy of any principles thus identified will depend on sev- eral factors. Obviously it matters a great deal how well the principles match or organize the data. It also matters how comprehensive or inclu- sive the data are to begin with. Further consultation with the communi- ty, which is planned in PEI, is an important means of testing the princi- ples thus arrived at.

However, even if the set of principles identified does capture the range of values held in the community of concern, issues remain regard- ing how these principles are supposed to "apply to" or "guide" decision making. Because such principles are general, and the particular circum- stances for which guidance is sought tend to be complex and rich in detail, their application may be a matter of some contention. When Queens Board members analyzed one of the cases presented for discus- sion in light of the values and principles identified, they came up with contrary conclusions about what should be done. Even when the appli- cation of a given principle is clear enough to yield a determinate decision, some other principle may also be relevant to the situation, and may guide it toward a contrary conclusion. When moral principles conflict—and such conflict is likely when a set of principles is drawn from a diverse popula- tion—questions thus arise about which principle should take precedence.

Furthermore, in virtue of their generality, principles also lend them- selves to use after the fact to rationalize decisions. If one is clever enough, and the situation is sufficiently ambiguous, it may be easy to justify whatever decision one takes (or wishes to take) by appealing to principles that, in truth, may have had nothing to do with the decision. In this event, the principles do not guide the decision maker toward a decision, but come later, justifying or rationalizing it.

How serious these limitations are will depend on what is desired or expected from an approach to managing ethical issues. If the primary reason for adopting a principled approach is to enable Board members to achieve greater clarity about ethical issues and to help frame and facilitate dialogue, these limitations will not be great cause for concern. To accomplish this much is certainly an advance over having no explicit principles.

If greater direction is desired, it will be necessary to further specify the guiding values or principles and to provide some basis for weighting them, or to adopt a higher-level decision rule identifying which principle should take precedence when two or more conflict. An extreme possibility along these lines would be a decision framework or procedure so directive that any two people using it would arrive at the same conclusion. This could be in the form of a complex flow chart with branches covering a wide range of contingencies, and branches upon branches upon branches. But it need not be terribly complex. For example, one ethical theory, utilitarianism, reduces to a single decision-making directive, namely, "accomplish the most good or health care possible with the resources available."

Thus it is possible to distinguish different approaches or procedures for ethical decision making according to how neutral or directive they are with respect to decision outcomes. Merely listing a set of principles to be considered without ordering them in priority may be useful for facilitating discussion, but beyond that provides very little direction. At the other extreme, a procedure approximating an algorithm may be extremely directive in its guidance, but at the price of being contestable for that reason.

The Queens Region Board was, at minimum, committed to a principled approach to ethical decision making. This much was required to meet its standards of accountability. However, the Board found that the ethical principles identified and structured in a coherent taxonomy did not provide sufficient direction. Deciding what principles to adopt was one thing; deciding what the region should be doing, and in what order of priority, was another. The Board understood that, as long as these latter decisions remained to be made, the status quo would continue with a powerful inertia. In effect, *not* to decide was to decide *for* the status quo, which was not acceptable to the Board. The status quo was neither sustainable, efficient, nor fair. One of the exciting things about regionalization—and this is true about restructuring in general—is that it creates a climate in which new ideas and new approaches can be put in place. The Board felt that, even within the difficult fiscal constraints within which it had to manoeuvre, regionalization opened a field of exciting opportunity.

Changing the system was likened to turning the *Queen Mary* around. Like the *Queen Mary*, the system the Queens Board inherited was moving with a powerful inertia, and would continue on its default, rudderless course unless or until the Board gave forceful and explicit direction to the contrary.

Although the Board was convinced that major changes in the system were necessary and desirable, it did not have a clear vision of what should be put in place of the status quo. The second ethics workshop mentioned earlier was convened to explore more directive approaches that the Board might use to guide it in its decision making. At this workshop, the Board was presented with various options and issues as concerns choosing a framework for decision making.

Ultimately, the Board decided on an option that incorporated some of the benefits of a maximally directive decision procedure, but without the disadvantage of being so value-loaded that it would not be acceptable. The framework it chose begins with the principle of utility, which counsels the decision maker to produce as much good as possible with the resources available. With respect to setting priorities among various health services, for example, this would mean comparing them in terms of how much benefit each would yield per unit of cost. Utility was a prominent value emerging from initial consultations, and moreover was consistent with the emphasis on disease prevention and health promotion so central to the health reform philosophy adopted in PEI. However, it was chosen as the beginning guiding principle not because it was deemed more important than other values or principles, but rather because it provides the decision maker with clear direction. This directiveness was thought necessary in order to help the Board win control of the "Queen Mary."

Thus the principle of utility is set at the beginning of this framework to get things moving, so to speak, and not in terms of importance. With respect to importance, the framework is neutral between various values and principles of relevance. It incorporates these other values as considerations in the form of a constraint on utility-based decision making.

More precisely, the procedure instructs that the principle of utility is to be the guide, unless the guidance it gives is seriously inconsistent with one of the other values of concern.

Conclusion

To discharge their mandates in an ethically responsible way and to be morally accountable to the communities they serve, regional boards will need to develop some facility in ethical analysis and evaluation and clarify the values and principles guiding their decision making. These values and principles must be open to public scrutiny and integrated throughout the various institutions and agencies under their jurisdiction, ideally in the context of an ongoing ethics program.

Different boards may very well approach the challenge of ethical decision making differently in light of local circumstances, culture, and traditions. Some boards may deal with this need by establishing an ethics committee; others may hire a staff person or consultant with ethics expertise; still others may form a network to share ethics resources.

The type of ethics advice required by a regional board will in part depend on its mandate. In PEI, regional authorities were assigned responsibility for both health and social services. In establishing priorities, boards need to determine and then compare the relative benefits and harms for many types of public services, from specialized hospital services (e.g., bone marrow transplantation) to rehabilitation programs for convicted criminals to job creation (arguably the best form of poverty relief). Early in its mandate, the Queens Region Board decided on a morally principled approach for establishing criteria for choosing one program over another and for ensuring that the process used to determine and implement these criteria is fair and open.

Another ethical task for regional boards is the development of codes of conduct for themselves and their staff. The Queens Region workshops did not deal with this task, but it was clear that the Board members are not exempt from the pressures facing all public servants, appointees and politicians. The projected move from appointed to elected Board members will exacerbate these problems, as individuals face conflicts between their accountability to specific groups of electors and to the community at large. Provincial conflict-of-interest officials may be able to assist in the development of guidelines for both Board members and staff.

The Queens Region Board adopted a framework for ethical decision making that was quite directive. Because this framework incorporates certain normative assumptions, they recognized that it was important to consult with the community and with various stakeholders in the system. It is too soon to tell how useful this framework will prove to be in practice, but at the very least it has helped the Board to focus the issues with which it is faced and to better understand its task.

10

Downsizing, Change, and Ownership

Vincent Di Norcia

"Knock, knock."
"Who's there?"
"Not you anymore."
　"Dilbert's world." (*Newsweek,* 12/08/96)

The Dilbert cartoon reflects the spirit of the downsizing trend at the end of the millenium. But second thoughts about corporate cost-cutting and the associated "jobless recovery" are now emerging. In Part I of this essay, I question the view that downsizing is management's only option in reaction to massive social and technological change and the view that it improves business performance. Rather, reactive downsizing seems to be a new version of older tensions between capital and labour. In Part II, I suggest an ethical approach to enhancing productivity and corporate governance. In it management would canvass the options and then prune waste with care for employee welfare and share productivity gains equitably with them. To ensure equity, I argue, corporate ownership and governance systems should include employees in their councils.

Part I: When in Doubt, Downsize

Since 1979, forty-three million jobs have been eliminated in the US economy, while only twenty-seven million have been created (Rifkin 1995, Ch. 1; Bragg et al. 1996). Canadian and European unemployment rates have hovered around 10 percent or more for years. Large corporations have cut their workforce, typically around 20 percent. Such cuts extend beyond industrial jobs to secretaries, cashiers, middle managers, and professionals (Norman 1995). Part-time work now constitutes about one-third of all jobs. Wages have been stagnant, work time is lengthening, and work is being deskilled, creating new class divisions in the economy, between owners and executives on the one hand and salaried employees, including managers, on the other, with a growing underclass of unskilled, low-paid labour (Sloan 1996, Downs 1996). Even in the most advanced economies, job insecurity has reached levels not seen since the Depression of the 1930s.

"What companies do to make themselves secure," The *New York Times* observed (March 3, 1996), "is precisely what makes their workers feel insecure." Indeed executive compensation, the *Wall Street Journal* reports, is reaching new highs, growing far faster than corporate profits (April 11, 1996). From an average of less than three hundred thousand dollars in 1965 and one million dollars in 1985, it has now reached five million dollars. Similar patterns are found in Canada's top firms (Lindgren 1996a, Ip 1996). In 1995, for example, "Chainsaw" Al Dunlap, CEO of Scott Paper, merged Scott with Kimberly Clark and cut the workforce by 35 percent, or eleven thousand employees, including middle managers (Sloan 1996). After similar job-slashing by Robert Allen, AT&T's chairman, "the wits at AT&T quip that the chairman would soon fire everyone but himself, and AT&T would stand for [CEO Robert] Allen and Two Temps."

Both Allen and Dunlap saw their compensation and the share price increase. Indeed, workforce downsizing is typically rationalized in terms of what is best for the shareholders and executives. When, for example, US employment figures improved dramatically on March 8, 1996 the New York stock market plummeted 171 points (3 percent), in perverse response to the good news (*Wall Street Journal,* April 11, 1996). Bay Street repeated the performance a few weeks later (*Globe and Mail,* March 9 and April 5, 1996). As a result of such stakeholder tensions, corporate capitalism is once more in question. Peter Cook, a *Globe and Mail* business columnist, wondered whether Wall Street agreed with Karl Marx that capitalist prosperity develops on the backs of the workers (Cook 1996). John Manley, the minister for Industry Canada, was moved to ask whether business would not just pay dividends to shareholders but also "reinvest a good portion of its earnings into expansion, growth, and the creation of jobs" (*Globe and Mail,* March 23, 1996), but the Chrétien regime has not acted on his concerns.

Reactive Downsizing

An unthinking reaction to change, many feel, is a key factor in the downsizing trend. Since labour is only a cost, technological innovations and related productivity gains lead to workforce cuts (Greenhalgh et al. 1988, Israelson 1996). Such notions reflect an old, adversarial "Theory X" approach to management–employee relations (McGregor 1960). Certainly, technological innovations in computers and telecommunications have increased productivity and reduced labour costs, in the office as well as on the shop floor. No wonder employees, and mid-level managers, too, see technological change as threatening.

Unfortunately, many managers see decision making in essentially conservative technical or accounting terms. They treat employees like numbers and demand constant, high productivity increases. Their quantitative, technical bias gives all too much credence to the myth of uncontrollable technological change (Di Norcia 1994). Reactive downsizing is in addition often driven by management fads such as corporate restructuring, total quality management, and re-engineering (Shapiro 1995). The resultant gains, however, are often not just ephemeral—they are non-existent. Less than half of the more than three hundred large US firms which followed the re-engineering fad and cut their workforce (by three hundred employees on average) improved their market share (*The Economist,* July 2, 1994; see Cascio in this volume).

In 1993, moreover, Chase Manhattan Bank began a corporate "vision quest" process, whose aim was to stress "customer focus, respect for each other, teamwork, quality, and professionalism," and of course to improve the stock price (*New York Times,* March 3, 1996, A26–29). Chase then merged with the Chemical Bank. By 1995, it had cut its workforce by 28 percent, while "corporate assets" grew by 38 percent. Chase Manhattan/Chemical Bank managers termed laid-off employees "saves," i.e., savings to the company. One manager who was proud of the fact that he had laid off hundreds with no lawsuits even boasted, "That record counts in my favour." Remaining Chase employees, on the other hand, are overworked, undervalued, and insecure. They sense their dispensability. Office staff feel industrial, punching in at nine and out at five: "It's 'Pay me, don't play with me.'" The company has become Hobbesian, with individuals, competing to keep their jobs. Many have learned to cynically spot the safest jobs and retrain to get them. There are signs of survivor guilt among remaining staff; as one said, "I ran into B today. He wasn't offered a job and is devastated. Any sense of joy I felt I had at being on the 'Schindler's list' of employees who've got jobs with our new parent corporation has been wiped out by experiences like this" (Ibid., A29).

Downsizing Costs

Doubts about the benefits of downsizing are growing fast. Not only does it worsen employee morale, it also results in productivity declines, loss of competitiveness and other costs (O'Neill et al. 1995). Nor does cost-cutting itself improve sales or increase market share. Lay-offs have costs too: severance payouts, the loss of employees with valuable corporate knowledge, poor morale, and lower productivity. A US chemical company, for instance, laid off an engineer who alone knew the design specs of a certain compressor, but could not later relocate him to hire him back (*Globe and Mail,* August 15, 1995).

Senior executives at Connecticut Mutual Life Insurance company reacted to lagging sales and profits (not losses, note) by soliciting voluntary resignations from employees to help cut costs (*The Economist,* April 3, 1993). They expected only 475 employees to choose their generous buy-out offer. Instead, 1,650 did. The executives then found themselves fighting a rearguard action to persuade valued, knowledgeable employees to stay. Ultimately, 890 left, including 220 whom management did not want to lose. Uncertainty about the future was one of the main reasons for the employee rush to leave, not the generous buy-out.

In sum, reactive downsizing represents a pathological management syndrome. As *The Economist* warned, excessive cuts and lay-offs produce "the anorexic corporation," a company so overworked and stressed out that it cannot respond to future market upturns (February 10, 1996). Being lean, mean and reactive is not the same as careful cost-control.

Part II: Downsize with Care

To the extent that managers rationalize downsizing merely as a reaction to inevitable change, they evade their responsibility as decision makers. Instead of downsizing reactively, management should act proactively. Cuts should be part of an overall, flexible strategic response to change. Careful downsizing involves foresight, responsible pruning, equity, and inclusion.

Proactive Planning

Executives who reactively replace people with hardware may be happy to take responsibility for the resultant productivity increases and profits, but they remain reluctant to accept responsibility for losses. Those are instead blamed on uncontrollable socio-economic forces—or on subordinates (Jackall 1988). If you're responsible for the gain, you're responsible for the pain. To take responsibility in either case is to take it in both. Executives should therefore explore all the options and mobilize all their resources when facing tough choices in response to external forces and changes. As in medicine, drastic surgery should be considered only as a last resort. Foresight and care are needed.

Change then represents an ethical challenge, one which calls for an intelligent and even creative response (Toynbee 1962). Responsible, proactive executives do not perceive change only as a threat. Instead, they not only track socio-economic and technological trends, they also try to foresee how business and work are changing. They look for new business and market opportunities and adapt as necessary. Instead of unthinkingly reacting to technological change, responsible management assesses innovations in terms of a wide range of capital investment norms, including consideration of their impact on stakeholder welfare (Di Norcia 1994). In the face of change, companies may have to redeploy their resources more productively and retrain staff (see Chrominska, this volume). In adapting to an ever shifting future, one should care for the welfare of the whole company and minimize the risk of harming the business. One must preserve the core strengths of the company. Good management, then, responds to technological change by nurturing the firm's strengths—that includes productive, knowledgeable employees.

Careful Pruning

On this reading, responsible cost-cutting is more like careful pruning than clear-cut logging. One should prune a healthy, overgrown tree, not uproot it. Even healthy firms need pruning now and then, like any growing organism. The only elements that should be cut are those that are excessively wasteful, such as unproductive costs, excess debt, poor investments, risky derivatives, excess capacity, inefficient plants, and unproductive divisions. Cuts should be designed to yield more value to the company than is lost. Significant downsizing tends to be required in older economic sectors and lower-performing, unproductive and bureaucratic firms, companies beset by low margins, old technologies, declining sales, excessive paperwork, etc.

Pruning means carefully reducing excess costs as part of an ongoing effort to maintain overall business performance and to enable corporate renewal (Brooks 1996). These are rich notions. They extend well beyond financial measures like profits and share prices, to sales, market share, growth and stability, productivity, customer and employee satisfaction, technology development, and environmental protection (Norman 1995). Pruning should in addition be combined with enhancing returns through

increased sales, revenue, productivity, and growth. Pruning should be
done with an eye to the overall welfare of the company and its stakeholders as a community of interests.

Many large companies might follow the lead of Hewlett Packard,
a company which treats its skilled employees as core assets. Lay-offs
therefore should be considered only as a last resort, after all other options
have been canvassed and prioritized. Even then they should be minimized and handled with care. There are many alternatives to lay-offs: cutting overtime, reducing/rearranging the work week, reducing benefits
and wages, days off without pay, redeploying and retraining employees.
Where personnel cuts are necessary, they should be distributed equitably
across the organization, beginning in the executive suite and moving
down, not the other way around. Where employees must be let go, attrition is preferable to lay-offs or resignations as a means of workforce
reduction. Even then they should be minimized (Nitkin 1991, Perry 1986).

People—that is, one's employees—should come first, in practice
and not just in vision statements. In 1985, for example, Stroh's had to
close its Detroit Brewery, and eliminate 1,159 jobs (Perkins 1987). Peter
Stroh, the president, felt that Stroh's should do all it could to help them.
Management, working with the union, announced the closure four
months in advance. A liberal severance package was developed with
union support, including an extensive outplacement program and transition centres for both salaried and hourly employees. There was an
intensive job search that generated 1,400 job offers. Seventy percent of
workers used the programs; the rest chose to retire. The result was that
all salaried employees and 98 percent of hourly workers found new jobs.
The program cost Stroh's US $1.5 million, plus six hundred thousand
dollars in state government support, or about two thousand dollars for
each worker. Peter Stroh personally monitored the program and wrote
and called to help former employees.

Share the Gains, not Just the Pains

Equity, Lester Thurow has argued, is as fundamental to a market economy as efficiency (Thurow 1980, 194, 206). The human fallout of the recent
restructuring and downsizing trends makes his words ring even truer
today. The productivity gains from technological innovation and reactive
downsizing seem to have been stockpiled by senior executives and shareholders, while they pass the burden of costs and risks onto line managers
and employees. But productive pruning requires equity as well as efficiency. Equity can help prevent the promise of technological change from

turning into a threat. Gains as well as costs should be shared equitably across the organization. The promise of technological progress always was that society would benefit from increased productivity, in the form of higher wages and shorter work weeks. The time has come for executives to realize that promise by sharing/the productivity gains of technological innovation with administrative managers and line employees. This would also make the organization more of a community of interests.

Some enlightened companies have shown that downsizing can be done without lay-offs, e.g., by sharing costs. One way of combining productivity and equity is to maintain jobs when technological change leads to improved productivity and decreased labour time. In the 1970s, a decline in orders led Hewlett Packard executives to consider a 10 percent cut in output and payroll, but they were determined to avoid lay-offs (Packard 1995, 132f). After discussing the problem with employees, it was decided to distribute the cuts evenly across the organization. In their "nine-day fortnight" strategy, everyone from the president to the lowest employee took every second Friday off, and they all took a 10 percent cut in pay. No one was laid off. Later, when times got better, they returned to full-time work. HP's approach not only preserved the company's stock of productive employee knowledge without overworking people, it also saved severance, buy-out and termination costs, and maintained employee morale and productivity.

Time is a central issue. Wherever possible, companies should try to reduce overall work time rather than lay workers off. Employees would likely prefer salary and work-time reductions to losing their jobs. This is not a new idea. In 1932, during the Great Depression, the AFL called on the US government to institute a thirty-hour work week. Large firms like Kellogg's, Sears-Roebuck, Standard Oil, and Hudson Motors voluntarily complied with calls for reducing the work week, so as to keep people working (Rifkin 1995, Ch. 2). W.K. Kellogg himself decreed a six-hour shift, which gave work to three hundred more families in the community of Battle Creek, Michigan. He also raised the minimum wage and increased hourly wages by 12.5 percent, to offset the loss of two hours each day. His view was that the goal of increased productivity should not only be greater profits for his company but also increased leisure time for his workers. As he said at the time,

> This isn't just a theory with us. We have proved it with five years actual experience. We have found that with the shorter working day, the efficiency and morale of our employees is so increased, the accident

and insurance rates are so improved and the unit cost of production so lowered that we can afford to pay as much for six hours as we formerly paid for eight. (Rifkin 1995, 27)

Today, the move to a four-day week has begun. Ending overtime has long been supported by the Canadian labour movement (in Craig and Solomon 1996, 175). Bell Canada reduced the work week to thirty-six hours from thirty-eight through discussions with its union, preventing lay-offs among 13,500 installers and technicians.

Part III: Inclusive Governance

In setting shareholders against bureaucratic (i.e., middle) management, the merger and takeover battles of the 1980s reinforced the power of the corporation's core owner/executive group, to the exclusion of other organizational stakeholders. The result is a structurally constricted, private-corporate ownership system that systematically excludes employees from any say in governance decisions. It not only reflects a Theory X, adversarial management–labour model of the firm, it also facilitates the inequitable distribution of costs and benefits throughout the organization. The inability of employees and line managers to resist the forced inequitable imposition of costs and risks on their shoulders explains the ease with which reactive downsizing has spread through the business world. The distribution of rewards and risks, cost and benefits throughout the firm parallels the distribution of decision making and corporate governance powers.

As long as the nineteenth-century legal anachronism of a private property right in the corporation is maintained, one may not rely on the good will of those at the top. For its employee-excluding governance system allows owners and executives to ignore employee concerns. Nor may one rely merely on the personal probity of senior people or hope for a Sylvia Chrominska or David Packard, for the system is structured to select those who fit its values. Indeed, talk of the inevitability of technological change and of downsizing responses might be read as a code phrase for the view that what cannot be allowed to change is the rigidly restrictive, stakeholder-excluding ownership and governance structures.

Today, however, the times may at least be ripe for change. One of the most obvious changes in modern societies is their unprecedented size and scale. Neo-classical economics and private property presupposed the small nineteenth-century, primarily domestic, joint-stock company, in which owners might do as they will, without inflicting too much harm on others. Today, however, the reality is one of huge markets of hundreds of millions of people, served by corporations with tens of thousands of employees, shareholders, and associated suppliers and retailers, organized into complex production, control, and communications networks. Even small firms do business in several nations. Instead of numerous individual shareholders, investors are more and more grouped into large organizations like pension and mutual funds.

Given their size and complexity, businesses are professionally managed, regardless of shareholder rights mythology. Large firms are run by large management groups, often involving thousands of administrative managers, and a small senior executive team, working closely with the board of directors. The feedback required from the fingertips of the organization in today's changing environment cannot be achieved as long as the old stakeholder-excluding ownership and governance structures are preserved. Without employee inclusion in the governance councils of the firm, those councils will not be responsive to its stakeholders' concerns or even to the changing socio-economic environment, and able to take them into account when making decisions, e.g., about cost-cutting and downsizing. Such an environmentally unresponsive system makes it unnecessarily difficult for the core governing group to determine and secure the common good of the organization and ensure its survival in turbulent times. It increases the risk of bad decisions, as evidenced in the high financial and organizational costs of reactive downsizing.

A business today, then, is a complex socio-economic network of interacting stakeholder interests, both inside and outside the organization. It is no exaggeration to say that the welfare of millions hangs on corporate decisions. It is rigidly unresponsive, therefore, to insist on preserving and maintaining a nineteenth-century system of corporate governance suited to small firms operating in small, local markets. Instead, corporate ownership, governance, and cost–benefit distribution systems must be restructured to reflect their increased size, by recognizing the interests of key stakeholders, like employees. Restructuring corporate ownership and governance along more inclusive lines is needed if firms are to respond to technological change and become more socially accountable. As we move into a "post-capitalist" society, the responsibility structure of the organization, Peter Drucker has argued, must become more socially accountable: "We now have to redefine the role, power, and function of both capital and ownership...we have to rethink the governance of the corporation." (Drucker 1993, 67) True, but this won't happen unless there are significant structural reforms, such as increased stakeholder involvement in corporate ownership and governance.

Accordingly, my proposal is that corporations should abandon the old private-ownership and restrictive-governance systems and move towards a more inclusive, common, truly corporate property system, supported by more participatory decision making. Since such a system welcomes employee input, it would consider their welfare when making decisions about technological change, cost-cutting, productivity, restructuring, etc. Given that salaried employees, including middle management, are most at risk from reactive downsizing, they have an overriding right to inclusion in corporate governance. It will indeed facilitate the equitable distribution of the costs/risks and gains of such decisions among all stakeholders. Stakeholder inclusion both provides needed feedback in decision making to both management and employees, and helps the organization become more responsive to change.

This argument rests on a stakeholder model of the organization. It not only recognizes the extent of risk to stakeholder interests in corporate decisions, it also calls for the informed consent of stakeholders like employees and managers to corporate decisions that affect their interests. Employees who face imminent job loss due to downsizing are exposed to risk equally as much as, if not more than, investors, owners, and executives. Given that risk exposure, they have a solid claim to participate in making the relevant decisions, up to and including ownership decisions, and a right to membership in the highest councils of the firm, the board of directors. Indeed, corporate ownership is already becoming more inclusive, inasmuch as owners work with management on an ongoing basis, and widespread share holding is institutionalized through mutual funds and pension funds.

Employee inclusion means a range of things, such as participation in the various councils from the bottom to the top of the organization, in both advisory and decision making capacities. Cadet Cleaners gives its drivers shares in the company, and treats them as owners of their distribution routes (*Globe and Mail,* March 6, 1996). The result is enhanced employee loyalty and productivity, high sales, and a strong customer base. Canadian Tire's employee management committees, with fourteen elected employee representatives and four senior management representatives, meet monthly to discuss a wide variety of issues that affect employees and the company (Nightingale 1982, 217f; *Globe and Mail,* June 1, 1992; Crane 1995). The committee operates on a consensus basis, without votes. Lincoln Electric of Canada, a subsidiary of the Ohio company, has a similar employee–management advisory council, composed of eight elected employee representatives, one for each division, and the company president. In Germany, employees are involved in both board and executive policy making in the highest councils of the corporation (Crispo 1978). Worker representatives sit on company supervisory boards, and on management–worker councils throughout the organization. They discuss company problems that affect employee welfare, such as production problems, workplace design, shift work, design and production links.

Unfortunately, in North America employee ownership is usually considered only as a last resort to enable the firm to survive, as in the 1992 five hundred million dollar employee buy-out of Algoma Steel of Sault Ste Marie. It is the largest employee ownership experiment in North America to date. The Algoma buy-out was well thought out beforehand, due to a cooperative partnership between the previous owner, Dofasco, the steelworkers' union, and the New Democratic (NDP) Ontario government at the time. Algoma has been well managed since, by an independent management group, which has invested $442 million in technological modernization. It saved the company from imminent bankruptcy. As Jack Ostroski, president of the United Steelworkers Local at Algoma Steel, said, "There's no blueprint. A lot of this is ad hoc, and the first two years are critical.... We've shaken up Bay Street, and now we'll be under a microscope for a while."

Today, Algoma employees have a 60 percent controlling ownership of the company (*Globe and Mail*, June 1, 1992, February 29, 1992, and August 2, 1991). They elect five directors. There is a joint labour–management corporate steering committee, consisting of four union representatives, the CEO, three senior executives, and a representative of non-union employees. Their mandate is to discuss workplace issues, retraining, restructuring, and worker participation. Joint management–worker task forces were created, on cost reductions and workplace redesign and technology. The employees have the power to approve a board decision to sell the company, to invest outside the steel industry or the local community, and to issue shares that would dilute their holdings below 50 percent.

The Algoma experiment seems to be working. The company has become the most profitable steel company in North America. Employees recently agreed to invest capital in technological modernization. In 1994, sales increased by 23 percent. Net income was up, to $127 million, while bank debt was down to sixty-seven million from $103 million. Capital expenditures have more than doubled. A new, simpler, high-quality steel strip mill is being developed. Steel shipments are up 5.6 percent. Algoma has become a low-cost, innovative, market-oriented, high-quality continuous improvement steel producer. Algoma was the third such buy-out under the Ontario NDP regime. The aim in each was to prevent shareholders from closing a still-healthy operation merely because their returns were unsatisfactory, to keep people working, help local communities survive, lower the related public welfare expenditures, and invest in the future. This cooperative partnership between business, government, and labour set employee inclusion within a broader stakeholder-inclusive model of common corporate ownership and governance (also see Van Deusen 1996). The overall message of employee inclusion, then, goes well beyond Algoma, as Leo Gerard, the Ontario director of the Steelworkers commented:

> My dad believed workers had made the wrong trade-off when industrial unions were created in the '20s and '30s. We needed to have influence on the methods of production, but we traded off our entitlement to a share of the control of the workplace to management.... It's not enough to say you don't trust management.... How can we make the economy stronger and improve the lives of workers? That's the challenge. (In Craig and Solomon 1996, 6)

Conclusion

In review, much downsizing has been reactive, and imposed serious costs on firms. It reflects an outdated, fundamentally adversarial corporate ownership and governance system. Social change requires a more responsible, strategic management response. It should involve an equitable distribution of risks and benefits among the organization's employees (and other stakeholders, too, but there is no room to develop this theme here). Much socio-economic and technological change reflects fundamental structural shifts in the business environment. They require equally structural adaptation from the corporation, notably greater responsiveness, equity, and inclusiveness. Employee-inclusive, truly corporate ownership and governance structures were suggested as part of the organization's response to change. If, as I suspect, the reactive downsizing trend has peaked, and restrictive corporate governance is in question, then the expectation is that there will be many more moves of all manner and scale to a more equitable and inclusive form of business organization.

PART V
The Process of Restructuring

Restructuring implies radical changes that dramatically affect the stakeholders of a restructuring institution. Though its relationship to the public which it serves is sometimes altered in drastic ways, the human costs of restructuring are especially evident in its consequences for employees, who may lose their livelihood and their careers and are in any case subjected to difficult periods of uncertainty and adjustment. Especially in view of the latter, the process of restructuring raises difficult ethical issues. In discussing methods of restructuring, a number of authors have already addressed the general question how restructuring decisions can be made fairly and reasonably (Groarke, for example, argued for arm's length restructuring boards in cases of large-scale restructuring). The three articles in this section continue this discussion, directly addressing the questions "How should the restructuring process be conducted?" And "How can it ensure that the different stakeholders it affects are treated fairly and equitably?"

In a short account of EBDM (Evidence-Based Decision Making), Sharon Dewey and Leo Groarke argue that the principles which are the root of EBDM in the medical arena can be transplanted to the context of restructuring and can in this way be the basis of a fair and reasonable restructuring process. Above all else, the process which results emphasizes that restructuring institutions have an obligation to rise above the politics and vested interest that can characterize decisions in this context, and must instead employ empirical evidence in an attempt to ensure a fair assessment of alternative restructuring strategies. Dewey and Groarke illustrate their four basic points with a number of references to other studies in the present book.

In the article that follows, David Drinkwalter provides a general overview of the responsibilities which should guide managers in their relations to employees during periods of major organizational change within a corporation or an institution. His account of these responsibilities stresses the existence of an implicit "unwritten" contract between employer and employee which needs to be recognized as a starting point when one attempts to understand the obligations created by restructuring. Good restructuring will recognize this contract and broaden it to adapt to new realities, recognizing the implicit obligations to those employees who retain their positions and to those who lose them.

Because equity policies are a central issue in ethical management, and because they can be very adversely affected by restructuring, the third article in this section discusses equity initiatives in the context of restructuring. In arguing for "fair change," Norma MacRae argues that the formation and implementation of equity policies provides a useful precedent for restructuring, that restructuring should be informed by the same kinds of concerns for excellence, and that the principles of equity need to be protected in the course of a restructuring.

11

What Restructuring Can Learn from EBDM

Sharon Dewey and Leo Groarke

What is EBDM and what can it contribute to debates about restructuring? One might answer that evidence-based decision making (EBDM) is simple common sense, but that common sense can take one a long way when one attempts to sort through the thorny issues raised by the process of restructuring. Formally, EBDM has been promoted as a new approach to medicine, but we shall argue that the principles it is founded on can be used (perhaps in an admittedly unexpected way) to provide a useful account of fair and reasonable restructuring processes in business, health, and education.

Research on EBDM takes one to "cutting edge" articles and editorials in medical journals, and to the heated responses they have generated, usually in the form of letters to the editor. These articles, editorials, and letters to the editor highlight three important features of EBDM as it has been advocated in the medical community: (1) it is rooted in medical practice, (2) interest in EBDM has expanded rapidly, and (3) EBDM has generated a great deal of debate and conflict.

Sackett et al. define "evidence-based medicine" as "the conscientious, explicit, and judicious use of current best evidence in making decisions about the care of individual patients" (1994). The Evidence-Based Medicine Working Group illustrates the approach that this implies with a hypothetical example. Imagine a junior medical resident at a teaching hospital who is evaluating the condition of a forty-three-year-old "previously well man who experienced a grand mal seizure." Alcohol and any recent head trauma were ruled out as factors and drugs were administered in

Notes to this chapter are on p. 305.

order to stabilize the patient's condition. Using the Grateful Med program, the resident "proceeds to the library and...conducts a computerized literature search." She finds a "directly relevant" paper, "reviews the paper, finds that it meets criteria she has previously learned for a valid investigation of prognosis, and determines that the results are applicable to her patient." Equipped with this information, she returns to her patient, conveys the risks of recurrence, and makes recommendations for improving the patient's chances of avoiding future seizures (Evidence-Based Medicine Working Group 1988, 2420).

Extended to the context of restructuring, EBDM suggests that restructuring decisions should be founded on the conscientious, explicit, and judicious use of relevant evidence. More deeply, it suggests that institutions should be restructured in a way that facilitates an EBDM approach to the decisions they must make. This sounds like common sense, but it is common sense that frequently gets lost in the difficult battles and debates that characterize many cases of restructuring. This is to some extent inevitable, given that restructuring has enormous consequences for those that it involves. It produces winners, survivors, and losers who lose a great deal (in the worst scenario, their livelihoods). In circumstances like these, the process of restructuring very frequently becomes a process of political manoeuvring in which political clout, aggressive rhetoric, battles between different stakeholders, and the attempt to protect one's territory and vested interest—not a judicious weighing of the evidence—determine the decisions that are made.

In the medical community, evidence-based decision making has been controversial because some medical practitioners and researchers see it as the imposition of one group's "evidence" on that of another—i.e., as favouring empirical research over clinical practice (Smith 1995).[23] We would answer that EBDM must be carried out in a way that respects different kinds of evidence, but also that one of the benefits of EBDM can be the way in which it forces a re-examination of existing clinical practice. Something similar can be said of EBDM restructuring, which forces a reconsideration of existing ways of doing business. Yeo et al. have something similar in mind when they write that "[o]ne of the exciting things...about restructuring...is that it creates a climate in which new ideas and new approaches can be put in place" (Yeo et al., 139).

That said, we accept some of the concerns that have been raised about evidence-based decision making in the medical community. We would argue that a fully adequate model of EBDM cannot restrict itself to rigorous scientific evidence, which implies an unduly narrow basis for decisions about patients' health. Instead, EBDM must make some room for clinical and work experience when it canvasses the relevant "evidence." This is even more important in the context of the organizational decisions restructuring implies, where evidence will rarely conform to rigorous scientific standards. Considered from this point of view, cases in which clinical or work experience conflicts with other kinds of evidence do not prompt the question "Should we proceed on the basis of a review and consideration of the evidence?" but rather "What *kind* of evidence should have more weight in our deliberations?" or, more generally, "How shall we resolve the differences between conflicting bodies of evidence?" These are important questions, but the important point is that they are questions which can be addressed without rejecting an evidence-based model of decision making.

In the present overview of what an EBDM approach can mean for the restructuring process, we want to emphasize four aspects of the evidence based approach which can usefully guide restructuring.

1. Evidence-Based Decision Making Implies a Formal Process of Evidence Collection

The crux of EBDM is an explicit process that collects and reviews evidence, and makes decisions on this basis. If a university engaged in restructuring decides to pursue certain kinds of programs in order to increase its revenue, then EBDM suggests that it should have collected and reviewed relatively hard evidence that suggests that this will be the result. If a corporation decides to downsize, it should be on the basis of good evidence that doing so in the way proposed will have the intended short- and long-term effects. The evidence collected and reviewed in such a case may include a look at other cases of corporate downsizing and restructuring, the corporation's internal strengths, the situation of its competitors, and developmental research. This will inevitably include a consideration of the kinds of cases that Cascio and Hostager et al. discuss in their contributions to this volume.

In the best situation, an EBDM approach may amount to little more than the formal articulation of a process that is already occurring. In such cases, EBDM probably means the "tightening up" of existing processes in a number of ways. Evidence may, for example, be guiding a decision, but in a more or less haphazard fashion. In such a case, evidence-based decision making seeks to focus and articulate the process of decision making in order to allow the decision makers greater facility in making and defending their decisions.

In other cases, evidence-based decision making requires more drastic changes to a decision-making process which is fundamentally wrong-headed. In this scenario, decision making is frequently informed by personal biases, political pandering, emotional appeals, and slanted arguments that favour this or that vested interest. Consider, for example, Yeo et al.'s account of the methods of decision making which are available to newly formed regional health boards that have been created in the context of restructuring:

> One option for managing ethical issues at the regional level would be not to explicitly address issues in any systematic way but rather to deal with them on an ad hoc basis as they arise. For the most part, that is how ethical issues were managed before regional boards were implemented. This does not mean that decision making in the previous system took place upon no grounds whatsoever. To be sure, it is difficult to determine what rules or principles guided decision making in the past, since there was no requirement to be explicit about these things. Nonetheless, "insiders" can identify a number of operative realpolitik principles, including the "that's how we've always done it" principle, "the principle of 'the squeaky wheel,'" and the "who you know" principle. (Yeo et al., 136)

Sometimes such forces manifest themselves under the guise of "evidence" itself. Here the "evidence" that is invoked in making a decision is heavily massaged or manipulated, or fails to be considered in light of other relevant evidence or constraints (community needs, budgetary realities, and so on). In many such cases, vested interests protect themselves with the presumption that evidence-based decision making is already occurring under an attitude of "Why of course—how else are decisions made?!" In all cases of EBDM, it is important to remember that the assertion of the values it enshrines does not prove that its principles have actually been invoked.

2. Evidence-Based Decision Making Is Teleological

Evidence-based decision making is by definition a "goal-oriented approach." By this we mean that it requires a clear articulation of desired ends and a system of checks and balances which is instituted to ensure that these established goals remain paramount. EBDM has a limited ability to challenge the ends it serves, which may be established on the basis of a variety of intangibles which transcend evidential measures. A college may, for example, decide to restructure in a way that makes its mandate a good liberal arts education because this is what it believes in, because this is its tradition, and so on. It is of course possible to ask for evidence that demonstrates that this is what it believes in (by polling its faculty, alumni, etc.) or that this is its history (by reviewing the historical record), but EBDM is in such circumstances predicated on a commitment to tradition and what the college believes in. EBDM cannot be used to prove that these commitments are correct. In this way, EBDM is subservient to the ends it serves. Once they have been established, it can then be instituted in deciding how one should restructure in a way that achieves these ends. In such a context it may do so by looking for evidence that this can best be accomplished by teaching in this way, by targeting this population, by saving money in this way, and so on.

It is important to see that EBDM does in this way make room for intangible values which must figure into an evaluation of any institution's operations. This is an important point, as the careless use of EBDM may allow it to be used in a way which squeezes out all intrinsic values which do not fit neatly into a category of "evidence." To do so is to lose sight of the distinction between the ends that an EBDM restructuring aims for and the means by which it attempts to attain them. It is primarily in the discussion of the latter that we propose the evidence-based mode of decision making.

All of this being said, there will be circumstances in which EBDM's emphasis on evidence may force a reconsideration of goals which are not viable. In attempting to downsize a particular social program, for example, evidence may emerge that demonstrates that the initial mandate was untenable. In such cases, EBDM demands a reconsideration of the initial mandate. Given the financial imperatives that drive most restructurings, it must nonetheless be said that in most cases, evidence-based decision making can only result in making restructuring transitions as effective and painless as possible. This focus highlights both a strength and a limitation of evidence-based decision making which underscore the need to use EBDM in combination with other critical processes which examine, challenge, and force a careful consideration of the goals adopted by those who make restructuring decisions.

Because evidence-based decision making must be directed toward some end or other, the first step in invoking it must be an attempt to make the goal of decision making explicit. It may be general or specific as the case requires: a new mission, a streamlined system of production, a new emphasis in an institution's operations, or simply as effective a continuation of previous goals as is possible in the wake of new fiscal realities. These initial goals may have to revised or amended during the process of restructuring in light of the evidence that surfaces. If the available evidence suggests that the initial goal is unrealistic, unattainable or unreasonable, then the goal must be reconsidered and replaced with some alternative objective.

The need for EBDM to operate within the context of some goal does not mean that a commitment to EBDM cannot have substantial consequences. Consider, to take a specific example, treatment and prevention models of health care. Here the goal is a very general one: meeting the health care needs of a community. In the context of this goal, one might easily argue for a restructuring of health care that emphasizes prevention rather than treatment services. If it is to be convincing, the basis of such an argument must not be wishful thinking or speculative hypotheses, but studies that provide empirical evidence for the claim that prevention is a more effective way to achieve our long-term health goals. Studies of socio-economic factors that affect health needs in Canada must be presented alongside analyses of current trends in health services in Canada, cost-effectiveness studies of prevention-based systems, and an examination of the results of attempts at prevention in other social infrastructures (Sehl 1996).

When considered from the point of view of our present system of health care, where the focus of health care is acute care, arguments of this sort recommend a radical transformation of the health care system. Without this transformation, restructuring will probably be implemented with a "logical," across-the-board reduction of services (or even with extra cuts for prevention, given the status quo's commitment to a treatment model). Such arguments thus provide an example of the way in which evidence-based studies can pose a useful challenge to the status quo and can guide restructuring. Without an explicit and concerted attempt to engage such evidence, the loudest voices in the status quo are likely to remain the loudest voices in restructuring, irrespective of the evidence. In the process, restructuring is likely to marginalize those who do not enjoy political influence.

3. Evidence-Based Decision Making Assumes an Integrating and Interactive Model

If it is to attain the best results in the context of restructuring, evidence-based decision making must function as a way of requiring and facilitating interaction between decision makers, researchers, experts, and stake-holders. Understood in the broad way we have proposed, it is not an attempt to "empiricize" all decisions to favour particular kinds of evidence and particular points of view. Instead, it is an attempt to give appropri-ate weight to various kinds of evidence. In dealing with empirical evi-dence this "entails three separate but interrelated steps: systematically examining the trustworthiness of...[a study's] conclusions; assessing whether its results are important; and considering its applicability to the local population" (Griffiths and Peters 1995, 1059–1060). In dealing with other kinds of evidence, EBDM will require a more general assessment of its reliability and its applicability to the case at hand. Evidence-based decision making in the context of restructuring thus requires that restruc-turers attempt to clearly articulate the *nature* of relevant evidence and its relative appropriateness. Often it is the clash of different points of view put forward by different interest groups that can best force this kind of examination. Because restructuring inevitably involves stakeholders with diametrically different interests, integrating different kinds of evidence is an especially important aspect of EBDM in contexts of restructuring.

This feature of EBDM highlights the fact that restructuring is a radical intervention—and often an abrupt one—in "business as usual." Often, it results in painful losses for labour and management, and has the poten-tial to fundamentally alter the way business is done and social services and education are provided. This probably implies a change in the assump-tions that are the basis of work and employment—a change which can rarely be accomplished without dissension, conflict, and debate.

In cases where vested or competing interests make it extremely dif-ficult to integrate conflicting points of view, it may be best to bring in outsiders who are more removed from the internal politics, conflicts of interest, and competition this implies. In restructuring the hospitals in a city, this might mean the use of a board composed of community mem-bers as well as managers, and employees in the hospitals (see Groarke, this volume). These community members are well situated to see past the internal politics and the vested interests that often play too large a role in restructuring decisions.

An alternative, though not always feasible, way of maximizing one's ability to integrate the evidence relevant to restructuring is by following Ford's example in the restructuring which Cascio (this volume) outlines in his discussion of responsible restructuring. Ford proceeded by con-ducting restructuring in a time of prosperity and security instead of wait-ing for a crisis to emerge. This allowed restructuring "without the threat of recession or corporate raiders, and without mass lay-offs, divestitures, or wrenching disruptions" (Cascio, 64). In such circumstances, the company was able to get "the whole company involved" and reorganize "in the open." Significantly, "[a]fter spending months studying other restructurings, CEO Alex Trotman concluded that a common mistake is that restructuring often is ordered by top management, but implemented by subordinates who poorly understand the objectives." In order to counter this, Ford included "hundreds of others in the process" (Cascio, 65). Whatever the circumstances, this "open" approach to decision making in times of restructuring has great potential for reducing the influence of "back-room politics," conflicts of interest, and other non-evidential sources on the decision-making process.

4. Evidence-Based Decision Making Asks Tough Questions

The fourth feature of EBDM we want to highlight might almost stand as a motto: EBDM asks tough questions. By this we mean that the strength of evidence-based decision making is the way in which it demands evidence for opinions, conclusions, and decisions. Among other things, it follows that EBDM refuses to assume the status quo. Claims to the effect that "this is how it has always been done," "we are opposed to…" and "the front office says…" have little market value in the discussion that EBDM demands. They gain value only to the extent that they are backed by evidence which can be produced. In the final analysis, EBDM need not result in a rejection of the status quo or accepted ways of doing things, but it does not tolerate the complacent presumption that they should continue. From the point of view of EBDM, any position on the way in which established goals should be accomplished must be tested by asking for evidence of one kind or another.

Hanly (this volume) presents a good example that illustrates the need to ask tough questions in his discussion of minimum wage laws which are sometimes weakened or eliminated in labour law "reforms" that accompany government restructuring. The call for such changes is often backed by claims that minimum wage laws have a damaging effect on the economy, employment, and especially on the worst off. Hanly cites a microeconomics textbook in which this conclusion is the end result of an exercise entitled "The Effect of Minimum Wage Laws." At first glance, this might appear to constitute evidence in favour of a decision to eliminate such laws, but closer examination shows that such effects are purely speculative and not backed by any hard evidence. In a situation like this, EBDM requires that we ask for evidence that backs such predictions. If one attempts to find it, one instead finds studies which refute the claim that the elimination of minimum wage laws has positive consequences for employment and the disadvantaged (Hanly, 46).

The kinds of broader forces that evidence-based decision making can combat are illustrated in Cecilia Benoit's study of "Paradigm conflict in the sociology of service profession: Midwifery as a case study" 1994). It uses a variety of critical perspectives—the "professional dominance approach," the "perspective of professional decline," and the "perspective of patriarchal control"—to challenge standard notions of health care decision making. We tend to assume that decision making in health care (and in business and education) is a purely rational process that proceeds on the basis of a straightforward collection and weighing of the relevant evidence, but this is a naïve view that ignores the many social, political, and economic agendas that have an impact on decisions in any institution. By forcing us to place more emphasis on evidence, an EBDM approach can be used to combat such forces.

The "tough questions" that EBDM requires are especially poignant in the context of restructuring, for they usually produce conflicting points of view and conflicting evidence which must be dealt with, one way or another. Among other things, this questioning requires that one first ensure that all stakeholders be consulted. If the goal of a health service has been redefined with a focus on community-based care, for example, then the community is quite obviously a major stakeholder and must be involved in consultations and providing evidence. Especially when redefinition occurs, one needs to make special efforts to include new players and stakeholders who have not previously been heard or have fewer resources and skills for negotiation.

In sorting through conflicting evidence, decision makers should recognize possible conflicts of interest and the degree to which this is a significant liability when one considers the integrity of the evidence. Even when this is not a problem, one should explicitly consider the veracity of the evidence—the rigour of the study that produced it, the trustworthiness of the source, and so on. While a thorough account of the validity of evidence is beyond the scope of this paper, it is clear that decision makers must adopt a critical attitude to research methods and should draw on the expertise of experts as required. In "Users' Guides to the Medical Literature: VIII. How to Use Clinical Practice Guidelines," for example, one finds a list of considerations that can be used in measuring the validity of medical data. The authors begin by describing "formal taxonomies" which present "levels of evidence" and "grades of recommendations" and go on to include as measures of validity "...sample size, recruitment bias, losses to follow-up, unmasked outcome assessment, atypical patient groups, unreproducible interventions, practical clinical settings, and other threats to internal and external validity" (Wilson et al. 1995). Other general benchmarks could easily be developed for assessing other kinds of evidence.

The significance of restructuring is a result, first and foremost, of its prevalence. It is no accident that restructuring has been called the "trend of the decade." In Ontario, it has been placed in high relief by the introduction by Ontario's Harris government of Bill 26, the Savings and Restructuring Act.[24] Similar trends are observable across Canada, ranging from the Klein agenda in Alberta to the radical restructuring reforms undertaken by New Brunswick's Premier Frank McKenna (on the latter, see the case study by Blanchard in this volume).

What can evidence-based decision making teach us in the context of restructuring? Above all else, it can teach us the importance of (1) an attempt to marshal evidence that bears on different restructuring alternatives, (2) a critical discussion of this evidence, and (3) an attempt to ensure that decisions are explicitly made in a way that is founded on such considerations. Looked at from this point of view, the principles of EBDM are implicitly at work in many of the proposals and discussion put forward by other authors in their contributions to the present volume.

Our concern has been a general model of the restructuring process which can be derived from the medical account of EBDM. This model presumes a set of values that should be served in such processes. It attempts to ensure that decision making pays attention to the evidence and is guided by it. This is no small feat, for it requires a fundamental reorientation of decision making. As Yeo et al. say in their discussion of regionalized health care, "in the past, with the continued growth in available resources and the institutional 'stove pipe' approach to service delivery, these issues had not been made explicit and addressed in a principled way. Vested interest groups, squeaky wheels, back-room politics, and expediency had driven these decisions. In the new climate of increased accountability and demands for greater transparency, decision making along these lines was not an option" (Yeo et al., 137). We do not suggest EBDM as a panacea for all restructuring woes, but we do believe that the values it enshrines can contribute to emerging processes which place greater value on accountability, responsibility, and integrity in policy formation.

12

Discharging Employer Responsibilities to Employees during Major Organizational Change

David Drinkwalter

During the past decade, the economic environment of domestic organizations has been fundamentally altered. Social, economic, technical, and political change have been unprecedented in their breadth, depth, and speed. The Cold War ended, the USSR disintegrated and underdeveloped countries have made major economic advances. Countries in Eastern Europe, Asia, Africa and South America have entered the world economic system on a scale, and with a rapidity, unimagined in the mid 1980s. Today, goods from South Korea, Singapore, Malaysia, Hong Kong, South Africa, Brazil, Venezuela, and Mexico are as readily available as those from France, Germany, Britain, New Zealand, Australia, Japan, and the United States a mere decade ago. The creation of the World Trade Organization (WTO) to replace the General Agreement on Tariffs and Trade (GATT)—which regulated trade between the "industrial" countries from 1946 until 1995—is but one reflection of this change. The demands for capital from the developing countries have fundamentally altered the world capital markets.

Advances in technology have touched us all in a variety of ways, both in our employment and in the way we spend our leisure hours. Today, "surfing the net" is a reality for individuals and organizations alike, and the "information highway" is expanding at a rate which outstrips our ability to understand its implications and regulate its sprawl.

Canadian firms in all sectors, including manufacturing, mining, agricultural, retailing, and services, find themselves facing worldwide competition within their traditional "domestic" market. Educational and health institutions are also being forced to dramatically alter the way they conduct their affairs. Many old, familiar and previously stable institutions have failed to respond in a timely manner and have disappeared; new organizations, and entire industries, have sprung up to take their place in the economic landscape.

Most organizations have responded to these economic pressures by unconsciously proceeding through three clear stages. The first actions are usually directed at cost reductions which centre on "downsizing" the employee body—on *getting smaller*. When it becomes evident that these actions are insufficient—many downsizing efforts fail to reduce costs—the organization frequently attempts to *improve efficiency* by reorganizing or restructuring and simultaneously empowering its people. Once this proves inadequate, organizations frequently attempt to become *different*. This third step appears to have greater success, although the jury is still out.

Through it all, the employee–employer relationship is altered in dramatic ways. This produces substantial internal conflict and is often described as becoming "lean and mean." It is telling that most managers I have met feel they are attempting to create an organization which is "lean and *keen*." Why this difference in perspective? It appears to arise from a failure, on the part of both parties, to recognize and appreciate (1) the responsibilities an organization has to its employees during a period of significant change, and (2) the limitations on its ability to discharge them.

This conflict arises from the termination of the traditional employee–employer relationship and the onset of a new relationship which has significant differences. Frequently, this change occurs through a process viewed by the employee as unnecessarily harsh and insensitive, and by the employer as necessary and appropriate. The concerns this raises are clearly evident in the case of public sector unions, which question government actions to redefine their delivery of services to the population because of large annual budgetary deficits and huge outstanding financial debt obligations. The ensuing internal turmoil is frequently accompanied by the workers' loss in faith in senior management's ability to discharge their responsibilities. In both the public and the private sector, a failure to address such conflict and consider the human element during these changes can severely affect the effectiveness, and ultimately the success, of any organization.

Concerns about employee treatment during these (often seemingly continuous) reorganizations have driven unions to formalize decisions on employees whose jobs may be eliminated or re-engineered. As a result, union leaders now speak of "job ownership" by the incumbent, and publicly question corporate restructuring in the presence of large, absolute profits. They adopt a two-pronged approach to such concerns. First, they attempt to secure a contractual job guarantee for their membership and attempt to back it with a formal job-search process which provides for retraining. Secondly, they attempt to establish a process that guarantees participation and input into decisions which affect the number and category of their members (the clearest instance of this approach is discussed by Vince Di Norcia in this volume).

Both of these approaches are reflected in the 1996 agreement between the Canadian Auto Workers and Chrysler Canada. Within the agreement, the union has gained a guarantee with respect to the total number and level of their membership, and a role in the decision process with respect to out-sourcing. In return, the union has agreed to ensure the good conduct and satisfactory performance of its members during the life of the contract.

Managerial action in response to the profound changes in the economic environment has fundamentally altered the way business is conducted. This includes changes to the employee–employer relationship. Both anecdotal experience and empirical evidence indicate that the success or failure of repositioning effort turns on the degree of commitment and dedication exhibited by the organization's body of employees. In those organizations that have successfully navigated these uncharted, turbulent transitions, management has recognized and addressed, in a positive manner, the human impact of the changes.

In responding to changes, managers have two key groups to whom they have responsibilities: the owners—shareholders of private corporations, and tax payers for public institutions—and the employees. It is the discharge of the obligations to the latter group which is the most frequent source of turmoil. The need for corporate change, downsizing, repositioning or refocusing occurs in the name of corporate survival and protecting and enhancing shareholder value. The importance of the desire to improve the working conditions of the employees, recognizing the value of their ideas, and giving them greater autonomy to discharge their responsibilities is, unfortunately, too often overlooked. In view of this I will, in the rest of this paper, outline some key ways in which this desire can be pursued.

1. Recognize the Unwritten Contract

Every employee's relationship with their employer is governed by a contract—terms and conditions of engagement—which has moral and ethical, as well as legal, implications. Very few of these contracts are explicit and comprehensive. Those which are usually confine themselves to the legal aspects, which are most often documented in specific contracts with a union or employee association formed to represent the employees, or in government legislation.

In contrast, virtually all moral and ethical obligations are implicit and unwritten, and derive over time from management actions observed under a variety of circumstances. The clearest and most obvious evidence of their existence and definition is provided by "corporate culture." It is these unwritten rules of conduct which demonstrate the moral and ethical obligations which have been assumed by management. Experience provides a view of the organization's response under a variety of circumstances and leads the employees to assume, and hence to expect, certain corporate obligations during a time of significant change. These expectations on the part of the employees are, when unfulfilled, at the heart of the greatest internal upheavals during corporate transitions. They have taken on particular relevance in today's circumstances because so much of the desired change turns on the need for all employees—from the most senior to the most junior—to undergo behavioural change. Flattened organizations require different behaviours from their managers; those driven by quality of performance and customer service depend on front-line staff who must change their behaviours in equally fundamental ways.

These internal cultural norms are specific to an organization, although the differences are often greater between industries than among organizations within the same industry.

In the vast majority of organizations, employees expect job security, the recognition of their value and contribution, fair access to evolving opportunities as they arise, and potential development, both personal and career, in return for a job well done. When change hits and the realization of any of these expectations is threatened, many feel betrayed by their employer.

For management to successfully lead the renewal of their organization and discharge their responsibilities to the employees with harmony, good faith, and the retention of trust, they must usually adopt an approach which differs from the norm. The existence of unwritten, implicit contracts affecting the moral and ethical foundation of the organization must from the start be recognized. The degree to which they have been affected and modified must also be appreciated. To be successfully realized, changes must be managed as they would be if they were explicit, written legal obligations.

To ignore these is to destroy the commitment, dedication, support, and loyalty of the employees which is so critical for the organization's ultimate success. Frequently, employees of organizations in transition feel they have been deceived by their employer and become bitter and distrustful. Successful transitions require the support of the employee body—with trust as the corner stone.

Hence, success begins with the understanding of the employees' expectations in the traditional order. These unwritten obligations will not disappear, but they will be altered.

2. Broaden Employee Interests

Organizational stress, challenge and success reflect an organization's respect and treatment of employees—the "corporate culture." Previously, many, if not most, organizations faced a more stable, predictable, and comfortable operating environment incorporating the prospects for a more certain future. In these circumstances, it was perhaps inevitable that the same degree of certainty and feelings of security would be passed to, or developed by, the employees. In the uncertain, unstable, and rapidly changing circumstances encountered by organizations today, it is similarly inevitable that these feelings will be passed to the workforce.

In this environment, job security, recognition, opportunity, and development often assume very different definitions and require different approaches if they are to be realized. Where they were previously defined within the boundaries of an individual organization, they must now be defined in terms of the employee, who may have several employers during his or her working life. Where the responsibilities for their achievement were mostly borne by the employer, they are now shared, with a major obligation residing with the individual employee.

Awareness of the change in this most fundamental of relationships within an organization is the starting point for the successful management of its transition to a form, structure, and approach geared to survival and growth. Management must also demonstrate through its actions that it has accepted these new obligations and responsibilities.

This will only be achieved, and be perceived to be sincere, if the organization adheres to the principles of the unwritten contracts. Any change in the actions necessary to achieve them should, therefore, be identified to the employees.

In recent years, London Life and Ontario Hydro have both attempted to discharge the unwritten rules with varying degrees of success. Both are large and have long histories of successful operation within their respective industries. In each situation, employees expected to remain with the company until they, the employees, chose to leave, either to join a different employer or retire. Each company, for very different reasons, was forced to disrupt this situation by reducing staff numbers in response to the pressures it faced.

Each demonstrated an awareness of its moral obligations by providing all employees—those it believed would be departing as well as those expected to remain—with considerable information and assistance for a job search in today's environment. All affected employees had the opportunity to attend seminars relating to the changes the organization was contemplating, and the reasons why; the preparation of an effective resume focusing on personal skills and desires, rather than previously held job titles or positions; and effective procedures to follow in order to find a new position. More senior individuals, whose skills were less portable, were given opportunities for training, and some were provided with individual testing, counselling, and assistance.

While the majority of employees in each case were shaken by the change, those who remained with their employer at least felt the organization had made the effort to fulfil the employees' expectations, albeit in a radically different way. For each employer, the future is more secure in so far as the employee commitment and dedication is concerned.

3. Manage the Conflicts of Transition

For new hires these new circumstances are easily implemented—they do not know, and have not experienced, the previous "culture." For existing employees, the task is more daunting. They have their memories, and usually place a substantial value on "the way things were." Now they face the uncertainty and insecurity they were previously shielded from, as well as the fear of assuming new roles and responsibilities should they be fortunate enough to remain employed after the transition.

In these circumstances, management must have a dual internal focus: the employees who will remain, and those who are departing. The treatment of each will do much to set the tone for rebuilding the support, dedication, loyalty, and trust which are essential for the organization's future well-being. The treatment of those who leave is as important for this rebuilding as the treatment of those who remain: each group is equally important and influential in the rebuilding exercise.

Managers have two responsibilities to existing employees: building a foundation for the future and a bridge to it for those employees who will be retained, and the fulfilment of their expectations as a consequence of the former relationship. While separate, these are intimately linked: the foundation for the future will be significantly better if those who remain feel their employer treated their departing colleagues in an appropriate manner—if, in other words, they believe that the employer lived up to the traditional expectations and can be trusted to do the "right thing" in the future with respect to their own job security, the recognition of their value and contributions, their access to new opportunities, and their personal and career development.

Job security will be in doubt—immediately, as the restructuring unfolds, and over time as the organization wrestles with the reality of the new, more competitive market. These insecurities will be reinforced by the continuing introduction of new processes and approaches derived from the relentless march of technological advances. The forces of competition will virtually force an organization to adopt new approaches and technologies in a timely manner. All will come to realize that the slow, steady advance of the past has been replaced by the quickening pace of change in the workplace.

4. Broaden Job Security and Outplacement

In these circumstances, job security must be redefined as financial security which may be achieved in a variety of ways for those who leave and those who remain. Departing employees face options which are more diverse and immediate. For older employees with longer service and greater seniority, it may be achieved through appropriate "early" retirement options. For shorter-term employees, it may mean having to increase their employability through training or retraining in order to upgrade and enhance their current skills or acquire new ones. For others, it may be achieved by means of severance packages, including the provision of "outplacement" services and techniques which afford adequate time and concrete assistance to secure employment elsewhere, perhaps to follow their entrepreneurial dream. For many employees, the appropriate efforts will be directed at their ability to find and retain employment.

As a result of the experience gained with, and the sheer numbers of, downsizings since the late 1980s, the techniques, approaches, and services available have changed and become more readily available and acceptable. Training has been broadened to put greater emphasis on more general abilities through education to supplement the traditional emphasis on specific skills for specific positions. Hence, educational assistance and leave packages are more widely available.

Similarly, outplacement services have expanded in scope. Where they originally were directed at the needs of specific individuals, usually more senior managers, they are now readily available for large, diversified groups. Greater emphasis is placed on developing an understanding of the individual's strengths and desires. Resumes are now developed by examining the tasks and assignments people have undertaken, not the titles of the positions they have held.

An outgrowth of these outplacement activities has been the broadening of management and supervisory training programs to include personal development. As a result, greater assistance is provided to help in the selection of an appropriate position, enhance job satisfaction, and career planning. All of these activities assist both the departing and remaining employee.

Those who remain in the workforce, either with their current employer or with another, will most likely achieve financial security through more specific awareness of the need to participate in ongoing training and retraining programs (lifelong, continuous learning) in order to enhance their employability through time. The employer must work with them to ensure they recognize this need and their new personal responsibility for its attainment.

This represents a substantial change in the employer–employee relationship for many organizations—for both parties. A shift to a shared commitment for personal development benefits the employees by making them more flexible in their career options. The employer benefits from having employees who take ownership of their development because it often results in better-trained, more highly committed employees who are more likely to demonstrate a positive attitude towards their current employment.

5. Provide Recognition, Fair Access to Opportunities and Career Development

The other factors, recognition, fair access to opportunities, and changes for personal and career development, are subject to less dramatic upheaval. However, they are also subject to redefinition and a change in emphasis. Their attainment through the period of transition will be equally challenging.

Recognition can be demonstrated in a number of ways, first and foremost by giving employees a chance at the remaining positions where it appears that their skills, abilities, and experience, with or without retraining, are appropriate.

Providing fair and appropriate access to new positions within the restructured organization is crucial to developing the support, commitment, dedication, and trust of the employees. Time is often the largest obstacle to the realization of this objective. Management's need to have the positions filled in a timely manner will be in conflict with the need to find the best person.

Some organizations have declared virtually all positions in the new structure to be vacant and invite employees to apply for positions which appeal to them. This appears at first blush to be a fair, open and democratic approach to this issue, but severe difficulties can arise. Immediately, the number of applications overwhelms the system and those making the selections. Given the uncertainties, most individuals apply for more than one vacancy in order to maximize their chances of attaining a position. If, on average, each applies for four vacancies, there are suddenly four times as many applications as there are people. If the process is adopted before the downsizing occurs, there will be proportionately more applications.

The pressure to make timely decisions frequently makes it impossible to conduct a thorough assessment of each application for each position. Selections are therefore based on previous, often less relevant information. Many candidates are selected to fill what at least look like their former positions. The changes in roles and responsibilities are often too subtle to be recognized by a wide audience; it therefore appears that only the title has changed and the incumbent was pre-selected. Many selections will be based on previous contacts with the applicant, leaving the impression that the "old boy's network" is alive and well.

As a consequence, what began as a process geared to demonstrating the new order, gaining converts, and building support, turns out to have the opposite result. The majority of employees, including many who were selected, feel the approach was a sham and they were manipulated. Suspicion and distrust soon follow.

A better approach fills the vacancies in the new structure with people who have proven performance records, and equally important, whose actions have clearly demonstrated the desired corporate values and approaches. This approach provides a smaller, more manageable list of candidates and reduces the pressure on management to make hasty selections. This allows more thoughtful selections. If the criteria for selection are clearly enunciated and followed, both the selected and non-selected employees are more likely to be supportive, even if the support is grudgingly given.

Once the appointments have been made, the non-selected, "redundant" employees should be offered "departure" packages which the retained employees will view as fair and reasonable.

Taking the time to understand the skills, abilities, and potentials of the existing workforce is a wise investment. Otherwise, the relief and euphoria first experienced by those whose employment remained unaffected will soon be replaced by anger and distrust, particularly if they feel they were passed over for an appropriate and more desirable position which was filled by a "favoured" internal candidate, or worse, by an inappropriate outsider—at this point, all outsiders will be viewed with hostility.

6. Communicate

Communication is an important ingredient in the transition process, but its role, significance and limitations are frequently misunderstood. The vehicles available range from the objective, detached organizational newsletter and directed memos, and their electronic counterparts, through town hall, department and section meetings, to one-on-one personal discussions. Their value ranges from clarity and certainty of facts to misunderstanding and misinterpretation of the basic message. As well, management staff are as susceptible to these misunderstandings and misinterpretations as anyone else. When this happens, it often leads to a failure to "walk the talk," thereby inadvertently causing further harm— do as I say, not as I do. The sincerity behind the efforts will be questioned and distrust will be reinforced, not diminished. The appropriateness of a vehicle will change throughout the transition and should reflect the requirements of the audience.

Frequently, too much is expected of the communications process. In reality, it is a dialogue which will, if properly conducted, achieve only three objectives. It will raise awareness and understanding of what is being done and why. It can give comfort: the employees not only understand what action is being proposed, why and how, but how they can derive personal satisfaction from these changes and from knowing that their particular circumstances are understood and considered. In addition, and perhaps most importantly, the communications program will legitimize the actions of an employee's supervisor both in assuming new roles and responsibilities and in asking their staff to undertake equally new and different assignments. If the employee recognizes that his or her supervisor has the organization's approval for their new behaviour, it will be easier for him or her to accept the changes being asked of them. This reinforces the fact that the closer and more personal the dialogue, the greater the awareness, comfort, and support instilled in the recipient.

The value of an effective communications program can be increased, and the possibility of clarity reinforced, if the communications plan adheres to a cascading process beginning with the most senior staff and proceeding through the organization's authority structure to the most junior. These messages can be further enhanced through the use of a full range of available vehicles.

Conclusions

The breadth, depth and speed of change which has occurred in the operating environment of domestic organizations has created new and significantly different requirements on the way business is organized and conducted.

Changes in the unwritten moral and ethical characteristics of the employer–employee relationship in the workplace are a major source of powerful resistance to the successful adjustment of organizations in response to this new economic environment. This is particularly true for the vast majority of organizations, in which a major factor in the changes is based on behavioural modifications.

The recognition and management of these moral and ethical realities is an important ingredient in the change process. By shortening the transition period and pursuing the strategies I have outlined, one can develop a high degree of commitment, dedication, and trust on the part of the workforce. This is not just the right thing to do, it is good business.

13

Fair Change: Employment Equity and Restructuring

Norma J. MacRae

> The fact that the economy is anaemic does not justify a listless response to discrimination. (Abella 1984, 1)

Background

Employment equity as it has been implemented in Canada refers to a comprehensive and active planning process used by an employer to ensure appropriate representation of designated groups within the workforce. Employment equity not only identifies and eliminates employment barriers and practices which may be discriminatory, but also applies special measures and accommodates differences in order to ensure fair treatment. At no point in either the federal or in the short-lived Province of Ontario legislation were there "job quotas." In short, "the Canadian response to inequality has sought to avoid the controversy and stigma attached to affirmative action, but more important, it is a much broader strategy that is designed not only to improve numerical representation through hiring, but to provide fair employment systems and supportive organizational culture for women, racial minorities, aboriginal peoples, and persons with disabilities" (Agocs and Burr 1996, 34).

Clearly, employment equity is concerned with recruitment and hiring, but the essence of equity goes *beyond* the hiring process. A typical employment systems review within an organization examines *all* policies for recruiting, hiring, retaining, training, promotion, and the determination of salaries and benefits, thereby identifying which policies, if any,

---

Note to this chapter is on p. 306.

are discriminatory in their effect. Such a review also recommends the introduction of policies which would be supportive to the maintenance of an equitable work environment for *all* employees. Examples of such policies would include flexible work hours, job sharing, harassment policies, training leaves, etc.

Employment Equity: Common Sense

It is not the purpose of this paper to present a "case" for the existence of policies and programs whose aim is fairness in the workplace. It is taken as given that if rights exist under the law of the land, then they must exist for *all* citizens, otherwise they are not rights. It is also taken for granted that history has shown that good intentions are not enough—there must be effort put forward to ensure people receive *equal* treatment in the application of those laws and the access to those rights, which often means receiving *different* treatment. If good intentions were enough to ensure fairness, we would not see the lack of proportional representation of various groups within the workforce: "It is not enough to be able to claim equal rights unless those rights are somehow enforceable. Unenforceable rights are no more satisfactory than unavailable ones" (Abella 1984, 10).

The *Royal Commission Report* also noted that in Canada there are four groups that share disadvantages disproportionately in regard to employment: native people, visible minorities, disabled persons, and women. The continued denial of equal access to employment because of sex, racial characteristics, and disability has the potential for preventing economic growth—both national and organizational—because skilled members of the four designated groups are hindered in their participation in the workforce.

Those organizations which have implemented employment equity successfully are the ones which have recognized that diversity in the workforce is part of excellence. This has been the case in the private, public and "broader public" (government-funded) sectors. The need for a corporation's sales employees to reflect their customer base, the helpfulness of having people in the public service who mirror the people whom they serve, the merit of diversity in the providers of education for the changing society which is Canada—all of these constituency-based needs are synonymous with employment equity. To put it differently, service in the broadest sense is to understand and reflect the needs of those who are served. To amplify the examples further, car dealerships have been increasing the number of women in their sales departments to reflect the growing number of women who buy cars for themselves and appreciate dealing with a woman. In the public sector, it is acknowledged that the presence of police officers who are themselves members of visible minorities in a community which has a high population of members of visible minorities has aided immensely in police–community relations. In the broader public sector, it is deemed important in postsecondary educational institutions to have a variety of perspectives and skills from which students may choose their career and life paths.

Increasingly, organizations are making the case that employment equity is not just good in terms of fairness and service but also in terms of financial planning in relation to human resources. It has been argued (Lynn 1996) that diversity is part of the "intellectual capital" of the organization, one of the crucial intangible assets. The difference between an organization's "bricks and mortar value" in a financial statement versus the marketplace value of the same corporation, it is argued, is the intellectual capital. It is the people who provide what is excellent about an institution. For this reason, getting the right people (including a variety of people) is part of compounding the intellectual assets of an organization.

A case can also be made (Lynn and Bazile-Jones 1996, 2) that a diverse workforce is essential for "establishing a business environment that fosters flexibility and innovation." Companies which depend upon innovative design improvement, such as those in the transportation industry, have found that a team comprised of a variety of backgrounds can cut new design development time by up to half (Lynn 1996, 2).

The challenge for those who would make the business case for employment equity is whether it is a program which can stand up to a cost–benefit analysis. Certainly there are costs in regard to managerial time (policy development and review) and front-line time (training and input). But one must balance these costs with the corresponding benefits:

> the payoff or benefit from such an investment shows up in improved employee morale, which can produce a number of spinoff effects, *also measurable*. One of these savings is the potential cost of dysfunctional turnover, including the learning costs of new employees, the halo effect of low effort/low performance/high reward on the productivity of the high performers, and the phenomenon of low productivity and minimal performance displayed by dissatisfied employees seeking employment elsewhere. Another identifiable cost saving from reducing turnover is out-of-pocket hiring costs, such as agency engagement, advertising, travel costs for recruiters and candidates, and orientation costs. At least

a portion of potential turnover costs may be saved by developing policies that train and reward employees equitably and that are geared to
recognize and enhance the individual's unique contribution to the organization.... A single complaint of inequity or unfair practice, such as an
harassment complaint taken through the courts or the human rights
commission, could cost the organization more than $50,000, not includ-
ing the damage to the organization's good will (i.e., its reputation with
its primary stakeholders). (Lynn and Bazile-Jones 1996, 16)

The Challenge of Restructuring

In recent years, organizations have faced the necessity of internal change
for a variety of reasons. Certainly one which caused (and continues to
cause) major ripples in organizational management is the impact of computer technology. Training (and retraining), departmental reorganization,
revision of job descriptions, renegotiations of collective agreements,
alterations in product design (sometimes a complete change of product)
have been extensive responses to technological change. The changing
financial climate also has provided organizations with a challenge which
may have even more sweeping implications: restructuring.

The restructuring process generally includes, but is not limited to,
the following:

• Consultation with client/customer constituencies regarding products,
  needs, and services
• Identification of core organizational values
• A study of the institutional/company human resource demographics
• A review of the organization's mission statement
• Options for optimizing current resources/maintenance of quality plan-
  ning
• Development of a plan for change
• Education of employees regarding change
• Implementing changes
• Continuous monitoring to ensure quality of results and meeting of goals

The key in restructuring, as in employment equity, is the skills of the
workforce: "what cannot be copied are people's skills, expertise, experiences, intelligence, and ways of thinking (a primary component of the
organization's intellectual capital) that can be applied in creative, innovative ways to meet the organization's goals and objectives" (Lynn and
Bazile-Jones 1996, 10).

What is striking about the steps in the restructuring process listed above is that they are in essence the same as those in the process for employment equity, including the employment equity census, the employment systems review, the setting of goals within the context of institutional values and objectives, education of the employees, and the monitoring of change. Similarly, it might be argued that organizations which have developed the capacity to incorporate employment equity into the workplace have thereby developed the same skill set which is needed to adapt to other challenges. Both employment equity and restructuring involve an open-minded and planned institutional response to change which makes the best use of a diverse institutional skills base. It can be argued that organizations which have successfully implemented employment equity are those which are in the best position to face the specific challenge of restructuring precisely because they have more flexibility through diversity.[25] Both restructuring and employment equity require that the organization put aside preconceptions concerning *what the workplace structure must be* on account of *what it has been* traditionally. Some practices now presented as restructuring, such as job-sharing, flex-time, voluntary reduced hours, first surfaced in many organizations as part of employment equity initiatives.

The University Case

Universities may face a particularly strong challenge in regard to restructuring because for the most part their traditional way of operation extends back for decades, sometimes centuries. With the advent of equity, however, change has found its way into the Ivory Tower. Those who would have been denied registration in a university one hundred years ago (such as members of the four designated groups) are now registering as students in increasingly large numbers. This is important because "[i]f universities are places where we value diversity of thought, places where we want to encourage creative debate, then they must be places to which all people with the intellectual capacity and interest have equal access and in which there is equal opportunity" (Council of Ontario Universities Status of Women Committee 1995, 1).

Change has been somewhat slower in regard to the employee profile, but even at the level of the professoriate there is movement in the last decade. Although it varies depending on the university, in the Ontario system it is reported that "about 10 percent of all full-time tenured full professors are women. On the other hand, women make up about 37 percent of the assistant professor category and 50 percent of the ranks below assistant professor" (Council of Ontario Universities Status of Women Committee 1995, 1).

There are a number of ways in which universities must be cognizant of the impact of restructuring upon equity in the environment. First, as they downsize through attrition and various early retirement initiatives, they must monitor their progress toward achieving their equity goals, just as they would other institutional goals. For example, because most of the change in the employee profile has taken place in recent years, early retirement initiatives directed toward long-term faculty will support diversity more than the alternative policy of "last in, first out." An informal survey of Ontario universities after the first round of restructuring in 1995–96 showed in fact that the universities which relied heavily on early retirement incentives came close to maintaining or improving the diversity in their workplaces while respecting issues of seniority.

Second, there are very practical aspects of restructuring which can be considered so that actions taken do not have a differential impact on various groups within the employee profile. A document from the Council of Ontario Universities made recommendations for restructuring in accordance with equity principles beyond the issue of the numerical profile. For instance:

- If staff are expected to take days off without pay, consider closing at times that coincide with school breaks, so that there is not a differential impact on people with children. Remember that child care expenses can't always be reduced on a per diem basis.
- If choices are made involving "tradeoffs" between salary and benefits, the differential impact of these choices on those with and without family responsibilities should be considered.
- Junior faculty are likely to find it especially difficult to do their jobs in the coming years. Workloads are likely to increase and granting councils are reducing their level of support. We need to ensure that junior faculty have equitable access to university resources. (Council of Ontario Universities Status of Women Committee 1995, 1–2)

Also, in accordance with the equity process, increased training is recommended: "In this kind of environment we must maintain the commitment to deal with frustration, complaints, and a potential increase in disruptive behaviour. This commitment includes both personnel and training. It should be noted that administrative staff (the majority of whom are women) are typically on the 'front line' in this regard and that female faculty report experiencing higher rates of disruptive behaviour than their male counterparts" (Council of Ontario Universities Status of Women Committee 1995, 2).

Another recommendation is the maintenance of support for orientation and mentoring programs since, as universities become leaner, more care must be taken to ensure the sustaining of morale and productivity and the avoidance of mistakes. The establishment of a favourable environment must remain an ongoing goal. A climate which is positive for equity groups will be good for everyone, as such equity initiatives such as the conducting of campus safety audits has shown.

Above all, universities need to adapt a stance which reinforces employment equity throughout *any* restructuring process. Indeed, it is argued that employment equity should in fact have a central role to play in restructuring: "It is important that these issues form part of the filter through which decisions are made and judged. At the very least when two strategies are approximately equal with respect to academic mission and cost savings, the choice should be made on the basis of least harm to equity/diversity objectives" (Council of Ontario Universities Status of Women Committee 1995, 1).

Conclusion

If fair treatment is part of an organization's self-definition in what may be called "good times," there are no reasons for it to be set aside during the difficult years. Instead there are, as has been shown, good reasons— both ethical and business—for the strong maintenance of employment equity programs during restructuring and beyond. To ask the simple question "Can we afford to keep practising equality in employment in these difficult economic times?" is deceptive, for in fact it calls into question far more than the application of a human resource policy within a single organization. It is better to ask who we are and what we believe: "No exigency, economic or political, can justify the knowing perpetuation of inequality in Canada. If we fail to rectify it, we guarantee its survival" (Abella 1984, 6).

PART VI
Pitfalls of Restructuring

Restructuring implies radical changes to the ways in which public and private enterprise conduct their business. In view of this, it raises serious questions about the ways in which we should provide health care, conduct private business, and run our education system. The two articles that follow address these issues by considering some of the common pitfalls that can accompany restructuring when it fails to properly consider the ethical (and economic) ramifications of the major structural changes it implies.

Conrad Brunk addresses the issues that are raised by a common tendency to accomplish the cuts that restructuring requires by treating the risk assessment that is a normal part of product testing and development as a dispensable corporate function. He warns of the dangers of this attitude—dangers which are both ethical and economic—and illustrates his point with a detailed case study of Dow Corning and the consequences of its failure to fully recognize and accept its obligations in this regard.

In the article that follows, Andrea Baumann and Barbara Silverman raise questions about the nature and effects of de-professionalization—the replacement of professionals with workers without professional training and qualifications—within the health care system. In the process, they argue that restructuring in health care has in reality been a process of "destructuring" designed "to remove millions of dollars from budgets" and chart the effects of de-professionalization on professional staff and patients.

14

Managing Risks in the Restructured Corporation: The Case of Dow Corning and Silicone Breast Implants

Conrad G. Brunk

After several decades of successfully marketing silicone breast implants to well over a million North American women, the Dow Corning Corporation announced in 1995 that it was seeking bankruptcy protection from any further claims being brought against it for damages caused by the product. The company was hit with unprecedented awards against it from judges and juries who were convinced by the testimony of women and their physicians that a whole range of health problems they suffered were caused by the implants manufactured by Dow Corning and several of its competitors.

One of the first of these lawsuits had been brought in 1984, when a California jury awarded Maria Stern $1.7 million in damages for illnesses it was convinced had been caused by Dow Corning's implants. The court found Dow Corning guilty of fraud in its handling of information the company possessed concerning the risks to women from its implants *(Stern v. Dow Corning*, 1984). The flood of litigation against Dow Corning did not really begin, however, until 1991, when a San Francisco jury awarded Mariann Hopkins $7.3 million because of its finding that Dow Corning implants were defective and that the company was guilty of fraud.[26] After the *Hopkins* decision, the US Food and Drug Administration announced a moratorium on the sale of the implants, reinforcing an avalanche of court

Notes to this chapter are on p. 306.

suits filed against Dow Corning. By the end of 1994, over 19,000 cases had reportedly been filed against Dow Corning.

The straw that broke Dow Corning's back came from a class action suit in which an Alabama judge approved a US $4.5 billion settlement between several implant manufacturers and women who filed injury claims with the court, the largest class action settlement in history. Dow Corning, which manufactured nearly 30 percent of the over two million implants placed in women's bodies, agreed to pay nearly half of this $4.5 billion. The Alabama settlement was not the end of Dow Corning's liabilities, however, since the court left the door open for claims from additional women. More claims were forthcoming, including actions on behalf of an estimated fifty thousand Canadian women, most of whom had been excluded from the Alabama settlement.[27] By 1995, over 440,000 women had registered in the global settlement against Dow Corning and the other implant manufacturers.

The Dow Corning experience with the silicone implants is a critical case study in business ethics, full of lessons in an era of business restructuring and a changing legal and regulatory environment. The company's bankruptcy declaration represented the near demise of a company as a result of litigation over a product that represented only 1 percent of the total sales of the company. It produced unprecedented court awards for alleged damages of which there was, and remains, little reliable scientific evidence. Despite the scarcity of scientific evidence for many of the alleged risks, the overwhelming public perception in North America is that silicone breast implants posed clearly unacceptable risks of a wide variety of systemic auto-immune and connective tissue diseases, as well as many other severe disabilities suffered by women. This public perception of the risk undergirded the willingness of juries and judges to find Dow Corning guilty of "injuring" countless numbers of women and to impose these high levels of punitive damages. Dow Corning is widely perceived as a company whose major failure was ethical—in failing to take seriously the known and unknown health risks of its product and manage these risks responsibly—though this was a company which, prior to the implant debacle, was judged to be a model of corporate ethics in North America.

The story of Dow Corning and its silicone breast implant products is a story about the critical importance of ethical risk management. The story is a graphic illustration of what happens when a company does not commit sufficient resources to the assessment of the risks inherent in its products, or fails to communicate accurately and candidly what it knows about those risks. This story is especially relevant within the current rush of business enterprises to "restructure" their operations in ways that lead to greater efficiency and cost-effectiveness. Risk management and communication are both costly and financially risky. The activities surrounding these activities are, consequently, among the most vulnerable to restructuring and downsizing. They are among the "first to go." When managers are faced with decisions about whether to hold a product back from the market for further assessment of its health or environmental risks, the temptation is to interpret the uncertainties in the existing assessments in the most favourable light (assume the minimum risk) and take one's chances in the marketplace.

The downsizing of resources and attention devoted to the management of risks inherent in the products produced by business enterprises is encouraged by a similar dynamic in the public, regulatory sphere. North American society is in a strong anti-regulatory mood, leading to the slackening of regulatory standards of acceptable risks to health and the environment (see Hanly, this volume). With the forces of downsizing affecting the public sector as much as the private, it is inevitable that the regulatory resources of government are the first to go, and that the result is weakening regulatory pressure upon manufacturers to insure that their products have acceptable limits of risk.

The effect of this restructuring of resources is predictable. If less attention and care is given to product safety at the production level and the regulatory level, the slack will inevitably be picked up at the level of the consumer—through litigation in the courts. If products impose harms upon customers or other stakeholders, or if they are *perceived* to impose these harms, the only recourse is to sue the manufacturer—the perceived risk producer—in the courts. In this legal forum, the people who are called upon to judge whether the plaintiff has been subjected to unacceptable levels of risk are not scientists, nor even persons who have an elementary understanding of science, to say nothing of the intricacies and nuances of risk assessment science. As a result, the evidence sufficient to convince judges and juries that a product poses unacceptable levels of risk may fall well short of that required to convince expert risk assessment scientists, and the burden of proof can easily shift from the plaintiff, who need not prove that he or she has been exposed to unacceptable risk, to the defendant, who suddenly has the burden of proving that the company's product does *not* impose this risk.

The Dow Corning silicone breast implant story illustrates precisely these dynamics. It also illustrates that the costs of a corporate failure to take the management and communication of risk seriously can be extremely high—indeed, suicidal—for a company. The moral of the story, and of other similar court settlements in recent history, involving the Dalkon Shield, asbestos, and Agent Orange, appears to be that restructuring a manufacturing company in ways that give less attention to the issues of product safety is not only questionable on evident grounds of business ethics, but also from the point of view of corporate self-interest, even corporate survival. And the most critical factor in both the public perception and the legal adjudication of the safety of the silicone breast implant is the public image of the company as an ethically responsible steward of the public health, safety, and welfare. In these cases, the ethics of a company and its self-interest appear to coincide closely.

Science and Public Perception of Breast Implant Safety

Since the wave of litigation against Dow Corning, the scientific community has mounted a vigorous defence of the company and the safety of silicone breast implants. A strong voice in this defence has been the editor of the prestigious *New England Journal of Medicine*, Dr. Marcia Angell. Soon after the controversy broke in 1994, the journal published the first major epidemiological study of breast implant patients, which found no significant differences in the incidence of connective tissue and other diseases among these women than among a non-implant control group of twice the size (Gabriel et al. 1994). In an accompanying editorial, Angell wrote that the study showed the decision of the US Food and Drug Administration to remove silicone implants from the market in 1992 to be "overly paternalistic and unnecessarily alarming." She also claimed that the FDA decision, which was based on the fact that the manufacturers "had not fulfilled their legal responsibility to collect data on the question" (not because implants were known to pose a risk), was construed by the public as an indictment of the implants. Frightening stories of auto-immune and connective tissue diseases swept through the public and were, she said, "reified by repetition." "The accumulated weight of anecdotes was taken by judges and juries as tantamount to proof of causation" (Angell 1994, 748).

Angell pursued this argument in a 1996 book, *Science on Trial*, in which she reported more recent studies strongly corroborating the Mayo Clinic findings.[28] In the book, Angell claims that the breast implant case is merely one graphic example of the way public risk perceptions are often manipulated into mass hysteria, which then becomes accepted as valid evidence in the courts. The courts had erred by ignoring the science, or worse, by allowing "junk science" in the courtroom.

Thus, in the period since the initial, devastating court settlements against Dow Corning, the science appears more and more to vindicate the company's insistence that it did not impose unacceptable risks of systemic disease upon millions of unsuspecting women. As a result of the growing consensus in the scientific and journalistic community, even the widespread view among business ethicists that Dow Corning had acted unethically has undergone revision.[29] The company has undertaken a vigorous public relations campaign to restore its image, and appears to be meeting with a great deal of success.

The lawyers and victims' groups have pointed out, however, that even the most recent studies have failed to rule out the possibility of significant risk of the systemic complications they believe are caused by breast implants. One of the recent major studies did find a slight increase in reports of connective tissue disease among women with breast implants. The most recent scientific review of all the epidemiological studies found that, while none has indicated a greatly increased rate of well-defined connective tissue disease or breast cancer in women with silicone breast implants, none has ruled out a moderately increased risk for these diseases, either. The study concludes that "[i]nformation is insufficient to adequately advise women who currently have or are seeking to obtain breast implants about the overall risk of these devices" (Silverman et al. 1996, 756). Thus, the most salient aspect of the science for these non-scientific groups is not the fact that the risks appear very low, but that this assessment itself is fraught with significant *uncertainty*. This, as will be explained later, is one of the critical factors in the finding among these groups that the risk is unacceptable.

The Erosion of Trust in Dow Corning

What explains this wide divergence between the public perception that the breast implants pose serious health risks to women and the expert scientific assessment that they pose little significant risk? These divergences between lay and expert risk assessments are not unusual in public debates about risk and safety. The experts usually attribute them to scientific naïveté among the public and especially the media, which profit from the mass hysteria created by stories of serious risks imposed upon unsuspecting victims by greedy and rapacious corporations. This, surely, was the view that Dow Corning and its scientific supporters took of the breast implant perception. But this account of the differences in risk perception is often based upon a misunderstanding of the way non-experts tend to think about risk and its acceptability, which is often quite different from the expert way of thinking of it.

In the case of Dow Corning's silicone implants, it is clear that what the public and the juries were paying most attention to was not the scientific evidence of the risk, but rather the way the company as the producer (and manager) of the risk was handling the safety questions surrounding its product. The judges and juries awarded the high settlements not so much because they were convinced that the illnesses of the plaintiffs were clearly and unambiguously caused by their implants, but because they were convinced that the company had not acted responsibly in handling the information, uncertain as it was, about the risks of the product. In effect, Dow Corning was found liable for the illnesses suffered by the many thousands of its customers because it was found to have acted *unethically* towards them.

The trials clearly indicate this. In the early *Stern* decision, Dow Corning was found guilty of fraud. The basis for this finding was the fact that Maria Stern's lawyers had uncovered internal Dow Corning documents which could be interpreted as showing that the company knew about the risks posed by the silicone implants and had deliberately chosen to withhold this information from the public, and possibly even from the regulators. Among the documents were memos from physicians to the company complaining about defective and ruptured implants, and detailing the effects of the leaked silicone on the bodies of the women. Some claimed there was evidence that the silicone was not biologically inert, and was causing severe foreign-body reactions in some individuals. Letters from surgeons complained about the poor quality of the implants. In response to the complaint that the implants felt "oily" with silicone when they were removed from their packages, salesmen were urged by their managers to wash the samples in washroom sinks immediately before using them in sales demonstrations.

In one memo, a salesmen who had heard many of the complaints wrote to his Dow Corning boss: "To put a questionable lot of mammaries on the market is inexcusable. I don't know who is responsible for this decision but it has to rank right up there with the Pinto gas tank" (Bryne 1996, 78). Another memo strongly suggested that a Dow Corning marketing executive made deliberately misleading assurances to complainants that the company was undertaking studies of the silicone migration and the contracture problems in response to complaints about the product. He wrote, "I assured them, with crossed fingers, that Dow Corning too had an active 'contracture/gel migration' study underway. This apparently satisfied them for the moment, but one of these days they will be asking us for the results of our studies.... In my opinion, the black clouds are ominous and should be given more attention" (Bryne 1996, 79).

Most damning of the internal Dow Corning documents revealed at the *Stern* trial, however, was a report on a study which had been published in a medical journal in 1973 (Robertson et al. 1973). It involved four dogs implanted with small implants and observed for two years. The published study largely reported the results at the end of the six-month mark (even though published after the end of the two-year period), and found only minor inflammation in some of the dogs. The internal report which had been kept within the company, however, revealed that at the end of the two-year period, one of the dogs had died, and the other three had varying degrees of severe chronic inflammation (Bryne 1996, 103–104).

During the *Stern* trial, an expert witness called by the plaintiff to comment on the study, pointed out the discrepancies between the published study and the internal reports. The judge compared the internal documents with those the Dow Corning lawyers brought into court, and noticed that the identifying numbers on the dogs had been altered on the documents Dow Corning had given the attorneys. It looked suspiciously like the company had altered the data to make it more difficult to get at the full two-year results of the study (Bryne 1996, 103–104).

The revelation of these internal documents, especially the allegedly misreported dog study, was the key reason why the *Stern* jury found Dow Corning guilty of fraud and awarded Maria Stern $1.7 million. Dow Corning, however, appealed the jury's decision, and during the appeal reached a settlement with Maria Stern for an undisclosed amount of money and an agreement that all the internal Dow Corning documents disclosed at the trial would remain confidential. This secrecy agreement won by the company may have been one of the most important contributions to its later troubles with the courts, for it made much more plausible the later charges that the company had withheld important risk information from the FDA as well as from its consumers.

In 1988, the FDA reclassified silicone implants as a "Class III" product requiring proof of safety to remain on the market, and asked the manufacturers to submit, by July 1991, Pre-Market Approval (PMA) applications which require the submission of scientific data showing their devices to be safe and effective. Dow Corning submitted 329 studies to the FDA in July 1991, and by September the FDA told the company that the studies were not adequate to show that silicone implants were safe (or harmful), and requested more data.

By this time, public concern for the safety of silicone breast implants was beginning to emerge in full force, prompted by the appearance in the media of rumours about risk information allegedly suppressed by the company. In December 1991, Mariann Hopkins was awarded the $7.3 million settlement against Dow Corning. FDA head David Kessler was under intense public pressure to do something in response to public fears. In the month following the *Hopkins* decision, Kessler received the information he needed to act. Hopkins' lawyer had won the lawsuit with the help of the internal memos and studies from the earlier *Stern* lawsuit, in addition to new studies he subsequently obtained from Dow Corning. By January these documents, still confidential, turned up in a package delivered to Kessler. Three days after receiving the package, Kessler asked the manufacturers to place a voluntary moratorium on the sale of the silicone implants. The Health Protection Branch of Health and Welfare Canada placed a similar moratorium on sales in Canada.

The FDA/HPB moratoriums further solidified the public perception, already well entrenched, that silicone breast implants were unsafe. It was clearly the widespread perception that Dow Corning had misled its customers, the FDA, and the public that led the courts to respond so favourably to plaintiffs claims that they had been subjected to unacceptable risks from their breast implants and to impose such heavy awards against the company. The company had lost a major public relations battle, due largely to the revelations of its apparent internal mishandling of the risks. The fact of this perceived disregard for the public welfare was the primary basis for the juries' judgment, not the actual scientific evidence of damage, which was slight.

Conclusion: Downsizing Risk Management Can Be Hazardous

What can be learned from the Dow Corning story about the ethical management of product risk? This is essentially a story about what can happen to a company that fails to manage the risks inherent in its products in a way that inspires public confidence. In the current atmosphere of downsizing in both public and private spheres, it is tempting for companies to cut back the resources allocated to this important function in the expectation that there is less corporate risk involved in paying less heed to product risks. After all, if the regulatory bureaucracies devote less attention to product risks, and if the standards applied to these risks are less restrictive, why should companies allocate increasing resources to risk management or impose more restrictive, risk-aversive standards to their products? Safety costs money, and the higher the safety standards the higher the costs—and the lower the corporate profits.

But the recent experiences of Dow Corning and other companies which have run into similar product liability disasters[30] strongly suggests that corporate self-interests, to say nothing of good business ethics, are best served by spending these extra resources, even under conditions of restructuring and downsizing. There are three points in the marketing process where product risk management can be exercised. It can be exercised by the manufacturer in the design and testing of its own products, where the company determines how extensive its risk assessments will be and what standards of safety it will adopt. Or, secondly, it can be exercised by government regulators who set the requirements for testing and the standards of safety. And, thirdly, it can be exercised much later by consumers taking their liability claims to the courts. In this third case, the courts will impose their own standards of risk management upon the companies. When they do, recent experience shows that they are likely to set more demanding standards than the regulators, and the costs to the company are likely to far exceed the costs of much more conservative and precautionary risk management at earlier stages, especially at the first stage.

The reasons for this are dramatically illustrated by the Dow Corning story. In the end, it was the public perception of the acceptability of the risks inherent in silicone breast implants that determined Dow Corning's liability. As the company has repeatedly pointed out, this perception of the risk greatly exceeded that which the science itself seems to support. The standards applied by the courts and juries were, consequently, far more strict than are typically applied by public regulatory bureaucracies. In the breast implant case, even the much criticized USFDA was never inclined to accept the risk assessments and safety margins ultimately imposed by the courts.

It is important to understand what lies behind the public perception of risk, which often differs significantly from scientific assessments. For only then can it be seen why it is so important for manufacturers to exercise extraordinary care in risk management at the first stage of the process, even before market approval is sought from the regulators. For scientists, the most significant factor in the acceptability of a risk is its *magnitude*. If the magnitude of a risk is assessed to be extremely low (and this is the current judgment of the best science with respect to the systemic health effects of silicone implants), then there is little reason to believe that the risk is unacceptable. Even if this magnitude factor is high, most scientists are inclined to withhold judgment on the risk's acceptability until other information about such factors as off-setting benefits are considered.

Non-expert perceptions of risk typically are strongly influenced by other, more qualitative, aspects of the risk which tend to be ignored, or considered irrelevant, by scientific experts. Among these are such things as the perceived voluntariness of the risk. Risks that people believe they are taking voluntarily are acceptable at far higher levels than risks perceived to be *imposed* upon them by others. This is a perfectly rational consideration in a society that highly values personal freedom and self-determination as well as the right to be secure from harms imposed by others. For very similar reasons, equally reasonable, lay people generally are much more accepting of risks produced and managed by agents they trust than by agents they do not trust. Just as people are notoriously willing to engage in high-risk activities like driving and skiing and sky-diving, because they trust their own ability to manage the risks (often with little justification), so too are they more willing to accept risks managed by others whom they trust to look out for their interests. A risk imposed by an agent whose competence and integrity one does not trust is far less acceptable than a risk posed by a trustworthy agent. The reason there is often wide disparity in the evaluation of risks between scientists and the non-scientific public is not, as is so often alleged, because the latter are misled by media fear-mongering or by their own scientific naïveté, but because the two are paying attention to two different aspects of the risk. The former are concerned primarily with its *magnitude* and the latter with the *integrity* and *competence* of the risk producer/manager.

This is why Dow Corning lost the battle in the courts—because it lost the battle for public trust and confidence. The evidence presented in the courts about the way the company had managed the *known* risks of local complications posed by its silicone implants undermined public confidence in the company so severely that it led to the firm and settled conviction that the other, weakly established, risks of systemic illness were unacceptable. Indeed, once public trust in a risk producer/manager is seriously undermined in public consciousness, the importance of the actual magnitude of the risk as established by the science becomes secondary. Dow Corning's defenders have often complained that the court trials turned into "morality plays" in which the juries looked for a moral villain rather than for a scientifically reliable cause of the plaintiffs' illnesses. When the internal memos provided the evidence of villainy— of a company that had failed to inform its customers of the known risks of silicone implants and had conducted little research to establish that the systemic risks were insignificant—this was all that juries needed to conclude that the plaintiffs had been exposed to unacceptable risks of the latter kind. It mattered little what the best scientific assessment of these systemic health risks was: they were unacceptable, because those who were doing the science were untrustworthy. If the company had proven itself to be untrustworthy in its handling of the known risks, why should it be trusted in the handling of the unknown (uncertain) ones?

The source of the distrust in Dow Corning lies in several perceived failures in its own management of the silicone implant risks. The first appeared to be a deliberate policy to keep information it had about flaws in the product (silicone bleeding, rupture, capsular contracture, etc.) "in house." Later, when it did make this risk information available, it chose to inform only the surgeons, and not the patients who received the implants. This constituted a second failure—a failure to consider as stakeholders of the company the ultimate users of its product who bore the risks of these complications. The third failure involved the company's decision not to engage in a vigorous study of the potential risks of systemic health effects—cancer, auto-immune and connective tissue diseases—which some of its early studies indicated might be a problem. This clearly was the view of the USFDA, which found that the data the company submitted in response to the 1988 request was insufficient to rule out the possibility of significant risks. The fact that subsequent research has failed to establish significant systemic health risks does not absolve Dow Corning of this failure. The research should have been done by Dow Corning *before* it was *forced* to do it by the litigation brought against it. The fact that the company was found to have withheld parts of its own studies when it published them did not help in the cause of image building as an ethically responsible company.

What the story shows is that Dow Corning chose to do the minimum in its assessment and management of the risks in its product. It interpreted the studies and market feedback indicating potential problems in the light most favourable to the product. It chose to err on the side of the potential risks in order to keep research and marketing costs down, rather than to err on the side of overprotecting the health of its end-users. It chose to put the burden of proof on those who alleged unacceptable levels of risk rather than to assume the burden of proof of safety in its product. And rather than adopt a policy of full disclosure to the ultimate risk bearers—those fitted with the implants—the company chose a path of minimum disclosure at best, if not outright suppression at worst.

That is to say, Dow Corning took the path that is most attractive to the streamlined, downsized, super-efficient corporation. It gave minimal attention to the management of product risk. It chose to be "bullish" with respect to the risks rather than "precautionary." Had it followed a "precautionary" approach, Dow Corning would have shouldered the burden of proof of safety and used the preliminary indications of possible risk in its early toxicological studies as a spur to invest in the additional epidemiological and other studies that would have strongly established the safety of the silicone implants with respect to the systemic health risks. The USFDA would have certainly found this scientific evidence sufficient to continue the market approval of the implants, and the moratorium on the product would never have been imposed.

Additionally, if Dow Corning had been candid in informing the public, and especially its patients, of the risks of the local complications, of which it was fully aware, it may have lost some potential customers, but the fact that knowledge of these risks has not significantly affected acceptance of the silicone implants in other countries,[31] and the fact that similar risks are posed by the new replacement saline-filled implants suggest that the silicone implants would have continued to enjoy wide acceptance. Had Dow Corning taken the "precautionary" approach, it would have been more costly in the short run for the company, but in the long run it would have avoided the harsh judgment of the public and the courts that the risks posed by its product were unacceptable. And it certainly would have avoided its own ultimate financial undoing—brought about by a product that represented a mere 1 percent of its total business. Instead, Dow Corning took a short-term "bullish" approach to the risks in its product, which left the judgment about the acceptability of those risks to the regulator, and ultimately to the courts, where the standards of risk acceptability proved to be far higher, and where the judgment was based on the largely non-scientific aspects of the risk. Ironically, Dow Corning's own failure to act with precaution with respect to the risks became the basis for a moral judgment of the company which made an otherwise acceptable risk unacceptable.

If adopting a "precautionary" approach to product risk is in the best long-term interest of a company, then the prudent company will not shortchange its commitment to risk management and its willingness to bear the extra costs of high safety standards. Reduced pressures from regulatory agencies resulting from public sector downsizing and anti-regulatory politics will not seduce prudent managers into the fallacy of thinking that product safety is an expendable option. Another irony of our time is that a public and a new economy which is currently in a strong anti-regulatory mood is at the same time becoming even more risk averse—demanding higher standards of health and environmental safety. If they do not find producers of risk meeting these standards, or regulators enforcing them, they will surely impose them in the courts. Such "third-stage" remedies for harm are much less economically efficient ways of allocating compensation for harm than are "first-" and "second-stage" remedies, as the Dow Corning story illustrates. They also result in the after-the-fact compensation for harms caused by unsafe products rather than the far preferable *prevention* of these harms. Precautionary risk management is also the ethical policy. The Dow Corning case shows also just how important the image of a company as an ethical manager of the public safety can be in the ultimate acceptance the public gives to the company's products.

15

De-Professionalization in Health Care: Flattening the Hierarchy

Andrea Baumann and Barbara Silverman

The hospital system has been undergoing restructuring at an unparalleled rate in the last five years. This process could as easily be called *destructuring*, as it is characterized by changes to traditional hierarchies. Much that has been written on restructuring during the past decade discusses a variety of activities taken on the part of managers or administrators to improve hospital efficiency and reduce costs. These include the downsizing and re-engineering of the working force in the hospital system. Few analysts of the process have recognized or acknowledged the impact of changes to professional staff. This paper explores issues raised by the de-professionalization of health care.

Much of the rhetoric surrounding restructuring supports cost efficiency, cost effectiveness, and improved quality of care. Underlying the rhetoric is a desperate attempt to remove millions of dollars from budgets while maintaining a viable service. What have health care organizations done to meet this fiscal challenge? In the 1980s, strategies included decreasing or eliminating services, joint ventures or shared services, and changes to long-standing practices governing length of stay and early discharge (Baumann et al. 1995). Initially, the hospitals achieved savings by decreasing bed size, changing the delivery of care practices, and improving general efficiencies in a way that allowed cost reduction. By the nineties, the magnitude of the savings required had increased to such an extent that hospitals were forced to undertake more dramatic measures.

There is little precedent for the measures hospital administrators have had to use to meet their targets. As a result, many salaried staff have been laid off, redeployed, and underemployed. In June 1996, 5,220 Ontario nurses were collecting Employment Insurance (Canadian Nurses

Association 1996). Those left—the survivors—include cadres of both regulated (professional) and unregulated workers.

The Phenomena of De-Professionalization

Different characteristics define different professions, as do the work environments many professionals find themselves in. But there is general agreement that by definition a professional has an identified body of knowledge, is autonomous, self-directing, self-regulating, and conforms to standards set by an association. In addition, Freidson (1986, 73) indicates that "Both public and private methods of professional credentialing assert as a prerequisite for qualification, successful completion of some formal training program associated with higher education." This credentialing or self-regulating function promotes some degree of predictability, uniformity, and understanding of what can be expected in the area of service to the public. When we lose professionals, we lose the rich expertise that experience and knowledge bring to highly complex environments.

The largest number of professional employees giving direct care in the hospital system are registered nurses, followed by other health care workers such as physiotherapists and occupational therapists. Professional practice takes place within a bureaucratic structure. Nurses, unlike physicians, are not self-employed; therefore, they have been the largest professional class highly vulnerable to reclassification, redeployment or unemployment. Within such a structure, professionals who are initially protected by contracts become vulnerable to displacement or redeployment. As organizational structures are altered/flattened, the standard professional hierarchies have been de-professionalized and "professional" heads of departments have been removed and replaced by managers without a health care background. We have to ask ourselves what an organization loses in the process.

What's in a Name?

Another restructuring phenomenon is the process of revising professional titles. There are twenty-four health care disciplines that are regulated in the province of Ontario. They have the legal right to call themselves nurses, physicians, midwives, etc. The term "registered nurse" is, for example, used to denote that someone is part of that cadre of regulated workers.

In the new restructured environment, professional staff have often been renamed. Registered nurses and physiotherapists are, for example, known as "clinical caregivers" (Hamilton Health Sciences Corporation 1996). Their role is explained to patients and families as follows:

> Clinical caregivers are formally trained individuals who co-ordinate the patient care you receive and manage others involved in your care. Clinical caregivers will be involved in the more complex components of your treatment and will evaluate those treatments as well as identify and assess any other health problems you may have. Most clinical caregivers will be registered nurses, but some may be from other regulated health professions such as occupational therapy, physiotherapy, social work, etc. (Hamilton Health Sciences Corporation 1996, 2)

The renaming of a role within an organization redefines the functions and increases the probability that this new role will be accepted. However, removing the word "registered" from a title could contribute to the de-professionalization of the nature of the role. In addition, when a client accesses health care services, roles and responsibilities can be obscured when it is not clear who is a regulated health provider.

The Diminishing Role of the Expert in the Context of Redeployment

Experts display special knowledge or skills derived from education and experience. "An expert performer no longer relies on an analytic principle (rule, guideline, maxim) to connect an understanding of the situation to an appropriate action. The expert with a background of experience now has an intuitive grasp of each situation and zeros in on the accurate region of the problem without wasteful consideration of a large range of unfruitful, alternative diagnoses and solutions" (Benner 1984, 31–32). With the diminishing number of professionals, there are fewer experts. Because of redeployment—defined to include substantive job redesign and the reallocation of workers to other clinical units due to factors such as seniority, substitution, retirement, and unit closures—many experts are carrying out different functions. In reality, this means a marginalization of expertise, the de-emphasis of explicit clinical knowledge, and a re-emphasis on a generic set of cognitive skills, such as problem-solving, administrative, and managerial skills.

The practice of moving experts from one area to another is a common aspect of downsizing. Often, the decision regarding who is displaced is based on seniority. This practice poses a dilemma—the organization has an employee who is now a novice. Although some knowledge is transferrable (e.g., procedures, policies), rich clinical knowledge is lost in the process. Experts have established schemata or patterns which allow them to assess processes quickly, move intuitively, and see a clinical pattern which they use as the basis of immediate intervention. These are critical skills in highly complex and uncertain environments. After redeployment, experts do not utilize their knowledge, skills, and experiences to the same extent since there is a new environment and set of skills and knowledge to be acquired; a professional expert becomes, in the process, a novice in the new setting.

It has been estimated that 23 percent of the hospital workforce faces redeployment or displacement (Metropolitan Toronto District Health Council, 1995). In organizations that are unionized, workers with seniority are moved—more junior workers are laid off. This results in difficult adjustments, raises insecurity, and disrupts the functioning of the organization (Lyall 1991).

Little is known about the effects of restructuring on displaced, redeployed or laid-off workers or the morale of remaining workers. Several articles have documented individual perceptions of the impact of restructuring on the system as a whole, or individuals (Armstrong et al. 1994; Baumann et al. 1995, 1996; Cameron et al. 1994a, b; Villeneuve et al. 1995). A survey of nurses from four hospitals which merged into two suggests that quality of work life, including job satisfaction, are negatively affected by restructuring (Cameron et al. 1994a). Other work life issues which are negatively impacted include job insecurity, reduced organizational morale, and lower commitment to the organization. Those who retain their positions may have their hours of employment altered in a way that has serious economic implications.

The Phenomenon of Underemployment

In the nineties, one consequence of restructuring that is not acknowledged is underemployment. Nurses who survive downsizing are sometimes required to change their work status, dramatically decreasing their number of hours of employment (Villeneuve 1996). At the beginning, the employee may have had the illusion that they are still employed and yet were changing status from full-time to part-time. This gradual change produces a workforce with a greater part-time complement. Though most hospitals have mission statements which include a commitment to continuity of care (i.e., care provided by the same workers), this cannot be achieved as the trend toward a high ratio of part-time staff proliferates throughout the organization.

Introduction of the Generic Worker

In order to fill the void left by the removal of professional staff, hospitals have introduced unregulated workers. Gill 1996 found numerous titles used to describe such generic workers: unregulated care provider (UCP), multi-skilled worker, personal support worker, nursing aide, nurse extender, and unlicensed assistive personnel. The implementation of UCPs is often done in conjunction with other organizational changes. This makes it difficult to assess the impact of introducing this class of worker.

Though decreased professional staffing ratios provide one way to cut costs, it is important to recognize the increased costs associated with the transition of past employees (laid-off and survivor) and the introduction of this new workforce. Before introducing generic workers into an organization, it should recognize:

- the increased technological support required to account for decreased professional staff
- the costs of training and retention
- that there are no regulations for UCPs, so patients cannot be assured of any standard of education or practice in this group of workers
- that continuous supervision of UCPs is needed to avoid large amounts of unproductive time (Gill 1996)

We need a rigorous study of the outcomes of using UCPs including costs and quality indicators such as mortality, length of stay, patient accidents, infection rates, and skin breakdown (Gill 1996).

What Does It All Mean?—Outcome Indicators of Quality of Patient Care

It is difficult to measure the impact of restructuring on redeployment. Even at the best of times, the outcome measurement of quality care is difficult to define. Quantitative outcome measures commonly accepted are indicators such as mortality, morbidity, and infection rates. The difficulty is determining cause and effect—do decreased ratios of professional staff lead to greater mortality and morbidity? Another important issue is staff morale. Common indicators to measure morale are commitment, absenteeism, retention, and productivity. The impact of a phenomenon such as de-professionalization is complex and the outcomes are as yet unestablished.

The Process of Restructuring

How does restructuring take place in health care? Often institutions hire outside or out-of-country consulting firms to facilitate the complex process. Employees are asked to work closely with the consultants to streamline the process. Schneier and colleagues advocate that the hands-on workers should be the ones asked to restructure the positions, as they know the work the best (Schneier et al. 1992). How can the organization on the one hand ask the employee for assistance, while on the other hand know that some of these same employees will be laid off or redeployed as a result of their input into the process? Rochon has shown that restructuring methodologies are not based on any previously studied determinants of the best processes (Rochon 1995). So much of what is documented in the literature has been applied from the private sector. "However, downsizing in the health care sector can have more life threatening and immediate implications than would be the case in most industries" (Baumann et al. 1996).

Anticipate the Future—Measure the Present

There is much concern that restructuring processes are not based on sound, tested methodologies. Instead, organizations are relying on models, frameworks, and structures that are haphazardly put forth as "today's method for restructuring." One result has been a dramatic reorganization of hospitals and the de-professionalization of health care workers.

What are the positives of this restructuring? It is hard to say, as the research has yet to provide enough evidence to answer this question. What are the negatives of de-professionalization? There are many anecdotal stories, but again, there is a dearth of research or information on this topic. Change can have positive and negative effects on the health care system. It is important to discern these strategies—to capitalize on positive aspects while minimizing the negatives. Changes based solely on fiscal restraint run the risk of undermining the purpose of the organization.

What Does the Future Hold?

This paper has reviewed some of the more dramatic effects of hospital restructuring on professional staff. One might argue that de-professionalization will lead to a re-organization that will improve health care—that is, the new roles will be assumed and more responsibility will be attained by professional staff. The leadership and management functions will be emphasized in order to supervise and guide auxiliary workers in the complex care of patients. There will be an increase in substitutions of one professional category for another (e.g., nurse practitioners and midwives will become more common in both high-risk areas and primary care). This will increase the opportunity for some professional categories to grow in numbers while providing efficient and effective care. However, the consumer of health care will need to attain a heightened awareness of the re-organization of the system and the professional roles as they evolve for the delivery of care. Organizations will have to pay close attention to factors such as staff morale and put in place a variety of incentives to help professionals cope with institutional change. Mission statements will have to be reviewed and resources put in place to carry adequate services to meet the prescribed mandate. The accountability will go beyond rhetoric in order to ensure a safe and effective delivery of care. The phenomenon of minimization of expertise should not be ignored, as it may have repercussions in the future that manifest themselves in poor quality care.

Conclusion

This paper has provided an overview of some of the issues that arise when one attempts to re-organize and downsize in the hospital sector. Organizational change is never easy, but the evaluation of that change is an imperative when the quality of health care is at stake.

This paper has raised more questions than it has answered. Restructuring is a process that will not disappear in the future, but it is important to identify trends that may impact on the productivity of employees and patient outcomes. Some of these changes are not negative, but these employees are in the business of providing direct care to an acutely ill population. Therefore, changes in delivery of health care services must be assessed closely, as it is not only the employees who are affected, but all consumers in the health care system.

PART VII
The Restructuring Economy

It hardly need be said that restructuring and the restructuring economy have tremendous social consequences. The new economy they are creating is one that is characterized by a new understanding of work and new social expectations that are in part the product of the widespread cutbacks in public spending that have been the hallmark of government restructuring. The three articles which follow discuss the nature of the new restructuring economy and the ethical issues which it raises, both in the developed world and beyond.

In their account of "Underemployment and the New Economy," Louis Groarke and Nebojsa Kujundzic discuss the issues raised by an ever-growing reliance on part-time (contract) workers who do not enjoy the benefits and the privileges of the full-time workers they replace. While they look specifically at the situation of part-time instructors within the university, Groarke and Kujundzic argue that the issues they raise in this context characterize other sectors of the economy and have become a major bone of contention in collective bargaining.

Like Groarke and Kujundzic, Robert C. Evans examines the ramifications of the contract economy. He considers it from the perspective of a long-time professional provider of "outplacement" services to employees who have been forced to deal with restructuring by ending one career and finding another. He identifies the loss of a sense of community as a major casualty in restructuring, suggests that this means that corporations no longer fulfil their obligation to provide one of the essentials of a good life, and ponders what this bodes for the future.

Darryl Reed ends this section's look at the consequences of restructuring with a look at the effects of restructuring beyond the first world. He argues the pressures created by the restructuring economy have greatly limited the range of viable social policies in developing nations and have undermined ethical social policy by not allowing equal opportunity for political participation.

16

Underemployment and the New Economy

Louis Groarke and Nebojsa Kujundzic

One phenomenon associated with restructuring is an increase in part-time employment which occurs when corporations attempt to cut their costs by employing part-time rather than full-time workers. This allows substantial savings because part-timers are not accorded the benefits, salaries and privileges of full-time workers. In the present paper, we look at the issues that this trend raises, looking briefly at the 1997 UPS strike and then focusing on teaching positions in universities, where the move to part-time workers is as significant as it is in any other industry. We argue that this move raises important ethical issues that have not been satisfactorily addressed. Though we emphasize hiring in the university setting, we believe that analogous questions arise when one considers the rise in part-time employment in other sectors of the economy.

Setting the Scene: The UPS Strike

At the centre of the brouhaha over the 1997 United Parcel Service strike lies the issue of part-time work. Part-timers account for about 60 percent of union employees at UPS and more than 80 percent of new employees hired over the past four years (Herbert 1992). Their complaints are numerous. They are paid less than half the hourly wage of full-time workers (Uchitelle 1997). They receive fewer benefits. They often work full time (Appelbaum 1997). And they enjoy little job security. Rachel Howard, a UPS employee, complains: "There are many weeks that I have worked 60 and 65 hours a week but UPS calls me a part-timer and pays

Notes to this chapter are on p. 307.

me part-time wages. I only qualify for a half-time pension.... I am now in my eighth year and still waiting for a full-time job (Lawsky 1997)."

Management representatives downplay the ethical implications of part-time work, while representatives of labour contend that part-time labour is the latest form of capitalist exploitation in disguise. A 1997 headline in the *Wall Street Journal* claimed that the "Part-Time Work Issue is Greatly Overworked" (11/08/97). The article cites some requisite authorities: Lawrence F. Katz, former chief economist at the US Labor Department, who points out that the percentage of part-timers in the US workforce has remained stable for the past fifteen years; Eileen Appelbaum of the "liberal" Economic Policy Institute, who concedes that about 75 percent of part-timers want to work part-time; economist Alec Leveson of the Milken Institute for Job and Capital Formation, who confidently asserts that "the part-time bogeyman is just a myth;" and Professor Rebecca Blank of Northwestern University, who complains, "I don't understand why there is as much discussion of part-time work as there is."

But many of the economic statistics used to dismiss the significance of part-time work are suspect. One can contest the way in which such figures are calculated. Most importantly, economists do not classify temporary work as part-time. An example can illustrate how misleading this can be. Suppose I work on contract; I spend the year working full time for five months, am laid off for three months, work full time another two months, and am again laid off for two months. At the end of the year, I have worked, on average, twenty hours a week. American officials consider anyone who works under thirty-five hours per week a part-timer. Statistics Canada sets the limit at thirty hours per week. I only averaged twenty hours per week, but I did not, technically, work part time. I was either fully employed or unemployed, so I will not show up as a part-timer in the official economic reports.

Workers naturally fall into two classes: those who enjoy full-time remuneration and benefits and those who do not. Both part-timers and temporary workers belong in the latter category. Both are, in a salient sense, underemployed. Surely they should be classified together.

There are further problems with the statistics. Labour economist Susan Houseman has argued that the official numbers are seriously flawed, for individuals who hold two part-time jobs and work enough hours appear in the official count as full-timers. At UPS itself, more than ten thousand full-time employees are paid part-time rates. These employees have the same working conditions, pay-rates, and benefits as part-timers, and should be classified correspondingly.

If government figures indicate that the proportion of part-timers in the US workforce has remained stable, the same figures show that temporary employment, although a smaller phenomenon, has risen 400 percent since 1982 (Jones and Waggoner 1997). Average daily employment at the National Association of Temporary and Staffing Services jumped 10.2 percent to 2,337,700 workers in the first quarter of 1997 as compared to the same period in 1996. These growing numbers of the temporarily employed should, like part-timers, be added to the ranks of the underemployed.

Exact rates of partial employment are hard to assess, but the numbers are significant. Even according to official figures, twenty-three million Americans, or 18 to 19 percent of the labour force, work part time. And a survey of 550 companies conducted by Susan Houseman at the Upjohn Institute in the summer of 1997 detected an increase in part-time employment. The situation at UPS in 1997 is instructive: 60 percent of employees were part-time, up from 54 percent in 1993 and 42 percent in 1986 (Uchitelle 1997).

One encounters part-time work in other industries as well. Forty percent of workers at the Bank of America are part time (Marshall 1997). According to the American Association of University Professors, almost 60 percent of faculty in American universities are part time or temporary (Westphal 1996, 151). And in the 1997 United Auto Workers strike, "The union...made the company's growing use of part-time workers the primary issue in the negotiations" (*The Detroit News* 16/07/97, B3).

The use of part-time help poses serious ethical issues. In a worst-case scenario, full-timers may be laid off, then rehired on a part-time basis. But even part-timers who have always been part-timers and always will be part-timers deserve fair remuneration, job security, good working conditions and proper benefits. Eileen Appelbaum argues that "part-time workers should not suffer a 'pay penalty' for working fewer hours, especially when they are providing the much-needed flexibility that companies seek" (Appelbaum 1997, 12A). Preston Conner, president of the National Association of Part-Time and Temporary Employees, claims that the UPS strike "highlights [a] growing disparity in wages and benefits" (Jones and Waggoner 1997, 1B). Louis Uchitelle complains of growing inequality in a two-tier job market where "part-timers, temporary workers and contract workers populate much of the lower tier" (1997, 22). And Professor Marick Masters comments that "the practice of using part-timer and temps is creating a two- or three-tiered class of workers that labour is reacting very strongly against" (Jones and Waggoner, 1997 1B).

Part-timers at UPS and elsewhere do face serious problems. Despite repeated claims that most part-timers do not want full-time work, a union-sponsored study conducted by Kate Bronfenbrenner at Cornell University found that three-quarters of former UPS employees were not satisfied with part-time opportunities there. Even those who want to work part time enjoy little job security. Of 180,000 hired by United Parcel Service in 1996, only forty thousand are still with the company, for a turnover rate of 150 percent (Herbert 1997). And they are paid much less.

Considered globally, across the US, the hourly pay of the average part-time worker is 64 percent of full-time pay. And the disparity increases when it comes to benefits. The US Bureau of Labor Statistics reports that part-timers in private industry averaged $1.82 per hour in benefits last year compared to $5.85 per hour for full-timers. According to CNN business correspondent Christine Negroni, fewer than one in five part-timers have employer-sponsored health insurance (Thierry and Negroni 1997). Only 19 percent have paid sick leave, only 42 percent have paid holidays, only 37 percent have retirement benefits, only 20 percent have life insurance options, and so on (Marshall 1997). The percentages are much higher for full-time employees.

Part-time, temporary, casual, "contingent," or limited-term work is an important and even a necessary part of economic restructuring. But as with other economic practices, it cannot escape moral scrutiny. In the rest of this paper, we will examine the ethical ramifications of part-time hiring in Canadian and American universities. We pick this example because we want to focus on a concrete case, and because this is one with which we are familiar. We emphasize that analogous questions can be raised about the treatment of part-timers in other sectors of the economy.

Partial Employment and University Hiring

In its 1995 newsletter, the American Historical Society decries employment trends in American universities. According to the society, "The increasing use of part-time, adjunct, and non-tenure-track faculty throughout colleges and universities in the United States has become a major crisis that threatens to undercut the entire post-secondary educational system" (Westphal 1996, 151). In a 1993 study entitled "The Status of Non-Tenure-Track Faculty," the American Association of University Professors (AAUP) reports that "part-time faculty now hold 38 percent of faculty appointments, and non-tenure track, full-time faculty hold 20 percent" (Westphal 1996, 151). This suggests that almost 60 percent of the teaching in American colleges and universities is being carried out by individuals who do not enjoy the salaries, benefits, and privileges of full-time, tenured faculty. A small percentage of part-timers do have tenure, but these figures do not include large numbers of graduate teaching assistants who teach at least one course in the process of completing their doctorates. One could therefore argue then that the number of part-time teachers is even higher than it appears.

The situation is essentially the same in Canada. As anyone who works in the university system will realize, Canadian departments regularly staff many of their undergraduate course offerings with non-tenured part-timers. It is nonetheless difficult to find exact statistics on the number of part-timer teachers in Canadian universities, for little attention has been paid to this aspect of academic employment. Though a 1991 Statistics Canada report suggests that almost 30 percent of workers in the economic sectors of education, health, and welfare hold temporary or part-time positions (Statistics Canada 1991, 31), Statistics Canada does not include figures on the number of part-time university teachers among its standard "educational indicators." It does, in contrast, keep figures on the part-time employment of elementary and secondary school teachers—figures which show a constant rise in the number of part-timers, from 31,619 in 1990–91 to 41,828 in 1994–95, an increase of 32 percent in five years (Statistics Canada 1996, 176).

For university teachers, underemployment is the result of financial pressures that have forced universities to limit the hiring of regular professors. The result is a growing number of teaching positions which do not enjoy the tenure or tenure-track status which has traditionally been the hallmark of permanent university employment. In 1990–91, for example, statistics available from the Canadian Association of University Teachers suggested that almost 50 percent of the faculty in Canadian universities did not hold a tenured or a tenure-track position (Riseborough 1993, 4). It is difficult to establish the extent to which these non-tenured faculty are part-timers, but a 1994 Statistics Canada study by Raynald Lortie concludes that the number of part-timers teaching in universities is growing, and that twenty-three thousand (in comparison with 37,300 full-timers) were employed in 1992 (Lortie 1994, 31). It is especially notable that women tend to be employed in the part-time category. Lortie's conclusions suggest that a substantial and increasing number of university teachers work part time, and that this situation is a direct result of the implicit and ongoing changes which have been forced by continuing budget pressures. From 1981–82 to 1992–93, the number of (full-time equivalent) students in Canadian universities increased 41 percent, but the number of full-time faculty increased only 15 percent. One (though not the only) way of compensating for this difference has been a steady increase in the hiring of part-timers.

Traditionally, there has been little concern for the plight of part-time, non–tenure track teachers in North American universities. Twenty or thirty years ago, career part-timers were a marginal element in the ranks of the teaching profession. Most members of the "baby boom" had little difficulty finding permanent teaching employment. Many, if not most, found employment before completing their PhDs. Ethicists nonetheless recognized that employment opportunities raised important ethical issues and focused their attention on debates about affirmative action and employment equity. In marked contrast, a vigorous public debate on the role of part-time, non–tenure track faculty in post-secondary education has only just begun.

The changing complexion of debates about the ethics of employment is seen in newspapers, magazines, professional societies' newsletters, and campus gazettes, which are increasingly punctuated with discussions or notices about "part-time faculty," "non-tenured faculty," "adjunct faculty," "early retirement," and "academic freedom." The May 1996 issue of *Proceedings and Addresses of the American Philosophical Association* published contributions to a special December 1995 session devoted to the role of non–tenure track faculty within the academy. In 1995 the journal *Teaching Philosophy* included a provocative "case study" on the ethics of part-time teaching (Pence 1995), and papers read at scholarly meetings increasingly have titles like "A New Model of Intergenerational Distributive Justice" and "Affirmative Action, Early Mandatory Retirement, and Intergenerational Justice."

In the present paper, we want to consider the ethical ramifications of part-time, non–tenure track university hiring. We will argue that however one analyses the situation, a great injustice is being perpetrated and that university administrations, professional organizations and all those involved in university hiring must try to rectify the manifest unfairness of hiring practices for part-time employees. Additionally, and quite independently from the interests of part-time and sessional teachers, we believe that there is a need to examine the impact of large numbers of overworked and underpaid part-timers upon students, especially over the long term, and especially in crucial first-year courses.

Though our detailed discussion looks only at part-time teaching within the university—which has relatively limited economic impact—we believe that analogous issues arise when one considers a growing army of part-time workers who are increasingly employed in other sectors of the economy. The case of university teaching is, in any event, an especially interesting one, for it is a case in which those workers who have to settle for part-time work are relatively accomplished professionals who have had to successfully complete many years of education. If professional workers of this sort cannot escape the problems of the part-timer, then one must wonder what the chances are for those whose work is inherently less skilled.

Before we can come to any general conclusions, however, we must try to understand, in some detail, the mechanism of part-time hiring. For the sake of simplicity, we will limit our discussion to part-time, non–tenure-track hiring as it occurs in Canada and the US. As PhD graduates, we know, in intimate detail, the deleterious effects such hiring practices have had on many of our colleagues. Though we will concentrate on that which we know best, we would emphasize that there is no reason to believe that the employment situation in most university departments—and especially in those in humanities and the social sciences—is drastically different from that in our own discipline (philosophy).

Defining the Term "Part-Time"

Before discussing university employment practices, we must define the term "part-time" faculty. This is a complicated issue, for the concept of part-time work has changed significantly over the years. The first serious discussion of part-time employment we have come across is found in economic literature concerning women. In the early sixties, part-time work was proposed as an ideal solution for the working mother. In *A Woman's Guide To Earning A Good Living* we read that "businesses and industries are coming to recognize the importance of part-time help and gradually will reorganize their schedules accordingly," and that "the great reservoir of potential [part-time] workers is among middle-aged women, most of whom want to work only part of the time, since they have home responsibilities" (Winter 1961, 53). The authors of *A Woman's Guide* propose part-time work as a viable alternative for women who lack the inclination or are unable (usually because of domestic responsibilities) to work full time.

In a *Few Choices: Women, Work and Family* one finds a definite change of tone. Although its authors are still able to say "Women who work part-time often feel that they have the best of both worlds" (Duffy et al. 1989, 74), they also recognize growing numbers of women are forced to work part-time because they cannot find full-time employment. They therefore distinguish voluntary and involuntary part-time work; between those who work part time because it better suits their needs, and those who work part time because they cannot find full-time work. If one looks at university hiring, one finds that part-time faculty are, in the vast majority of cases, engaged in involuntary part-time work.

But even the concept of "involuntary part-time" work does not adequately describe trends in university hiring. To be a part-time employee is, traditionally, to spend less time working. The standard full-time work week is forty hours. Statistics Canada then defines "employment as part-time if the hours worked are less than 120 per lunar month or thirty per week" (Lin 1995, 9). If one works appreciably less than forty hours, one is a part-time employee. But in part-time university teaching, the number of hours worked is not a salient issue. Pence 1995 describes a (fictional?) encounter between a part-time teacher who is teaching six courses with a tenured professor who is teaching two. The story illustrates a very common fact of life in the contemporary university: especially in the case of teaching, part-time university faculty often work more hours than permanent, tenure-track faculty. They often teach more students and mark more papers while trying to carry on research activities at the same time. In a university setting, "part-time" working has become a euphemism. It does not mean that one spends less time working, but that one is given compensation and benefits that traditionally accrued to part-timers. The term "part-timer" frequently means full-time work and part-time remuneration.

Traditional stereotypes suggest that part-timers are less qualified than full-time workers. But this is misleading. In the first place, we use the term "part-time faculty" to refer to those university teachers with PhD degrees who have failed to secure either tenure or tenure-track employment (though many of our remarks apply equally to graduate students who lecture during their PhD programs, we will not include them as part-timers). In the second place, generalizing about part-timers' qualifications in comparison with faculty who hold tenured or tenure-track positions is simply untenable. Though part-timers tend to be at the beginning of their careers, individual part-timers can have better publishing records and better student evaluations than at least some of their tenured colleagues, for older colleagues were awarded tenure-track positions in much less trying circumstances, often before they finished their dissertations. In our experience, it is difficult to find a department in which all full-time faculty are better qualified than all part-time faculty.

If part-time teaching faculty really were substandard, why would university departments hire them in such large numbers? As Robert Badillo observes, in his article in *Proceedings and Addresses of the APA*, "the quality-control issue…is largely a red herring, a defensive device used to cover up the more urgent problem found in maintaining a cheap labour force oriented to performing the more menial tasks of the profession at deploringly substandard levels of compensation" (Badillo 1996, 153). The real motivating force behind part-time hiring is economic. From the administrators' point of view, the advantages to part-time hiring are tremendous. Ben Fine writes (in a study of women's work in England), "The demand for part-time labour is dominated by considerations of cost…. In short, it is low pay that employers are pursuing" (Fine 1992, 154). In a university setting, part-timers are paid much less (often one third, one quarter or even less in relation to regular faculty), they do not have and do not expect any fringe benefits, and can be laid off at any time. In view of substantial cuts to university budgets, part-time teaching will, in all likelihood, continue to spread across North American universities. Hiring large numbers of part-timers is, from an economic point of view, the most efficient and the most economical way to cope with large numbers of undergraduates.

On the basis of such considerations, we offer the following sketch of part-time faculty. Part-timers have their PhD. They are not necessarily less qualified than full-time staff and may, in individual cases, be more qualified. They may or may not work long hours, depending upon the availability of work. They would like to work full-time, but lack tenured or tenure-track status. Instead, they are hired piecemeal on a temporary, course-by-course basis. They do not receive a yearly salary. The university and the department they work for do not recognize any long-term commitment to their employment. In most cases, they are not accorded priority when tenure-track positions arise. To be a part-timer is, effectively, to exist outside the tenure-track system with perhaps the hope that one's status will one day change.

The Fate of A and B

We appear to be witnessing a gradual imposition of a two-tiered system of employment at North American universities, one composed of part-timers, the other of tenured and tenure-track faculty. Consider a hypothetical example. Imagine that A has just been awarded a tenure-track position at the University of Opportunity and B has just begun teaching sessionals at the same institution. Let us compare the economic and professional progress of A and B ten years later.

Consider, first, the financial aspect. We will use the pay scale from the University of Waterloo for the 1995/96 financial year (*University of Waterloo Gazette* 12/06/96, 1). Assume, for the sake of simplicity, that there are no salary increases due to inflation over this ten-year period. Minimum salary for an assistant professor is about $39,000 at the University of Waterloo. After a period of ten years with regular "merit" increases, the average faculty member will be earning approximately $62,000. In ten years of teaching, then, A will make approximately $505,000.

Calculating the amount of money B will make is a more complicated matter. The sessional rate at Waterloo per course is about four thousand dollars. Assume that B manages to teach an average of four courses a year. Some years he teaches six or seven; some years two or three. There are no "merit" increases for sessional teachers, regardless of how well they teach or the quality of their student evaluations. Raises are almost non-existent. Over a period of ten years teaching, B will have made approximately $160,000. That is, he will have made $345,000 less than A. This, it goes without saying, is a substantial difference.

But the differences in A's and B's circumstances are not only monetary. In a five-year period, A will (if all goes well) be granted tenure. B, even after ten years of devoted teaching, can be laid off at the end of any semester. A also enjoys fringe benefits—for example, dental and medical insurance, a basic research budget (a professional allowance of $7,440 over ten years at the University of Waterloo), access to other research funds within and outside the university, a sabbatical leave every seventh year, a private office, extensive secretarial assistance, the possibility of promotions. If B is lucky, he will receive an office (often shared) and limited secretarial assistance.

A has some choice of the courses he wants to teach and, at the very least, he will always know beforehand what his teaching assignment is. B will have to take whatever is available and may have to prepare courses on extremely short notice. Badillo, who has been a part-timer at several American universities and colleges, relates his own personal experience:

> In all except three institutions, I have never known whether I would be teaching at all until registration, days before the beginning of the classes. Since the only responsible thing to do in such a situation is to prepare as if one were going to teach the course, I would have a syllabus,

reading material, etc., ready for the first day. In three cases, I was informed that the class had been cancelled due to low number of registrants; in another two cases I was asked to teach another course for which I had not had the opportunity to prepare a syllabus or to select course texts. (1996, 154)

In terms of numbers of students, it may be that B teaches more than A. If there is a graduate program in place, A will teach graduate students. At the very least, he will teach upper-level undergraduates. Typically, part-timers teach lower-level courses. This usually means that they have to teach classes with large enrollments, typically taken by non-majors; they may have more students clamouring for their attention outside class, and they have much more marking to do.

Consider next the professional success of A and B ten years later. In North America at least, it is very difficult to carve out a scholarly reputation as an independent researcher. As Badillo remarks, young scholars "need to be affiliated with the academic community for the purpose of, at the very least, keeping their credentials updated" (1996, 154). Status in the scholarly community depends on things like books, articles, conference presentations, membership in professional societies, attendance at specialized symposia, networking, university affiliation. Chances are that over this ten-year period, A has considerably more opportunities to advance his prominence in scholarly circles. "Raw ability" is only one factor in this situation. A has been able to teach at least some courses that are linked to his research interests. He has enjoyed research funding, secretarial help, and is welcomed as a peer into the scholarly community. B has had to pursue research on his own, without outside help, as something largely separate from his teaching duties. He must pay any costs incurred, dedicate his spare time to an endeavour for which he receives no tangible professional recognition (there are no "merit" increases for part-timers), and confront the unspoken prejudice that his work is substandard.

It is not hard to imagine the contrast between the morale of A and B. A has every reason to be satisfied with himself. He has a permanent job; he is respected by society; he has fulfilled his financial obligations to his family; he has authority at the university and prestige in the scholarly community. B is, in most cases, a bitter soul who continually wonders whether he should quit. He does not have a steady job; after ten years, he has not been promoted; he cannot help comparing his own lot to that of his tenured and tenure-track colleagues, whose paths he crosses in the university corridors every day. Being a part-timer exacts a heavy toll on B's morale.

Ethical Analysis from Various Points of View

We can consider the ethical implications of part-time university hiring from different points of view. We will consider the practice from the point of view of notions of fairness, of proportional value, "a living wage," exploitation, comparable worth, and discrimination.

John Rawls (1971) equates justice with fairness. But the most elementary notion of fairness tells us that it is quite unjust to treat two people who hold similar qualifications and perform generally similar work in a radically different manner. If, however, part-time hiring is unfair, this unfairness is not a personal or an individual phenomenon. Rather, it is political or systemic; it has to do with the way in which society, and in this case the university environment, is organized.

Consider next the situation of part-time faculty from the viewpoint of an Aristotelian notion of proportional value. Aristotle identifies just exchange with proportionality. He also argues (or assumes) that things have an absolute value. If, for example, a desk is worth six pairs of shoes, then if I pay you less than six pairs of shoes for the desk, I am treating you unfairly. In our previous example A and B provide similar services. A is (on average) paid $11,222 for a course; B is paid four thousand dollars for the same course. If what people are paid for particular goods and services must be proportional to the value of what they do, then these arbitrary differences are immoral. One cannot reconcile the fact that two people doing more or less the same job in the same economic environment—indeed, in the very same university department— should be paid such different rates. Either A is vastly overpaid or B is vastly underpaid. At the very least, there should be some consistency in their benefits they earn.

An older edition of *Websters' International Dictionary* defines a "living wage" as "A wage sufficient to live on; that is, generally, to meet fairly well the reasonable mental, moral, and physical needs of a person in his station in life, or, as stated by some, to maintain a good grade of efficiency in his work." One might argue that part-time hiring is immoral because it does not, in this traditional sense, provide part-time faculty with a living wage. Perhaps single students can survive on part-time wages, but anyone who is married and has children will find it very difficult to support a reasonable lifestyle for any lengthy period of time, even if both parents work "part-time." Buying a house, paying for life insurance, paying for your daughter's root canals becomes a very precarious, if not impossible, venture on the wages of most part-time faculty. If there is some moral obligation on corporations to pay employees a wage which allows them to live in reasonable comfort, then it seems clear that part-time university hiring is, at least in many cases, seriously immoral.

According to Statistics Canada, the average yearly income for all families was $52,504 in 1992. The average for dual-income families was $62,663, and the average for single-earner families was $41,838 (Cat. 13-208). In 1994, the poverty line for a family of one, two, three, and four persons living in an urban area was, respectively, $16,511, $20,639, $25,668, $31,072 (Cat. 13-207). A part-timer who teaches six courses a year at the University of Waterloo will make $24,000. A part-timer who teaches four courses a year will make $16,000 a year. For older students with families, part-time work may mean living at or below the poverty line. It might easily be argued that universities which tend to envisage themselves as a progressive force in society contribute to the problem of poverty.

But money is not the only ethical concern. Psychological studies suggest that the two strongest predictors for longevity are (1) job satisfaction and (2) happiness (see Shaw and Barry 1995, 320). Dissatisfaction at work may affect not just quality of life but literally, how long you live. To provide someone with "a living wage" is not to provide them with work which will make even the morally heroic chronically unhappy and dissatisfied. It is to provide benefits and conditions that provide some reasonable probability of happiness. Among part-timers there is, in contrast, a very high rate of dissatisfaction, bitterness, rage, frustration. They do not, in other words, receive, in the full sense of the term, a "living wage."

Consider next the possibility that part-time hiring is a form of exploitation. We might distinguish between three different views of exploitation: (1) Marxist, (2) Roemerian, and (3) non-technical. Marxists define exploitation as "the appropriation by a class of non-workers of the surplus product of a class of workers," where "the surplus product" is "the quantity of goods produced minus the quantity of goods necessary to sustain that workforce, where this difference is positive" (Arneson 1991, 203). In simpler language, exploitation is an economic relationship between non-workers and workers with the non-workers expropriating the surplus value produced by the work of the workers. But this is not a good description of part-time hiring. In this case, we do not have a class of non-workers directly exploiting a class of workers. What we have are two classes of workers, one advantaged, the other disadvantaged by a system (financed by all taxpayers) that is already in place. The exploitation that takes place is indirect and systemic. If full-time faculty are to be faulted, it is not so much that they individually take advantage of part-timers. If they are to be faulted, it is only that they passively acquiesce in a system that is patently unfair.

Roemer has suggested an updated definition of exploitation. He identifies as an exploited agent someone "who expends in production more hours of labour than are embodied in the goods he can purchase with his revenues from production" (Roemer 1982, 90). Exploitation, in this sense, reduces to an unequal economic transaction. The exploited agent produces goods or services of more value than the goods and services he can purchase with his wages. That is, he gives more to society or the employer than he gets back. Calculating the exact value of part-time teaching to society as a whole would be a very difficult feat. One can nonetheless plausibly argue that part-time faculty give much more to the university than the university gives them in return—i.e., that the value of the teaching they provide far exceeds the value of the benefits they receive (if this were not the case, then full-time faculty would have to be exploiting the university). They are, in this precise sense, exploited by the university as an institution. What keeps them working is not adequate remuneration but the hope that they will one day garner a tenure-track position with all the privileges that such a position entails.

Consider philosophy as an example. According to the yearly publication *Graduate Programs in Philosophy*, compiled by the Department of Philosophy at the University of Manitoba, sixty-one students were awarded doctorates in philosophy at Canadian universities during the 1995–1996 school year (129 more were awarded MAs). It is reasonable to assume that most of these graduates will look for work in Canada. To this number of eligible graduates, one must add the backlog of unsuccessful candidates from years past, those Canadian graduates who attended university elsewhere, as well as students who attended unlisted universities. All told, the number of PhDs looking for work during the 1995–1996 school year probably numbers in the hundreds. In the same period of time there were, at last count, five tenure-track jobs in philosophy awarded at Canadian colleges and universities (more jobs were advertised, but roughly half were cancelled). In such trying circumstances, universities can afford to hire recent graduates at unfair wages with minimum benefits, for these graduates have no choice but to accept part-time teaching if they want to remain within a university setting. Given the lack of opportunities outside the academy, this is a situation where graduates are forced to accept unfair work because they are in a situation where they have no opportunity to go elsewhere. In this sense, at least, one could argue that graduates are being exploited.

Having argued that PhD graduates are being exploited by the university system, we need to note that the situation is even worse than first appears, for it is the universities themselves that are creating this vast oversupply of PhD graduates. Why? Because PhD students are a desirable commodity for philosophy programs. They add prestige to departments, give tenured faculty graduate students to teach, increase government funding, help with teaching, and so on. Granting that it is in a department's interest to produce significant numbers of graduate students, it is not in the individual's interest to be directed into a workforce for which there is already a huge oversupply of cheap labour. Philosophy departments must, therefore, accept that they are, with their uncritical enrolment policies, actively contributing to a situation in which exploitation may be the inevitable result.

Consider next the notion of "comparable worth." It is difficult to define, but we can compare part-time and full-time teaching, for this involves a comparison of kind to kind. Part-time teaching requires essentially the same education, skills, and experiences as full-time teaching. It involves similar responsibilities and, at least in particular instances, a greater workload under poorer working conditions. If, then, there is any plausibility to notions of comparable worth, part-time hiring, as it is currently practised, is clearly wrong, for part-time teachers do not receive equal remuneration for work of equal value.[32] In 1990–1991, the median salary for university teachers paid on a regular salary scale was $65,799 (Statistics Canada, Cat. 81-241). Part-timers must often get by on less than twenty thousand dollars a year.

Finally, let us consider whether part-time hiring can be classified as a form of discrimination. If there is discrimination in the university workplace, it is directed towards younger members of the profession— call it the Generation X phenomenon. The older, already well established contingent of university faculty were hired during times of relative economic prosperity, favourable demographics, and employment stability. Many had a relatively easy time obtaining positions. Younger members of the profession have had a much more difficult time finding adequate employment. They must meet standards of excellence and scholarship that are much higher and more stringent than those which were faced by their older colleagues. One could then argue that younger members of the profession are being discriminated against on the basis of age. They are being treated in a drastically different manner than their older colleagues simply because they were born into a different age-bracket.

According to Statistics Canada, the number of new appointments of teaching staff in Canadian universities has declined significantly over the last two decades. Whereas in the year 1970–71 new appointments made up 17 percent of the teaching force in Canadian universities, in the year 1991–92, they made up less than 7 percent of the teaching force (Cat. 81-241, 14).[33] Observation of the dwindling number of full-time positions advertised each year suggests that this number has decreased even further.

Given that there are fewer and fewer jobs available for younger scholars, there has been a progressive ageing of the Canadian professorate. "In 1973–74, the percentage of [full-time] university faculty over 40 was 45 percent; in 1981–1982 this figure rose to 64 percent and in 1991–1992 to 78 percent" (Groarke 1996, 361). Younger age groups are under-represented in university teaching, at least when one considers regular, full-time positions. This is because they are not awarded tenure-track positions. They are hired on a part-time basis.

If, however, part-time hiring might be thought of as a form of inter-generational discrimination, it is not discrimination in the traditional sense of the word. In *Moral Issues in Business* Shaw and Barry argue that employment discrimination "depends on three basic facts: (1) whether the [hiring] decision is a function of an employee's or job applicant's membership in a certain group, rather than individual merit; (2) whether [it] is based on the assumption that the group is in some way inferior and thus deserving of unequal treatment; [and] (3) whether the decision in some way harms those it's aimed at" (Shaw and Barry 1995, 419). In the case of part-time hiring, one could plausibly argue that the individual in question is being "discriminated" against because they belong to a certain age group (1) and that the decision harms the individual in question (3). On the other hand, hiring decisions in these cases do not seem to be based on the assumption that the group is in some way inferior and thus deserving of unequal treatment (2). As one part-timer puts it, it is not that "tenured faculty are conspiring to keep part-timers out of full-time positions. They simply have a good thing going, and there is no incentive on their part to change it. In fact there are a lot of disincentives to changing it." It is not that university departments stereotype younger scholars as inferior; it is that they acquiesce in a tenure-track system which radically disadvantages them.

In so far as the hiring of part-time faculty involves discrimination, this discrimination cuts across racial boundaries and gender differences. It is a Generation X phenomenon. There does seem to be an age component that must be recognized. In the contemporary workplace, younger employees are often disadvantaged. Union policies, for example, typically emphasize the importance of seniority. When employees are laid off, it is younger employees, those without seniority, who must go. There seems to be little concern for the unfairness of the situation. It seems ironic that unions, including faculty unions, which traditionally portray themselves as the defenders of the disadvantaged, should be actively contributing to this Generation X phenomenon.

What Should be Done About Tenure?

What is the proposed solution? Many part-timers have a succinct and forthright answer: "Get rid of tenure."[34] We propose a more mitigated solution which combines revisions to both part-time status and tenure. The goal of these revisions would not be to eliminate the job security that tenure provides, but to bridge some of the gap between tenured and non-tenured faculty.

To begin with, part-timers should not be remunerated on a course-by-course basis. They should be salaried, at the very least on a yearly basis and, if at all possible, for two to three years at a time. Furthermore, they should receive salaries and benefits placed at least close to the lower end of starting tenure-track levels. They should enjoy some form of job security.

In conjunction with such moves, part-timers should be granted access to minor promotions and modest increments in salary, and if they prove themselves to be capable teachers and scholars, they should be given priority when competitions for tenure-track positions arise. The funds for their pay could be made available by a combination of moderate reductions to tenured faculty salaries and voluntary retirement.

It is equally important that tenured faculty be subjected to much more serious peer reviews and reevaluations. As W. Brehaut writes: "Despite the strong arguments set out by academics in defence of a system of tenure...it has on occasion offered refuge to those who have ceased to meet the high standards of scholarship expected of them by colleagues and by the public" (Brehaut 1995).[35] Defenders of tenure argue that tenure does not permit a faculty member to flout the rules and regulations of his institution and that research and teaching records of tenured faculty are subjected to "rigorous scrutiny." This is not the place to debate these claims, but it should be said that it is arguable that such standards are rarely enforced.

Proponents of tenure usually insist that it is a necessary condition of academic freedom. According to Jamie Moore, the president of the South Carolina Council of the American Association of University Professors, tenure "is a safeguard which society has devised in order to protect its long-range interest in free critical inquiry from the chilling effects of censorship of and reprisal against unconventional thoughts and ideas."[36] But the real effect of tenure is economic. Very few professors tout views controversial enough to be genuinely in danger of university censorship. Tenure may be about free inquiry in theory, but it boils down to job security in practice. To suggest that there should be no serious tenure review is to suggest that those who have been admitted to the company of tenured professors do not have to be held accountable either from a teaching or a scholarly point of view.

In North America, intellectual culture has developed around the universities in way that highly privileges tenured faculty. Opening up the arena of scholarship to all those who are qualified would help to rejuvenate intellectual debates and restore a sense of purpose to legions of graduates who have little opportunity to pursue academic work. It may turn out, as in the debate about the rise of the part-time economy, that they have something important to say.

The situation with respect to the hiring of part-time, non–tenure track university instructors represents a microcosm of the new economic realities that are prevalent today. If there are serious economic challenges that must be met, justice requires that changes in the marketplace and in society as a whole be carried out in a conscientious and reflective manner. The welfare of those who teach is inextricably linked to the welfare of those who are taught. If we want to have high-quality post-secondary education, we must treat the people who staff our institutions in an equitable manner. To blindly follow "market forces," to provide the bare minimum, to supply part-timers with as little as we can get away with, is in the long term to make victims of us all.

17

Losing Community

Robert C. Evans

This essay is a polemic included in amongst a number of finely researched articles. I make no apology for that. I wrote it on the presumption that I, as someone who has worked as an employment consultant for many years, could be a voice from the business community. I want to begin by turning to the tumultuous years following Newfoundland's entry into the Canadian Confederation in 1949.

This was a time when Joey Smallwood's government moved to eliminate many of Newfoundland's 1300 outports. This was in the interests of efficiency, it was said, but probably it was more in the interests of supplying cheap rural labour to the industrial and mining towns. One of the outports was Parsons Harbour, a tiny community that had clung to the inhospitable southern coast for hundreds of years. One resident forced to relocate was Theodore Symes. He recalls his leaving:

> When we left the wharf it was thick with fog there. I said to myself in my mind, I don't want to see it. And in the fog and stuff, I didn't.
> Leaving behind your home that you built with your own hands and your fishing gear that you'd worked with all your life—left behind, gone. You were coming to another place and you weren't going back no more. All the years gone by simply hove away.

The recollections of an old outport fisherman are vastly removed in time and place from the contemporary ethical and governance issues that generate solemn books like the present one. We need books and conferences on these topics because we are well down the road to a calamitous mess. But equally, we need the old fisherman to bring to our thinking a humanist sensibility that might suggest some better ways to deal with the wrenching changes now afoot in our economy.

Theodore the fisherman speaks of his visceral need for a sense of place, of community, of belonging. He knew in his guts that these things informed and enriched his life. He knew that these things, in some magical way, made him a better father, husband, fisherman, and friend. He knew in his guts that these things gave him the courage to face the sea, kept his back straight and helped him honour his gods. The spiritual side of these things is heard in the poetic cadence of the words he uses to grieve his loss: "...All the years gone by, simply hove away."

In urban, industrialized (and increasingly bloody-minded) Canada, our sense of community and place, our sense of belonging is all but dead and gone. Save in Newfoundland and a few other remote places, "community" is a quaint and largely meaningless word. As we changed from a rural and agrarian society to an urban and industrial one, communities died, and with this the concept of community. The only tangible things that took the place of community—to provide that fundamental need for belonging—were business and government. The churches, mosques, synagogues and shamans, locked in ideology and tradition, were unable or unwilling to be the basis of community in a changing, troubled, and almost entirely secular world.

And so our business and government organizations became the basis of community.

In good economic times, which we enjoyed from 1945 to the late eighties, our myriad public and private sector organizations did a passable job playing the community role. Importantly, they avoided firing people as best they could. They spent extraordinary sums of money on assorted benefits and perquisites without much concern about the pay-off. The rhetoric—"our strength is people," for example—became part of our mythology. Even at their worst, labour–management relations seemed a somewhat troubled but essentially stable marital relationship marred only by an occasional loud obscenity or perhaps a thrown dish.

In the seventies and eighties, the corporate ethic was founded on Milton Friedman's motto that organizations—mainly profit-making organizations—have but one duty, and that duty is to maximize shareholder value. This did not make a great deal of difference because growth was predestined. There was cash in abundance and it was possible to buy labour peace without putting a visible dent in the bottom line.

Milton Friedman would argue that corporate North America never intended to become the major contributor to the welfare state that he abhorred. This may be true. You cannot find this intention written in the charters of incorporation of many companies. The simple truth is that we—workaday Canadians and Americans—demanded their support and forced organizations to provide it. We did not do this out of a desire to be taken care of, as the David Frums of this world imagine, but because we needed and wanted community. We looked to private and public organizations the way we might look to a grumpy but decent parent who can be cajoled into fulfilling the needs which are the basis of community.

There was a flaw in this. We failed to understand that human organizations, unlike individuals or families (families being a natural model for rationalizing human interaction) are not naturally inclined toward morality. The bigger the organization, the closer it is to complete amorality. This is neither a good nor a bad thing—it is just reality. This doesn't mean that you should not work for a big organization and enjoy the pace, complexity, political interplay, and largely decent people with whom you live, day to day. But it does mean that one shouldn't buy well-intentioned rhetoric to the effect that such a corporation is a feeling, caring organization with everyone's best interests at heart. This just isn't so, and to this extent, Milton Friedman was right.

Toward the end of the long period of prosperity I have already mentioned, things began to fall apart. The Soviet Union collapsed, to the astonishment of almost everyone but the Soviets. The Balkans re-Balkanised. The world economy was re-engineered and the competitive playing field began to look and sound like the Donnybrook Fair. The recession that came with the change persisted like an infected tooth.

In these ambiguous times, both business and government organizations decided they could no longer afford their relatively gentle and paternalistic ways—or so they thought. They panicked. Led in too many instances by gaggles of self-anointed consultants and academics, organizations proceeded to re-organize, restructure, re-engineer, downsize, right-size, rationalize, rejuvenate, re-align, re-this, and re-that, all of which amounted, in the final analysis, to letting employees and middle management go, by the carload.

The problem is that owners, shareholders, and corporate officers do not share with employees a common understanding of their organizations. The view from above is that the private sector organization is an economic engine and the public sector or not-for-profit counterpart is an administrative engine. The view from the trenches is rather different. Employees experience their organizations as communities to which they belong, in which they work at tasks that they frequently enjoy, in return for which they receive the dollars they need to care for themselves and their families. For most workers, the organization is the place where they find friendship, stimulation, recognition, some identity, and a sense of purpose as well as a pay cheque.

It is fascinating to realize that both views are correct, and bleakly amusing to observe that the quasi-profession of human resources management (human resources, or HR, might aptly be described as personnel management with attitude) has yet to discover how to bridge this perceptual gap. If it does so—and it may—it will finally occupy a respected place in organizational life. If it does not, it will go the way of phrenology and other well-intentioned but ill-considered efforts to understand and influence the human condition.

Given this unbridged perceptual gap separating the two organizational solitudes, it is not surprising that many restructuring organizations break faith with employees by terminating so many of them and by requiring the "survivors" to work harder. In the process, termination is used as a threat, and most middle management is terminated on the hopeful assumption that their role is superfluous and that this will produce organizations capable of dealing effectively with tomorrow's ambiguities and threats.

Many of those in the consulting/academic world believe that these Draconian measures actually make sense. But one might instead describe them as the business answer to Jenny Craig: "Special! This week only! Lose 300 employees for only $300,000! You too can have the lean, mean, flexible flattened look! Be the envy of your competitors! Call now!"

But what you get if you go to the businessperson's Jenny Craig is an organization staffed by a disloyal, dysfunctional, angry workforce. You get an organization that, because it is lacking the supposedly superfluous middle management group, has no sense of its history, little corporate wisdom, and no useful sense of right and wrong. Such a corporation suffers from a truncated communication and problem-solving ability, and has little capacity for self-renewal because a solid, experienced middle management bureaucracy provides the framework for the training and development of future senior managers and leaders. In such an organization, the executives have no time for dealing with external publics, no time for planning, and no time for reflecting on their critically important leadership responsibilities because they have been sucked into an operational whirlpool and are doing all of the things their long-departed middle managers used to do. The result is an anorexic organization in which the heart muscle is atrophied and the electrolytes are mortally out of balance.

All of this provides the context that informs the steady growth in the numbers of part-time and contract employees (for a detailed example, see the paper by Groarke and Kujundzic in this volume). The evisceration of organizations is almost over. There is a great deal of hiring going on. The recruiters I use as my bellwethers report boom times. And they report that many organizations are looking for contract, part-time, and short-term employees at every level from the plant floor to the executive suite. These organizations need help; they need people who will enthusiastically buy in to what they are doing and put some sweat in to making it happen. But they are asking for, and consequently hiring, people who do not care about their organization because the organization clearly does not care about them. The people who are hired in such capacities are prepared to work for their mortgage payments, but they do not expect to be around for long and do not buy into the organizational environment at any level. They do not care about the organization's tomorrow, let alone next week. In a world of increasing complexity and ambiguity in which a corporation needs to be thinking several years ahead just to break even, this may not be the best workforce.

My good friend Dr. Carlos Frewin has spent most of his adult life turning his knowledge of education theory into programs and processes that make for better training and development in industry and produce a more effective, graceful, and civilized workplace. He reports sourly on a high-technology company that believes it a virtue to have a 40 percent contract and part-time workforce. As he puts it, "There is a notional sign on the front door that says, 'Salespersons, Pedlars, Servants and Contract/Part-time Employees Please Use The Rear Entrance'" (personal communication). He comments on yet another anorexic organization much enamoured of its current healthy balance sheet and oblivious to its dark future. All of the wonderful brainpower it is now able to access will one day take a walk and will not come back—at any price—because price is the only reason it is there in the first place.

In my own experience, I am familiar with a little company called the Osborne Group, founded by two former clients of mine, Don (Osborne) Wood and John Stewardson. It operates with great success as a mercenary clearing house. It is a collection of about thirty experienced managers and executives who hire themselves out as part-timers. They are not consultants—they are hired guns. They prosper because corporate and bureaucratic Canada wants and needs their know-how but either cannot afford it (as is the case with many small- and medium-sized enterprises) or is gun-shy about commitments that have a time line greater than three months.

In this latter situation, corporate Canada has a serious problem. It is afraid of marriage but wants all of the benefits. The big surprise for employing organizations is that the employees and managers whose skills they need increasingly feel the same way. Ten years ago, my clients—executives and managers between engagements—often made noises about some form of self-employment, but they did not really mean it. Today, most of them talk about it seriously and nearly half of them go this route.

The breach of trust is complete, and the Osborne Group therefore flourishes. In December 1996, it began expanding into a national organization. As corporate Canada recites a tedious litany of cost control aphorisms and then refuses to establish long-term commitments with its employees, the people it wants to hire have concluded that community, a sense of belonging, a sense of affiliation and place are not found in our human organizations as they now comport themselves. People therefore turn to alternatives that seem to promise what they need.

Humankind's triumph of hope over reason causes us to inquire whether there might be a positive side to the rise of the part-time economy. I suspect that this is the wrong question. In the short term, the part-time employment contract is a given, whether we like it or not. We need to work sensibly with this reality.

There are many practical, essentially technical things that can be done that can make the short-term employment contract a better arrangement for all parties. Given the increasing numbers of part-time and contract workers, is there not a clever insurance company able to make a buck by providing a reasonably priced benefits package? If an insurance company can sort out a way to provide a long-term disability plan for unemployed people—and at least two of them have—then they should be able to cover all of the necessary bases.

Could not the federal government improve RRSP opportunities? Could not the bureaucrats who concern themselves with human rights, employment equity, and the like produce some guidelines for the drafting of short-term employment contracts? Some excellent employers in this country are already finding, or at least thinking about, better ways to treat their non-permanent staff. They are investing in training for these people and are funding coaching in job search skills. They are making efforts to keep some of their part-time employees and are quietly promoting their availability to other employers. These are not altruistic gestures; it is that they correctly see merit in becoming known as good employers of part-time and contract people.

The technical question how we deal responsibly with contract and part-time—non-permanent—employees is the easy one. The hard questions arise when we consider where we are going as a society. If we end up with an adult population that rejects corporate employment in the public or private sector as a reasonable option, and opts for some form of self-employment as so many of my clients are doing, is this not suggesting that we have a grass-roots social change under way, the result of which we cannot estimate? Doesn't this suggest that the big, monolithic and paternalistic organization that has been our economic cornerstone may be on the endangered species list?

If I were a corporate or government executive, I would be worried. As a consultant, I *am* worried. I thank the eloquent Ervin Duggan of PBS in the United States who reminded me of a song from the Grateful Dead. It has to do with a locomotive engineer who stops for a break and leaves his pet monkey in the cab. While the engineer is gone the monkey takes control. The chorus of the song goes:

> Big locomotive going down the line,
> Big locomotive runnin' right on time,
> Big locomotive number ninety-nine,
> Left an engineer with a worried mind.

I would describe myself as a man with a worried mind. I believe that the so-called part-time or non-permanent economy is an indicator of things to come and not a problem in itself. I believe that our human organizations are not functioning as though the humans are in control, and that baffles me—who left the monkey in the cab?

There is much that we need to do about the new, no-loyalty, no-commitment, and no-benefits employment contract. I (like others in this volume) have suggested some reasonable possibilities. But before we commence analyzing and tinkering, we must assess any new arrangements in light of whether they answer our basic human need for contact, affiliation, and community. If they do not meet that minimum standard, they are bankrupt and must be rejected by all of us who desire a graceful, principled society.

I have spoken of the need to preserve and strengthen our society and make a better place for those who follow. I hold to no ideological position save that we all in our own way attend to a moral foundation, speak with a clear moral voice, and listen to one another in hope that as the train rolls down the track with the monkey at the controls, we can view the event with an unworried mind and know what we must do.

18

Restructuring beyond the First World

Darryl Reed

Over the past two decades or more, processes of restructuring have fundamentally altered economic, political, and social activity in all countries around the globe. One of the major concerns surrounding these changes involves the fact that they have significantly reduced the viable social policy options available to states. This has important implications for social policy ethics, especially with respect to the non–First World states which are most severely affected by these changes. In taking up this problematic, we will start by offering an account of processes of restructuring and how they have affected social policy in developed nations. We will then go on to examine the situation of non–First World nations, first arguing that restructuring has had an even more restrictive effect on social policy in these countries and, then, suggesting some of the structural reforms necessary to allow for an ethical public policy that is financially viable.

Restructuring is a complex notion that can refer to a range of processes. In the present context I use the term to refer to changes that have occurred in relations of production (see Hanly in his contribution to this book). One can understand these changes by drawing a distinction between core and peripheral aspects of the production process. Increasingly, large firms permanently retain only the core aspects of the production process (viz., research and development, finance and accounting, etc.). More peripheral aspects (e.g., production of component parts, maintenance, etc.) are contracted out. The basic goal is greater flexibility in accumulating profit. It results in tremendous efficiency gains for large firms and increased profits for shareholders, but it has significant disadvantages for workers. They are reflected in declining union membership, a greater reliance on part-time workers, less job security, downward pressure on wages, and so on.

These changes are not merely the result of technological and organizational developments. They have also come about because of political activity. One might say that there has been a dialectical relationship between changes in the political and economic realms. On the one hand, technological and organization developments have increased the mobility of capital and given capital increased power over states— power which is exercised by threatening to move investment. On the other hand, political influences have promoted changes in the relations of production (e.g., privatization, deregulation) as well as other concessions (e.g., a significant shift in the tax burden from firms to individuals, investment incentives, etc.). States "willingly" make such concessions in the context of an increasingly integrated global economy which is itself in large part the result of processes of restructuring. In this new global economy, states must compete, not only to sell foreign exports, but also to attract foreign capital.

Different states have reacted to the pressures of the new global economy in different ways. Two basic trends characterize developed countries. A "hyper-liberal" approach (in, for example, the US and the UK) advocates a clear separation of the state and the economy, and actively promotes changes in the sphere of production (e.g., privatization, deregulation, etc.). It adopts a confrontational attitude to labour and uses populist appeals to traditional values in its attempt to find a new basis of legitimacy.

A second trend which has emerged endorses a "state-capitalist" model of the state (e.g., Germany, Japan) which is characterized by a consensus-based adjustment to the realities of the emerging new economy. It still prescribes a strong role for the state in the form of industrial planning and as a mediator between the principle social forces of production (forces whose participation must play an essential role in the implementation of industrial policy). International competitiveness is promoted by exposing sectors of the economy to international competitive pressures, at the same time supplying subsidies and orientation which support innovation (Cox 1987).

Such developments have important implications for social policy ethics. A central concern is the way in which restructuring limits the range of viable social policies available to governments. In the emerging global economy, individual countries are forced into new accommodations with investment. The result has been a major shift in the tax burden away from firms and towards individual taxpayers, and (as middle classes resist this shift of the tax burden) a decreased ability to raise tax revenue. The resulting fiscal problems place increasing pressure on governments to cut spending. To the extent that this induces fiscal crises, it has the effect of limiting the range of feasible social policy options. Governments in all parts of the globe and of all political stripes have therefore been forced to (1) implement programs of economic liberalization and (2) cut social programs.

While restructuring in this way decreases state autonomy with respect to economic and social policy, it has not, in the case of large, developed states, resulted in the complete elimination of the state's room for manoeuvre. This is reflected in the social policies of both "hyper-liberal" and "state-capitalist" forms of state, though they are character-ized by significant differences.

In hyper-liberal states, there has been a much greater emphasis on private alternatives (e.g., health care, pensions), coupled with moves to eliminate universal programs, restrict eligibility for other programs, and decrease benefit levels (both in terms of payments and length of eligi-bility). New social control has been exercised by introducing (or con-templating) a variety of new measures: by placing restrictions on life style (e.g., man-in-the-house rules), by subjecting welfare recipients to surveillance (e.g., fingerprinting), by forcing beneficiaries to contribute in some way for their benefits (e.g., workfare), etc.

State-capitalist states, by contrast, have not tried to cut spending on social welfare programs to the bone. They have instead attempted to link the "balancing of the welfare of social groups" to the pursuit of com-petitiveness. This explains why, while all industrialized countries remain committed to maintaining key universal programs (e.g., health care), there are still significant differences between the traditional social wel-fare states (e.g., Sweden, Denmark, Norway, Finland) and other, more corporatist states (e.g., Germany, Japan) in terms of financing (with dif-ferent emphases on contribution-based and state-financed schemes) and the extent of benefits.

Figure 1 illustrates how restructuring has forced states to make changes to their social policy. Two points are worth emphasizing in this regard. First, in all cases and in all three aspects of social policy, the movements are all in the same direction—toward privatization, towards means-testing, towards social control. Second, there remain significant differences between social policy regimes which make for substantial differences in the quality of life of different sectors of given populations.

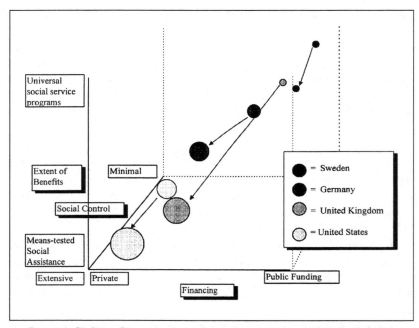

Figure 1: Shifts in Representative Social Policy Regimes (1970s–1990s)

While there are still significant degrees of difference in developed states, in non–First World states there is an increasing homogenization with respect to social policy as state after state has accepted the new neo-liberal orthodoxy. In Third World states, social policy has never been extensive. As a result, the effects of the new pressures arising from processes of restructuring may not be so evident as there was very little to cut to begin with. Still, restructuring will continue to ensure that nothing beyond the most minimal levels of benefits (necessary for legitimacy) is maintained.

The effects of restructuring are perhaps most evident in the former state-socialist countries of Eastern and Central Europe and the former republics of the Soviet Union. Because they once had well-developed social programs, the changes to social policy that restructuring has brought about are more evident in the situation of the former communists states. Whereas these states previously had extensive and relatively generous social welfare systems, the switch to a market economy (a transition itself in large part due to changes in the international economy) has forced them to make drastic reductions. To some extent, cuts were inevitable in the transition to market economies. What is telling is that these countries, against the tide of internal popular opinion, have not only had to make cuts, but to implement the more "hyper-liberal" approach to social policy advocated by multilateral economic institutions such as the IMF and World Bank. In part this is because debt problems allow such institutions to exert pressure on the nations in question (see Hanly in this volume). The recommendations of these institutions reflect the logic of the new global economic order, which overrides national preferences. This is why governments which are not ideologically sympathetic to the IMF line (e.g., the socialist-led government in Hungary) have also adopted it. In the new order, there are no real alternatives.

Such states have correctly seen that the only way to be able to guarantee even the most minimal social policy is to have a well-functioning economy which reduces the demand for social programs. In order to develop such an economy, it is essential to attract foreign capital. This in turn requires major concessions (e.g., tax cuts, tax holidays, deregulation, etc.) and, as a result, massive cuts in government spending. This is a logic which individual states cannot successfully oppose. The effect of this logic for these countries is to effectively limit all social policy options to one, viz., an absolute minimum social safety net which implies that large proportions of the population subsist at levels well below the poverty line. In the process, pragmatic discourse subsumes all ethical discourse under its domain.

In dealing with broader ethical concerns, it is essential to recognize that legitimate social policy implies certain minimal standards must be met in order to allow for equal opportunity for political participation. The problem is that restructuring undermines these conditions. The increased pressures to cut government spending undermines the provision of basic welfare rights which are necessary to guarantee people the ability to effectively exercise the right to participate in public discourse. The increased structural power of capital increases its ability to successfully violate the principle of the separation of state and society. With increased mobility and an absence of effective regional and international political and regulatory organizations, firms are able to make more effective use of (the threat of) capital flight to gain concessions from governments (Strange 1994). In so doing, they can, in effect, hold capital-starved countries ransom. This is especially true of poorer and smaller countries which are desperate for foreign capital and have very limited bargaining power. They are not in a position to offer an educated workforce, large domestic markets, and so on. As a result, law (and social policy) is established not on the basis of public discourse and democratic procedure, but rather as a bargain between firms and the state. The increased structural power of capital re-enforces its ability to dominate public discourse, especially through control over the media (Chomsky and Herman 1988), and thereby undermines the substance of the equal right to participate in the political process.

More than fifty years ago, another broad historical process of restructuring was documented by Polanyi in *The Great Transformation* (1944). He describes how, in the first moment of the Great Transformation, capital in nineteenth-century England was able to elicit the support of the state in the construction of a "market society." He goes on to show how, in a second moment, organizations representing those most afflicted by the processes of creating a market society were able, through the democratic process, to impose controls on capital in a process that led to the development of the modern welfare state. Some contemporary political economists (see Gill 1994 and Cox 1992) have seen a parallel between the creation of a market society in nineteenth-century England and present processes of restructuring which are creating a "global market society." The implicit suggestion is that in this new global society, capital once again needs to be brought under democratic control.

It should now be evident that the restructuring of the world's economy works to undermine popular determination of social policy and, indeed, any meaningful social policy ethic—first, because restructuring increasingly limits the range of possible social policy options; second, because the structural power of capital systematically undermines the possibility for the generation of legitimate law and social policy.

In order for social policy ethics to be meaningful, capital needs to be brought under democratic control again. In the new, restructured global economy, this can no longer happen at the level of individual states, as its increased structural power enables capital to play states off against each other and, in effect, bid down the costs of doing business. It is only by working through regional and global political bodies (e.g., the European Union, the United Nations) that control (in the form of social charters, regulatory standards, etc.) can be imposed upon capital and the conditions for social policy ethics realized. Without such control, it becomes increasingly meaningless to speak of "ethics" in the context of social policy decisions. Rather, it is more appropriate to speak, especially in the case of non–First World countries, of "triage."

PART VIII
Case Studies

In keeping with its name, "applied" ethics emphasizes real life situations and the issues they give rise to. All the articles in this book share this emphasis on the concrete rather than the abstract, and on real rather than hypothetical situations. In earlier sections, this is often evident in theoretical analyses which are founded on an in-depth look at concrete examples of restructuring and the restructuring economy. The articles in the present section are intended as shorter "case studies" which can shed additional light on what restructuring and its effects mean in human, social, political, and economic terms. They have been selected to reflect different interests and different points of view.

The case studies begin with the Honourable Edmond Blanchard's account of New Brunswick's restructuring experience, gleaned from his vantage point as the province's finance minister. Mary Sylver then discusses the restructuring of a small community hospital, J.L. Kachur and Derek Briton raise questions about the restructuring of Alberta schools, Monica Collins looks at the negative side of Bell Canada's restructuring from its workers' point of view, and Sylvia Chrominska defends responsible restructuring as an alternative to downsizing in the context of the dramatic changes which characterize business in the banking sector.

The aim of these case studies is not a definitive treatment of the restructuring they discuss, much less a fully developed theory which incorporates a comprehensive account of ethics as it applies to the new economy. Rather, the goal is a more modest collection of "reports from the front line" which can inform our reflections on the ethical aspects of restructuring, and which need to be provided by different voices which represent different interests and different points of view. Though they provide many valuable insights into the ways in which ethical concerns may inform particular restructuring situations, these reports are intended not as an end in themselves but as substance for further discussion, debate, and ethical analysis.

19

Rebuilding the Province of New Brunswick[37]

The Honourable Edmond P. Blanchard, QC

It is difficult to describe succinctly the profound change New Brunswick has undergone in the past ten years. It is especially difficult because I think that there are two issues I must focus on in this discussion: the first is the restructuring of the province itself, while the second is the restructuring of government. Many times you'll find I cross over between the two, and I think that is how it should be. I think too often people inside governments get too compartmentalized in their thinking, forgetting that the goals they are trying to accomplish must be placed inside the concept of the larger whole.

Over the past ten years, we have created twenty-five thousand new jobs. By pursuing and attracting businesses, we have increased awareness in the province and have increased the likelihood that people who lived in the province would also begin to look at the world in a new light. Ethically speaking, the decision to do that was made without hesitation, for we knew that many of the traditional, cyclical industries on which New Brunswick has relied—forestry, mining, fishing, and agriculture—would no longer support the workforces they once had. We didn't abandon those industries, but we have focused our efforts in those sectors on creating more value-added products. We knew that high-technology industries were not areas our population was actively exploring.

No matter how we may feel about the changes to our society—good, bad or indifferent—it serves no purpose to ignore them or to pine for the good old days of yore. To suggest that restructuring was not required—as some in our province would have us believe—or that we

---

Note to this chapter is on p. 307.

must continue down the same roads we have always followed simply because "we always did things that way" is to suggest that we must delude ourselves into feeling that time will reverse and that the world in which I grew up could somehow come back.

There were obstacles beyond the poor image our province had both inside and outside of our borders: our working-age population had a high percentage of people who were not literate, our drop-out rate from high school was unacceptable, and for those jobs we did have available, our colleges and universities were not providing people with the skills required by growing industries. So we started reworking our education system from the first day of school to the return of an adult student. We instituted free, non-compulsory, full-day kindergarten, so that now 95 percent of our five year olds are able to access this important educational step. This, at a time when other jurisdictions were *reducing* accessibility to kindergarten.

Then we worked to cut our drop-out rate, so that where over 2,300 students left school before graduating in 1991, fewer than two thousand left early in 1995. And we're working even harder to cut that number yet again, because we know how important education is in today's world. The most important efforts we've made are in the work we've done to promote literacy. In 1996 we harmonized our provincial sales tax to the federal Goods and Services Tax, a decision we were only able to make when we reached an agreement with Ottawa not to tax books in our jurisdiction. We were able to convince our federal counterparts to set up a 100 percent rebate on book purchases by our libraries, so that every cent they spend buying books goes to pay for the reading materials.

That commitment is just another part of our plan to improve literacy, something we've been working to do since 1987. In that time period, we have set up over 650 Community Academic Standards Programs across the province. Those programs involve volunteers, supported by the province and by the business community, working to help those who cannot read or write to learn those basic, fundamental skills.

We have restructured our school system by eliminating the boards that had governed our districts and by replacing them with two boards— one English, one French—which are now in charge of our education system. In place of the old boards, we have set up school–parent committees which give parents more input into the concerns they have about their schools by giving them an advisory role to the principal.

For the sake of our future generations, we have ensured that New Brunswick students have access to computers so that they may all take their first steps down the information highway while they attend school in New Brunswick. Microsoft was so impressed by New Brunswick's experience in developing and delivering education electronically, it chose us as the kindergarten to grade 12 content development and certification site for its new world-wide on-line institute.

We have recently announced, through my department, a rebate program for computers purchased for home use, where the province rebates the provincial sales tax spent on home computer purchases up to $250, provided the computer has the capability to access the World Wide Web. We did this to ensure that our province remains at the forefront of new developments in computer technology in the world, so that generations yet to come are not prevented from reaching their highest potential because "we didn't see the need at the time."

To those who call our investment a waste of money, I ask them only this: what would you have us do? Stick our heads in the sand and pray the future doesn't happen? We have learned that it is not ethical to pretend there are easy solutions to these questions. We believe that, as a government, we have responded to the changes society has presented us, because we know that to not do so would leave our population lagging behind at a key moment in history.

We believe that we have helped our citizens get the retraining they need if they find themselves unable to return to the workforce after a lay-off or an unexpected change in their circumstances. Programs offered through the New Brunswick community college system have been phenomenally successful at getting people back on their feet, and programs such as the NB Jobs Corps Program, NB Works, and NB First Start are helping New Brunswickers join or rejoin the workforce by helping them get the experience they need.

Through the community college system, we are able to respond to employer's needs more quickly than in the past, by working with them and discussing what sorts of training they require. That flexibility has been a big help in the telecommunications industry, where constant improvements make flexible training essential. We have recognized that New Brunswickers need a multitude of training options and experiences to compete successfully in the new economy. So we have worked to make those options available.

How did we start on this road? We started by identifying our strengths—strengths which include a dedicated bilingual workforce, a great quality of life and our magnificent geography with its wealth of natural and technological resources. Those assets were seldom emphasized, but all of us in New Brunswick had taken them for granted and had forgotten that they could be used to attract new investors looking for those attributes.

Next, we identified our weaknesses and tried to improve on them. We are working with business and consumers to cut red tape and to streamline the regulatory environment as much as possible. We're not doing that to try to avoid responsibilities, but we are trying to make sure every one of our regulations makes sense. We set up the new Service New Brunswick concept, which took sixty government services from sixteen departments and put them under one roof. Now, New Brunswickers can pay phone bills, renew driver's licences, and apply for student loans all in one convenient location. We were among the leaders in setting up one-stop centres for businesses looking at New Brunswick as a possible destination, so that all the paperwork they needed would be available in one place. We are increasing our information highway capabilities thanks to some two hundred community access centres planned for the province.

But no amount of money can replace New Brunswick's biggest asset: its population. If we have succeeded in attracting new investment, it has only been because our citizens have a reputation as hardworking, loyal employees who put in an honest day's work for their pay. That's why the province's latest initiative—the Service Quality Initiative—has been so successful. It puts an emphasis, both in government and in the private sector, on improving our quality standards by empowering our employees so they can bring better service to our customers, the taxpayer.

We've done many things—including seeking partnerships with the private sector to cut costs and improve service. Some of those partnerships were the first of their kind in Canada. We have just begun operating Canada's first privately built public school, the Evergreen Park School, in Moncton. We have a contract with Wackenhut Corrections to build, own and maintain our new youth detention centre in Miramichi, and we have partnered with many private-sector firms as we try to find the best ways to serve New Brunswickers. One of the most important of those partnerships was with Andersen Consulting, as our Human Resources Development department has transformed itself into a flexible, more client-centred department. The new program to be implemented—NB Case—will alleviate the burden of paperwork and allow staff more time to deal with clients, which is where we all believe their energies should be focused.

Helping clients by offering better service will also help our health care system, since those in the lower-income bracket need more health care services. And health care, after all, is the most important government service to Canadians. Survey after survey has shown that medicare, more than any other program, is one that Canadians hold sacred. But these are not easy days for our health care system, particularly in New Brunswick. We have an aging population in our province, and, unlike Ontario or provinces west, we did not have an "echo boom" once the baby-boom generation began having children, nor do we attract immigrants in the same percentages.

So we will face a situation, over the next quarter century, where the pace of increasing health care costs may outpace the growth in our revenues if we don't work hard at containing them. Consider this: in 1994, there were 93,400 New Brunswickers aged sixty-five and older, representing about 12 percent of the population. In 2009, that number will increase to 112,900, and it will stand at 179,300 by the year 2024. In more blunt terms, there are 341,000 people in New Brunswick today who make up the province's workforce, which means there are almost four people working for every person sixty-five and older, a four-to-one ratio. By the year 2024, if the size of the workforce does not increase, there will be only two New Brunswickers in the workforce for each citizen over sixty-five (though we're confident our workforce will increase in size so that those numbers are resolved in the natural course of human events).

We don't use those numbers to frighten people, but we need to be honest with ourselves, as citizens and as policy makers, about what those numbers mean. Otherwise, we may come to the point where young New Brunswickers will leave the province not because they can't find work but because they cannot afford the taxes to preserve our social safety net.

What we have done so far is to restructure our province's hospital system, replacing the fifty-one former boards which operated individual hospitals and health service centres with eight regional hospital corporations in 1992. That change has allowed us to expand extra-mural hospital services to the entire province, so that all New Brunswickers could take advantage of a service which both saves taxpayers' money and helps patients heal in their own homes.

These were difficult decisions, and there were many opposed to any bed closures or to the creation of the hospital corporations. But to have allowed the situation as it existed before 1992 to continue would have bankrupted the province without improving services to the population, an option that simply was not considered.

Now we have placed our emphasis on prevention and on creating a system that is more responsive to changing situations without so much need for bricks and mortar. Many of our top success stories come from the new mobility we have given such things as our MRI machine and our nation-leading experiments with tele-medicine, where a specialist in one area will offer a diagnosis for a patient in another doctor's office.

Individually, these things would not have worked, but when taken together as a whole, the restructuring of our health care system is creating a viable system which will survive in the next century. The province still spends one-third of its budget on health care, a proportion which has steadily increased over the years since Medicare was introduced. But now we spend that money where it is most needed: on patient care and on services, not on administration or on a thousand new buildings.

That's not the end of the New Brunswick story. We are also establishing a new, integrated justice system, where courts and Crown prosecutors will be on-line with police and corrections officials to deliver justice to New Brunswickers in the most efficient way possible. And we hope to have social service providers in that electronic loop eventually. We are downsizing our provincial corrections facilities as we move toward a system of community corrections, in which non-violent offenders will serve their sentences in the community rather than in jail. In so doing, we are implementing a more rehabilitative philosophy while we save money.

Inside government, we have restructured our public service. Since 1990, almost three thousand positions have been eliminated, with a further reduction of 750 full-time equivalents by the end of fiscal 1996–97. To achieve those reductions we relied in large part on our Workforce Adjustment Program, which consisted of severance and early-retirement incentives to encourage voluntary exit from the public service.

We didn't cut positions just to cut, but rather we made decisions based on ways we could streamline the civil service. Efforts like the creation of Service New Brunswick helped by showing us we could find new ways of performing the services our population expected. At the same time, the changes let us save $560 million to date on administration costs.

We've done all that without having to issue many lay-off notices by not filling vacant positions and by redeploying staff within the public sector. In addition, we are continuing to promote our voluntary work-time flexibility program, which allows people to work part time, job share, take pre-retirement leave or work fewer hours per week in a very innovative way.

The key to our success was that we didn't treat the public sector workforce like the enemy. Instead, we sought their input and invited them to participate in the task. Their professionalism has continually impressed all those who work with our public sector employees.

What does all this mean for other governments, be they federal, provincial, or municipal? Are there any lessons to be learned from the New Brunswick experience that can guide other provinces down the road? I can't say if these are lessons that can be applied to all situations, but I can say that I have learned that a thoughtful, deliberate approach is better than a short-term solution when it comes to restructuring anything, whether it be government or a professional baseball team. I think many people view restructuring as an evil without realizing that what we call restructuring has always been called "life," "progress," "the inevitable passage of time," or some other such manifesto of change. I have also learned that community spirit is alive and well in Canada, and that presented with an opportunity, people will work together toward a common goal with ease. And finally, I have learned that the most ethical stance there is puts the emphasis of a government, or of any organization, on the job of improving the lives of its citizens, collectively and individually.

20

Community Health at the Willett Hospital

Mary Sylver

Discussions of restructuring and new economic realities often focus on large institutions in major urban centres. But they also affect small institutions in small communities. Across Ontario, small hospitals are an integral part of their communities. In addition to providing health care services, they provide employment which stabilizes the economies of their small towns and villages.

But the Ontario health care system is in flux. Its paradigm is shifting, from a "focus on illness" to a "focus on wellness." Demographic changes, new medical and information technology, and more informed consumers are bringing about radical changes in the health care system. Even if there was no financial imperative—and indeed there is—hospitals would need to re-examine their roles in the face of these changes.

If we are to establish a health care system that promotes health and well-being, what role will small hospitals play? If such hospitals do not change, will we simply disappear? How can we re-invent ourselves to do the right things for our community?

Just a few years ago, the Willett Hospital was planning for renovation and redevelopment. It included a twenty-bed expansion of our chronic care unit. A number of new positions were created to staff a growing inventory of programs and services. The anxiety, which had plagued the hospital since 1976 (when the government threatened to close it), was diminishing. We were to become the major provider of chronic and geriatric care for the county. The future looked bright.

How quickly things change. In 1991, the plans for redevelopment were preempted by a planning process that looked at the county-wide rationalization of hospital services. By the following year, the hospital experienced the impact of a recession that was felt throughout the health care sector. For the first time in its seventy-year history, the hospital was faced with a financial deficit as a result of increasing costs and declining revenues.

Like many other hospitals across the province, the Willett embarked on a process of deficit elimination and "downsizing."

Initial reductions were designed to have minimum impact on programs and services. Several management positions were eliminated, six chronic beds were closed, and non-nursing duties performed by registered nurses were reassigned, resulting in a reduction in nursing staff. In an organization of about two hundred employees, where staff often referred to the "Willett family," these cuts were painful. Unfortunately, the financial situation did not improve, and the next budget cycle brought a further round of cuts. The Urgent Care Centre was reduced from twenty-four to twelve-hour service. The Day Surgery Program was reduced by 50 percent.

The workload of the remaining employees continued to escalate. Staff were increasingly concerned about the future of their jobs. Although it seemed that everyone was working longer and harder, signs of uncertainty and frustration were evident throughout the organization. The hospital would not survive if we continued to nibble away at the organization by progressively closing beds, tinkering with service reductions, and laying staff off.

Continued "incremental downsizing" would eventually undermine the hospital. Clearly, radical change was required if we were to continue to serve our community. The county-wide planning process had called for the Willett to develop a "non-traditional role" serving Paris and the surrounding community, but how would the new role be defined and implemented?

To guide the hospital through these uncharted waters, we needed a framework for decision making, a set of tools to ensure that we were making the right choice.

The framework we developed has similarities to the one elaborated by Yeo et al. in their contribution to this volume. It included six major elements:

I. Guiding Principles
II. Creation of a Shared Vision
III. Clarification of Mission, Goals and Values
IV. Revitalization of Staff

V. Developing the Infrastructure
VI. Transforming the Vision into a New Reality.

Each element of this process is described below.

I. Establishing Principles

As the hospital proceeded to develop a non-traditional role, the Board adopted underlying goals for service provision, including: "person-focused care"; quality and efficiency; enhanced primary care; strong linkages to ensure access to secondary and tertiary care; close to home service; a rural focus which serves the "natural community"; a willingness to be flexible, collaborative, and cooperative; and links to physicians.

II. Creating the Vision

Board members, physicians, and managerial staff worked together and developed a shared vision for the hospital which stipulated "a non-traditional hospital role in a vertically integrated continuum of care, serving the natural community of Paris and the surrounding rural area." The process included an examination of the needs of the community, the external environment, the hospital's capabilities, and the gaps that must be spanned to achieve the desired future.

III. Clarifying the Mission

Members of the corporation, governors, patients, staff, and representatives of the municipality helped articulate a new mission for the hospital. A commitment to put the community first is evident in the new mission statement: "To provide quality and accessible services that meet the changing health needs of the people within the community we serve."

IV. Energizing the Staff

As a first step in re-energizing staff, the board and management made a commitment to empower employees throughout the organization.

A process of continuous quality improvement was developed, based on William C. Byham's book: *ZAPP! Empowerment in Health Care* (1993). After initial training, ZAPP teams involving staff from all levels of the organization were formed to improve processes, solve problems, and promote interaction and communication. Through this process, employees developed increased self-reliance and a mutual commitment to work together to strengthen the organization.

The hospital also recognized the real stress and pain that employees were experiencing, and introduced strategies to promote healing within the organization. Straight talk, fairness, staff participation, and an honest recognition of the feelings experienced by the "survivors" of the changes were part of an intervention to help the staff through a difficult transition period. Too often, restructured organizations boast of being "mean and lean." Instead the Willett has tried to be "streamlined and sensitive."

V. Developing the Infrastructure

Once the hospital refocused its vision and mission, we began a process of internal restructuring and organizational redesign that would help the organization to move toward the desired future. We identified core services or programs, the needed support services and capabilities within the organization. The result was a flatter organization structure, building on a program management approach. The number of managers in the hospital was reduced from twenty-four to thirteen, and reporting relationships were simplified. In program areas, a similar approach was used to ensure that service is provided by the person with an appropriate level of skill and expertise. The result of the internal restructuring is a smaller and more responsive team which supports the core services and addresses the needs of the community.

VI. Moving from Vision to Reality

Perhaps the greatest challenge in the restructuring process was creating a model that would transform the vision into reality. The county-wide planning process supported a "non-traditional" role for the Willett, but the scope of that role was not clearly understood and needed definition. A Willett Future Directions Committee was formed, with representation from the various towns and communities within our natural community. The committee has developed an innovative model of an integrated system for a rural community.

An integrated system is defined by Stephen Shortell as "a network of organizations that provides or arranges to provide a continuum of services to a defined population, and is willing to be held clinically and fiscally accountable for the outcomes and health of the population served."

Key elements of the model include a hub which integrates a range of service networks, a process for facilitated access and coordination teamwork, a rostered population, and a primary-care physician network. The model is intended to provide members of the roster with improved access to a broad continuum of health and health-related educational and social services. The focus is on service and care, and not bricks and mortar. The model is based on the notion that services are delivered at, through or by the Willett. Integration—not ownership—is the fundamental issue.

As we move toward the implementation of the model, the Willett will go through a further radical transformation. During the transition, staff will need to continue to develop new and expanded skills. New partnerships must be developed to ensure the appropriate range of service to meet the unique needs of our community.

The Willett is ready to face the challenge of changing times. By focusing on the well-being of the community rather than the survival of the hospital, we have developed a model that truly will address the community's needs, will revitalize the Willett, and will ensure its ongoing relevance in the health care system of the future.

21

Alberta Education: Retooling through Deschooling

J.L. Kachur and Derek Briton

Until the recent election of Mike Harris's conservatives in Ontario, the siege mentality of economic crisis in Canada was nowhere more apparent than in Alberta. Haunted by the costly limitations of diversification strategies undertaken during the 1980s, Alberta's Conservatives rejected the statist conservatism of the Lougheed and Getty years in favour of a new form of neoliberal conservatism under premier Ralph Klein. This neoliberal conservatism, otherwise known as New Right politics, combine laissez-faire economics with cultural and political conservatism (King 1987, Laxer and Harrison 1995). Alberta's Progressive Conservatives are, therefore, committed to both a dismantling and restructuring of government. In keeping with the tenets of neoliberalism, their call is for a smaller, noninterventionist state when it comes to economic policy, but at the same time, in keeping with the tenets of conservatism, they call for a stronger state when it comes to issues of social control and cultural regulation.

Consequently, Klein and Alberta's new breed of conservatives have committed themselves to a process of "reinventing government" in order to establish an "Alberta Advantage" in the world market. The result: a transformation of the province's public sector according to a logic Osborne and Gaebler refer to as an American perestroika (1992). Klein's initiatives have won praise from the *Wall Street Journal* and support from the foremost promoters of neoliberal state policy in Canada: the Fraser Institute and Canada West Foundation (Kachur 1995). But Klein's predecessors—Peter Lougheed and Don Getty—have publicly criticized Alberta's new breed of conservatives for divesting themselves of traditional Tory social obligations. Such criticisms are confirmed by more comprehensive reviews that describe Klein's social and education reform in Alberta as a revolution, a deepening Americanization of Canada, and a corporate assault on Canadian schools (Lisac 1995, Barlow and Robertson 1994, Laxer and Harrison 1995).

Under the aegis of the New Right, the provision of schooling in Alberta has been re-envisaged as a "quasi-market" delivery system that unleashes the free-wheeling logic of the private sphere into the public sphere of education. In abandoning the vision of providing education through autonomous regional boards, Alberta's neoliberal conservatives have chosen to restructure the province's schooling system around a centralized administration, but with the promise of increased parental autonomy and choice in the guise of alternative programming and school-based management. It is within this socio-economic context that Alberta's chartered schools were first legislated into existence. Charter schools are part of the New Right's solution to the educational dilemma facing governments throughout the Western world. The problem focuses attention on how public schooling can help a nation develop a competitive edge in the global market *and* provide—in a cost-effective and accountable manner—educational services to an increasingly diverse group of "clients" within an increasingly complex socio-economic system.

This paper attributes the restructuring of Alberta's education system around market-based provision, and the subsequent emergence of charter schools, to an overwhelming deference to neoliberal thought. The rationalization of education services and the marketization of education has resulted from the strategic choices of Klein's Conservatives, envoys of privatization who have taken the leap of faith that will supposedly let the market work its magic. The vision of charter schools promoted by Klein's neoliberal Conservatives is part of a much larger picture drafted by a New Right state committed to "retooling through deschooling" Alberta's social contract in preparation for the province's entry into untrammelled global competition.

Charter Schools in Alberta

Charter schools have proven to be the vehicle to introduce market competition between diversified and specialized forms of educational provision to Alberta. They must be approved by the minister directly or in conjunction with a school board. They are created and run by parents or non-profit societies as registered companies or corporations. They cannot deny access to any students, except on the basis of limited space and resources. Unlike private, independent, or home schooling, charter schools are public institutions that the government funds on a per-pupil basis. They are allowed to charge fees only if they are in keeping with the fees charged by the public boards of education. Religious or denominational schools are not permitted unless affiliated with already existing Catholic districts (Alberta Education 1996).

It was through such a charter with the Elk Island Public School Division that Alberta's minister of education established the province's first charter school in September of 1995. The New Horizons School is operated by the Education for the Gifted Society of Strathcona County. The school's eighty students initially occupied three rooms on the second floor of an office building in Sherwood Park (a suburban community to the east of Edmonton), recess took place in a park across the street, there were no sports teams, and no school band; parents then, as now, dominate the board, hire and fire teachers (who are certified but non-unionized), and help run the school; the curriculum is certified by the education ministry.

Since New Horizons opened, seven other schools have been granted charters to operate in the province by the fall of 1996. These schools include (1) The Centre for Academic and Personal Excellence for gifted students (grades 1–9) in Medicine Hat and chartered in conjunction with the Medicine Hat Public School Board, (2) Action for Bright Children (ABC) for gifted students grades one to three in Calgary and chartered in conjunction with Calgary Public, (3) the Suzuki Elementary School specialized in music for grades K–4 in Edmonton and chartered directly by the minister of education, (4) the Boyle Street Community Services Co-op for inner-city students aged twelve to nineteen years in Edmonton and chartered directly by the minister of education, (5) Almadina school, specialized in English as a Second Language for grades 1–9 in Calgary and chartered directly by the minister of education, (6) the Aurora school, focusing on high academic expectations for grades 1–8 in Edmonton, chartered directly by the minister of education, and (7) the Global Learning Academy, specialized in independent learning for grades 1–12 in Calgary, and chartered in conjunction with the Calgary Public School Board.

In response to Alberta Education's charter school initiative, the province's public school boards have committed themselves to compete in the emerging quasi-market for education services. For example, the Edmonton Public School Board (EPSB) has long promoted a variety of programming choices to meet the diverse interests of parents and students. In addition to their "regular" and "special" programs for students with special learning needs, EPSB offers a menu of at least twenty-two "alternative" programs. EPSB has responded to the appearance of charter schools by increasing its alternative programming in an effort to attract clientele from the province's independent-, private-, and home-schooling community.

EPSB developed its own form of "charter choice" in 1995 by offering three new alternative programs. This offering was increased by two in 1996. These changes bring EPSB's charter-like programs to five. The Nellie McClung Alternative Junior High Program is for girls. It is premised on the belief that girls will achieve better academic results in a single-sex environment, especially in mathematics and science. The Edmonton Public Professional School of Ballet, for grades seven through twelve, and the Sports Alternative Program, for grades four through twelve, are each designed to provide flexible scheduling for students involved in extensive training and competition. The Cogito Alternative Program, for kindergarten through grade six, is defined according to basic educational values and traditional approaches. Finally, the Logos Program has opted to allow religious-based instruction.

Implementation of the Logos Program has resulted in strong resistance from the Alberta Teachers' Association (ATA) and has proven to be the most controversial program. Unlike charter schools, the Edmonton Logos Society and a lay board of directors operate a program that is both publicly funded and religious-based in what was a "non-denominational" system. In the Logos alternative program, instruction is grounded in Christian principles in a Christian environment. Teachers in the program are expected to establish a Christian viewpoint on issues and topics in the curriculum. They are also expected to adhere to the curriculum prescribed by Alberta Education and to respect the established standards of assessment for each grade level. Parents are asked to sign a commitment of support for the objectives of the program (Edmonton Logos Society 1996).

Along with Edmonton Public's foray into the public charter business, other urban centres, Calgary in particular, have initiated similar responses to the charter market. Rural communities, however, have expressed some reservations about delivering any new programs, given the financial cost of maintaining existing programs and their declining student population base.

Consequences of Charter Schooling in Alberta

The provision of education services through quasi-market mechanisms in Alberta has had four consequences. First, it has introduced a new kind of schooling based on parental choice and increased the differentiation and specialization of existing school practices. Second, public school boards have responded by further increasing the permeability of their school boundaries and intensifying the delivery of alternative programming, including an accommodation to ethno-religious diversity. Third, it has challenged the economic livelihood and professional status of teachers. Finally, decentralization at the local level has been accomplished through increased re-regulation at the provincial level as well as the centralization of financing and policy making at the ministerial level.

The quasi-market has increased the diversity of programming, and by definition, further fragmented the possibility of a "common core curriculum." The quasi-market has increased the differentiation and specialization of existing school practices and introduced new status distinctions among existing alternative programs. It is within public schooling, then, that a new kind of schooling has emerged. This new variant of public schooling retains the marks of "state subsidization" but remains in the shadow land of "privatized education." This private-like education is not based on a voucher system as neoliberal theorists imagined, but rather on "funding envelopes," or what is more properly termed "policy-based lending." Money follows the student and is tied to specific state requirements and parental demands, thus fostering the expansion of the most marketable programs.

The province's public school boards have responded to the emergence of a quasi-market in education provision by further increasing the permeability of their school boundaries and intensifying the delivery of alternative programming. They have embraced the competitive model in a modified form in an attempt to temper the individuating, competitive impulses of the charter school movement and to entice parents traditionally interested in private schooling into the public system. Public boards, engaged in more aggressive marketing of their already diverse programming, have instituted new curricula that allow them to compete directly with charter schools. Furthermore, the search for market share has pushed public school boards to accommodate lay-mediated denominational interests, and in so doing, to radicalize the original Alberta charter regulations that prohibit the chartering of religious schools. In the non-Catholic public system, the resulting mix of new denominational and non-denominational programming challenges the principles of inclusive civic pluralism, threatening to reinforce the development of separatist forms of ethno-religious pluralism. Although Section 93 of the 1867 *BNA Act* does not discriminate against denominational schooling, the variants of religious programming emerging in

Alberta sidestep normative regulation by the state via contractual oblig-ations and consumer demand.

Teachers' organizations have reacted to what they perceive as a threat to teachers' livelihood and status, and interpreted the minister's sanctioning of charter schools as an attempt to directly challenge the value of teacher labour. The use of non-union labour has created a mechanism to weaken the collective bargaining process and to drive teacher wages down. In terms of professional status, the introduction of "charter-like" schools and schools committed to denominational interests has reinforced ethno-religious splinter groups and established local con-tent standards for "quality schooling" that challenge universalistic princi-ples of civic-nationalism. For teachers, this challenge to civic-nationalism is also a challenge to their gate-keeping function as transmitters of civic-based morality. In addition to further fragmenting and politicizing teach-ers' gate-keeping functions, the new provisions compel teachers to rede-fine their role as professional public servants. In this case, professionals no longer represent the public good but rather sell a product to the high-est bidder. In this quasi-market, professional legitimacy is marketized and professional status is constrained by the logic of educational entre-preneurship, including the real possibility for the "McDonald's-ization" of education services.

Finally, deregulation at the local level has been accomplished at the cost of increased state regulation at the provincial level. As touched on above, the government has changed its tactics for intervening in the labour market. In 1994, the province's "anti-interventionist" government orchestrated a 5 percent rollback of teachers' wages. In 1994 and 1995, this same government established—again in a highly interventionist man-ner—an educational market (Alberta Education 1995a). Ironically, it seems that only such a political commitment to the expansion of charter schools will allow the price mechanism of Adam Smith's "invisible hand" to achieve the desired effect of moderating teachers' demands for wage stability. By unleashing the logic of the marketplace into the public sphere, charter schooling appears to decentralize educational regulation and strengthen local control through charter societies. It also appears to regulate the delivery of education provision through quasi-market mech-anisms. But such fundamental restructuring has been accomplished through the exercise of anti-democratic, managerial power.

We emphasize that the new charter market in education services has required the interventions of a more powerful executive arm of govern-ment to create *the conditions for the possibility* of charter schools. First, the government openly orchestrated the neoliberal and managerial discourse of reform. Don Getty initiated the reform strategy in 1991–92, during the *Toward 2000 Together* round tables and conference, and "contracted out " the coordination of the circuits of power of Alberta's elites to the Banff Centre for Management. The business community was treated as the universal stakeholder with expertise on *all* issues, especially education, and the consultations excluded all but a neoliberal approach to educational service. Though eighty-seven of the 164 recommendations in the 1992 moderator's report focused on education, it purported not to be about "economics" or "education." *Toward 2000 Together* was a carefully orchestrated public consultation process that precluded the discussion of education reform that did not fall within narrowly prescribed "economic" parameters (Barlow and Robertson 1994, Lisac 1995, and Kachur 1995, Ch. 6, 7).

Second, the Klein government introduced various bills that have concentrated the tools of governance in the hands of a select few confidants appointed to publicly unaccountable advisory committees. The *School Amendment Act* was given assent on May 25, 1994 and Alberta Education thereafter released the *Charter School Handbook* and established the target of fifteen charter schools for the fall of 1995. The *School Amendment Act* also included legislation to regionalize school districts, thus shifting power away from locally elected officials to provincial bureaucrats. But even more controversial than the process of centralization was legislation in Bills 41 and 57. Bill 57 was intended to allow every minister to hand over power for government programs to private corporations without parliamentary debate. After stirring up controversy by prematurely tipping its hand to the opposition, the government withdrew the bill and proceeded with Bill 41. This bill allowed for a similar kind of transference of power, allowing the government to proceed to contract out social services to private providers at the discretion of the minister (Robertson et al. 1995, 103). The legislation effectively circumvented legislative debate on the issue of privatization.

Third, included in the rationalization of this anti-democratic trend was the increasing use of policy-based lending to tie funding to the implementation of specific programming and the initiation of a centralized program of school evaluation through standardized testing, polling, and the publication of performance indicators.

The implication is clear. Once power is taken from citizens and given to technical experts, an ethical debate about educational goals simply cannot arise. Society is reduced to a collection of atomized consumers whose freedom consists in making consumer choices based on purchasing power. The charter school market was facilitated by a plethora of new laws, regulations, and state interventions. While implementation and delivery of educational service remained at the local level, conception and evaluation of those same services was shifted to the offices of a smaller educational bureaucracy consolidated under ministerial control. The government of Alberta and the ministry of education justify this authoritarian necessity in the name of "effective internal administration of the government of the province" (Alberta Education 1995b). This smaller but more powerful state bypasses local- and school-based democratic decision making mechanisms. Education delivery in Alberta has thus been reconceptualized in terms of a "bottom line" that subordinates the democratic decision-making processes of local citizens to the "quality control" of "outputs." Consumer choice thus supersedes citizen choice, and school administrators are compelled to perform as strategic managers in search of market niches.

Retooling through Deschooling

What a closer inspection of the charter school phenomenon reveals, then, is that under Ralph Klein a variant of conservative politics emerged—the politics of the New Right—to orchestrate the delivery of education services in Alberta through quasi-market mechanisms. This orientation is readily identifiable in the writings of neoliberals such as Hayek (1944), Friedman (1980), Douglas (1993), Lawton et al. (1995), and Osborne and Gaebler (1992), theorists who call for the market provision of education through vouchers or charter schooling. Klein's new breed of conservatives has successfully articulated neoliberalism with at least three forms of conservatism: (1) benevolent conservatism and managerial corporatism (Berle and Means 1932, Drucker 1993), (2) authoritarian conservatism of the religious Right, and (3) small-property populism. Klein's politics is a hybrid of liberalism and conservatism, and its New Right bloodlines remain incontestable. What holds the coalition together is *resentment* expressed as populist antipathy for the welfare state.

In promoting charter schooling as a means to further rescue civil society from the iron cage of state bureaucracy, Ralph Klein's neoliberal conservatives certainly appear to share some of the radical democratic and left libertarian sentiments promoted by Ivan Illich in the 1970s in *Celebration of Awareness* (1970), *Deschooling Society* (1971), and *Tools for Conviviality* (1973). These texts had a major impact on thinking about education in the 1960s and 1970s. How, then, does the notion of deschooling promoted by Alberta's New Right differ from that promoted by Ivan Illich?

Illich's primary criticism of liberal reform measures is that welfare state reforms deepen the state's power, allowing instrumental rationality to penetrate the logic of everyday life and objectify students in terms of system "outputs." Illich contends that in capitalist societies, the state's rationalization of schooling is implicated in the reproduction and deepening of class power. Consequently, Illich is critical of professional monopolies, state and corporate bureaucracies, and the commodification of schooling through the pursuit of credentials in a market economy. His proposed solution to this perceived dependency is to "deschool society," that is, a process of deinstitutionalising major areas of social life, especially the mass public education systems. Illich's proposed disestablishment of bureaucracies and construction of convivial education includes, however, the transformation of all bureaucratized institutions, including capitalist corporations (Morrow and Torres 1990, 17).

It cannot be denied that Alberta's right-wing populism bears a remarkable resemblance not only to the left-wing populism of the 1960s and 1970s but also the leftist critique of professional monopolies, state bureaucracies, and instrumental rationality. Both variants of populism also exhibit the same naïveté regarding social transformation. They mistakenly reduce the capitalist economy (a set of property relationships) to an industrial economy (a set of technical relationships). They also limit the challenges of social transformation to changes in consciousness.

What most readily distinguishes Klein's right-wing populism from its left-wing variants, however, is the content of its ideal future and its significantly different critique of political and cultural liberalism. While the New Left idealized the radical extension and deepening of political and cultural freedom, Klein's vision, in keeping with the principles of the New Right, idealizes traditional values, effective technologies, and economic anarchy—under the direct supervision of a strong state. The present crisis in governability is directly attributed to too much democracy and free thought. According to proponents of the New Right, professional social service elites have taken control of society, used the state and clients of the state to feather their own nests, monopolized credentialing as a bulwark for a false professional status, and subverted the truth of human nature through the myth of progressive morality.

On questions of power, both movements mobilize populist appeal against educated elites: the left against business technocrats, the right against public servants. The New Left, based on a critique of the centralization of economic and political power, called for the empowerment of the people, and disavowed the status and privilege accorded to professionals and educated elites. It was especially critical of the organization of capitalist corporations, the private ownership of the means of production, the regulatory power of state bureaucracies, and the power of the social engineers to subvert authenticity. While the New Right also uses the language of empowerment, it employs it toward a markedly different end. The New Right mobilizes the *resentment* of the middle and working classes against state and professional power but without any commitment to blunt the discretionary power of corporate executives and strategic managers who shape the workplace and state policy.

The New Right came to power in Alberta on December 5, 1992, when Ralph Klein defeated Nancy Betkowski for the PC leadership and effectively shifted power to rural Alberta and Calgary. Under Klein's command, old-time Tories, those who believe in communal solidarities and paternalistic obligations, have found themselves set adrift in a sea of neoliberalism. It is such traditional Tories who have both expressed public concern about the negative consequences of Klein's socioeconomic reforms and chosen to distance themselves from the neoliberal imperatives that have served to restructure the province's education and health care systems. Consequently, given the extension of the capitalist market and new production methods in the delivery of social services, given the increasing partnerships between schooling and the corporate sectors, given the deepening influence of the state controlling program delivery, and given the ethno-religious fragmentation of national civic standards, it would be a mistake to argue that education reform in Alberta exemplifies the deschooling of society.

We suggest, rather, that education reform in Alberta is more accurately a "retooling of society." The restructuring of social service provision in Alberta, as exemplified by the introduction of charter schooling and quasi-markets in education services, does not challenge the existing bureaucratic order, but rather complements and deepens its perpetuation. The inversion of the New Left's deschooling thesis into its opposite may well serve as a warning to contemporary ethical critiques of restructuring. Samuel Bowles and Herbert Gintis offer an interesting critique of Illich's deschooling thesis, and their thesis applies equally well to the New Right's "retooling through deschooling" effort and the growing number of pragmatic ethical adaptations to globalization that do not seriously consider the empirical social forces that actually exist in contemporary society (1977, 260).

Illich's formulation, the two argue, overlooks how instrumental and consumer consciousness is grounded in the production process, and how any
strategy for change that does not recognize and address existing economic structures is doomed to failure. The promotion of market-based schooling is no exception.

22

Bell Canada—from the Bottom Up: An Employee's Perspective

Monica Collins

In debates about restructuring and the new economy, statistics, numbers, and the bottom line tend to render faceless the people affected by downsizing or supposed "right"-sizing. The following is the story of two long-term Bell employees and the effects of Bell Canada's restructuring on them. It provides a glimpse of the lives behind the numbers and, in the process, a vivid illustration of the ways in which individuals' attitudes are changed, and the culminating effect of these changes on company productivity, workplace cooperation, and community involvement.

George Brown[38] has worked more than twenty-five years with Bell Canada. He estimates that only two of the first ten years were spent at home with his family. For the rest, he was on the road. But he was not unduly concerned. He knew that the Bell family would take care of and support his wife—who also became a Bell employee—and children in his absence. As a worker, he felt significant, a pioneer, a proud ambassador for his company. Some fifteen years later, he finds himself wondering whether his sacrifices for the company were worth it.

In March 1995, John McLennan, the president and chief executive officer of Bell Canada, announced his plan to eliminate ten thousand jobs by the end of 1997. He described this "slashing" as "inevitable" given decreased revenues, declining profits (46 percent over three years), and expenditures of twenty-three billion dollars on technical upgrading.

George recalls that this announcement changed the company overnight. Bell employees felt betrayed, frustrated, and uncertain of their future. Too many questions remained unanswered for too long and

---

Note to this chapter is on p. 307.

rumours fuelled the fears of already disgruntled workers. Support systems like health departments were dismantled and significant changes were made to maintenance departments, but few facts were shared with employees and no strategy was unveiled. The long-awaited video announcement by the CEO on the company future was postponed several times.

Finally, in June 1995, McLennan advised employees of their options over closed circuit-television. Workers could volunteer for an early retirement package by September 30, 1995, or have the career action centre find them other jobs somewhere in the company. After September 30, 1995, the value of buy-out deals would be halved and other "options," including lay-offs, would be examined.

Details remained unclear. The Browns and other employees watched and waited helplessly as immediate supervisors communicated front-line workers' questions to managers and received incomplete answers weeks later. They soon concluded that there was no well-thought-out plan in place. Instead, the company's prime aim seemed to be to alleviate investors' and shareholders' concerns about the company's ability to compete globally.

Workers concluded that their union's hands were tied if they were to save jobs. They read *Globe and Mail* reports of Bell's transfer of assets, its moves to set up distribution subsidiaries, its planned services spin off through the formation of two new companies, and its closure of operators' offices. Some workers left voluntarily to join the new companies. One thousand inside-wire maintenance workers voluntarily left Bell to join Entourage Technology Solutions Inc., a new company owned by the Quebec Federation of Labour's Solidarity Fund. Bell now contracts out its inside-wire maintenance work to Entourage. Then came critical CRTC rulings which denied Bell permission to test a potpourri of new services, a request which was hotly contested by the cable firms, and opened up the doors for new phone-line firms. According to the Browns, "The government gun had been pointed to the company head."

Workers could not get proper answers to their questions from management and were hard pressed to arrange for a chartered accountant to advise them on their severance package or pension during the regular work week. No on-site seminars were offered to explain the options, and most workers would not risk taking a day off work to seek advice they badly needed. Only those who accepted the severance package were eventually offered any adjustment assistance (a three-month resume writing/job search skills course).

With only incomplete information, bewildered and frustrated workers watched Bell diversify and create new companies. Front-line workers were not consulted or asked for their opinions. In a period of six to eight months, managers lost credibility as they frequently changed their minds, repeated rumours, and proved incapable of interpreting the various options which were offered to employees. Employees with long company service, such as George, felt they had insights to offer directors who had no hands-on experience, but their opinions were not taken seriously. As the number of first-line managers decreased, communication worsened. A family-like working environment quickly degenerated into one of rivalry and uncooperative relationships. Colleagues who had worked well together and thought of themselves as "ambassadors of the company" now competed fiercely for the new jobs in newly formed companies.

Workers perceived the whole process of rehiring as suspect. It was as though a few favoured employees had been hand-picked for choice jobs while others were slotted into "bum jobs" in different departments of Bell or, worse, laid off.

In order to keep a job with the company, employees were forced to make difficult decisions concerning relocation (including costs, benefits, their tolerance for extended absences from family, and their ability to adapt to new cultures and environments). As local offices were closed or their closures planned and work was centralized in major centres like Toronto, more and more families were faced with such dilemmas.

The Browns' only real option was to sell their house in Thunder Bay and move to the Toronto area. Leaving family and friends behind was traumatic, as were the initial battles with their two teenagers, but the Browns decided that Mary should take an option offered her. This meant relocation to the Toronto Ontario Control Centre, where she would perform support work for the repair department and full billing for damages or repairs for which customers were liable.

The family bought a house in Newmarket and have again assumed a large mortgage, due to the much higher cost of housing in southern Ontario. Every day, both Mary and George, who is now working shifts on a temporary, ninety-day contract, commute to Toronto, adding between two and four hours daily to their eight-hour work schedule.

The intangibles have been difficult to deal with. It has meant struggling to adapt to the faster pace of life and to a new social situation. It has meant rebuilding a social life, something difficult in a community where people do not greet each other as a matter of course on the street. The family has lost the joy they once experienced fishing after less than sixty minutes on the road in tranquil, relatively isolated northern lakes, which cannot be replaced by the tension and long delays on major highways needed to arrive at polluted lakes. George is trying to substitute wood-working for his passion for fishing. Mary wonders why the Thunder Bay office is still open, long after the date it was due to close. She wonders whether she made the right decision.

On the positive side, the children have adapted well. They enjoy the wide choice of post-secondary educational institutions available to them in southern Ontario. George believes he has more opportunities to work with and to learn about advanced technology thanks to the move south. He believes that he will consequently be in a better position to get new work or to become self-employed when he retires in two years.

But financial concerns are taking their toll on the Browns. They now have a high mortgage and two children to put through college and uni-versity at a time when fees are increasing by leaps and bounds. Mary in particular cannot reconcile the need to leave Thunder Bay and her friends. She does not understand why the company did not offer a tech-nologically feasible and less expensive work-at-home option. She is fed up with the "forked tongues" of managers who espouse team work and employee empowerment, but practise back stabbing, favouritism, and despotism. She cannot see the savings in centralization given the drop in employee productivity and constant technological breakdowns and delays. She believes that commuting and relocation have left employees bitter, without any sense of community, and exacerbated inefficiencies.

In the absence of a clearly understood restructuring strategy, voice-less Bell employees who had taken pride in doing their best and who had enjoyed their work, have adopted a "why should I bust my ass if the company is going to shaft me again?" attitude. The work ethic has changed dramatically and productivity has declined sharply. Workers' interest in on-the-job training in new technology has also declined as their sense of isolation has increased. They find it difficult to place much confidence in the abilities of the new, younger, "book-trained" managers with no "hands-on experience," and effective communication has decreased in consequence. Rather than face long commutes, those working overtime sleep at the office. In silent apprehension, they watch for the company's next move, wondering where the justice is, given that managers have been transferred to other close positions while techni-cians and operators have been forced to make heavy personal sacrifices to relocate to large centres like Toronto, or to take other jobs in new companies.

George is unwilling to sacrifice anything more for the company. He, like many of his colleagues, feels spurned. Their input was only sought after the fact, so what can they possibly offer now?

Management remains uncertain of labour and worker reaction and a wait-and-see attitude prevails. "There is a big pendulum around the world," George says, "and in two years' time the whole communications field will be revolutionized." In the meantime, nervous workers monitor the press. In an August newspaper report, Bell's plan to contract out 3,500 operator jobs was reported and Ms. Koen, Bell spokeswoman, was quoted as saying, "the company is reviewing operator services as part of a larger, $1.7 billion program to restructure and cut costs in preparation for full competition in local and long-distance telephone markets" (*Globe and Mail,* 21/08/96, B5).

According to the Browns, the company has paid a heavy price for the uncertainty of the last two years. It has lost employee commitment and is losing potential customers daily because the company no longer has the right personnel in the right jobs to provide responsive, quality service to the customer. Whatever the future brings, it is hard to believe that demoralizing workers in this way is the best way to build a solid foundation for a secure future.

23

The Banking Sector: Avoiding the Pitfalls of Restructuring

Sylvia D. Chrominska

I've been asked to address the question of how downsizing and restructuring are managed in the banking sector. To begin with, I'd like to make an important distinction between these two terms. "Restructuring" means employing your workforce in order to adapt to changing work. "Downsizing" means unemploying your workforce because work has changed.

The banking industry is facing huge challenges. Restructuring to meet these challenges is simply good business. But how each organization plans to respond to these challenges—or fails to plan—is the key point. I'm going to talk about the issues impacting banking, about what's happening in the industry as a whole. Then I'll touch on Scotiabank's experience and its approach to managing these issues and the changing needs of our workforce.

The banking sector has been undergoing tremendous change— change that is revolutionizing the financial services workplace. And it's largely driven by three things: technology, consumer demand, and new sources of competition.

Technology has opened the doors for banks to deliver—and for customers to demand—more convenient services: picking up the telephone to pay a bill, using a debit card to pay for groceries, or accessing a commercial account from your PC at work. In short, the traditional bank branch is no longer the only place to do your banking.

Consumer habits and demands have changed, too. We now expect convenient twenty-four hour access to services, we expect to check our account balances over the phone or pay with a debit card over the counter, and we expect more service. We want financial advice—such as mortgage advice or retirement planning advice—but we don't want to stand in line to get it.

This combination of new technology and changing consumer habits is dramatically shifting workloads. In Canada, between 1990 and 1994, the number of automated banking machines (ABMs) increased from about 7,400 to 12,700—a 72 percent increase—while the number of branches increased by less than 9 percent. During this same period, electronic transactions more than doubled, to six hundred million transactions per year. But the proportion of transactions handled by branches is dropping substantially. An Ernst and Young 1996 study predicts that retail banking transactions done at branches will decline from 38 percent of all transactions in 1995 to 21 percent of all transactions in 1998.

Now that the computer is fast becoming a key access point to banking, we have a unique new breed of virtual bankers. These are the information service providers, among them, Intuit and Microsoft, which use networks like the World Wide Web to provide access to financial services. These new players are joined by a wide variety of others: insurance companies, private pension funds, mutual fund firms, and credit unions. Each of these new competitors is finding ways to provide traditional banking services without the costs of a branch system. In fact, technology allows them to circumvent the use of branches.

For instance, the Vancouver City Savings and Credit Union, popularly known as VanCity, announced in 1996 that it is launching a completely branchless national bank, where all services will be offered over the phone, by PC and ABM. Foreign banks, such as Citibank, are also making more aggressive moves into the Canadian market. In August 1996, Citibank announced that it was joining forces with AGF Trust to offer full banking services. Other "branch-less" financial services include the financial arms of major manufacturers such as General Motors and General Electric, which provide everything from car leasing to credit cards.

This new competition, consumer demand and new technology all represent major structural issues in Canada's banking system. At the centre of it all is the branch network, the place where most bank jobs reside. Maintaining a branch infrastructure is an expensive proposition, and one that new competitors don't have to contend with. This raises the fundamental question, how can we manage the changes due to increasing competition and dramatically shifting service demands? How can we manage to compete successfully with competitors who can reach our customers via the Internet?

One way—and I believe it's the wrong way—is downsizing.

A 1996 report by Deloitte and Touche states that the number of staff in the Canadian banking industry will have to be cut by thirty-five thousand within the next ten years. That's roughly 20 percent of the industry workforce. They say deregulation, new technology, and more competitors will force sweeping changes in how banks conduct business.

Undoubtedly, many jobs will change or disappear over the next few years, but I think the Deloitte prediction is overstated. It assumes that the competitive pressures now being identified are new and unanticipated, but they are not. These pressures have existed for the better part of the past two decades, although they are speeding up today. The prediction doesn't recognize that the loss of some jobs will be offset by the creation of others. It doesn't account for the banking system's equipping its current workforce with the new skills and knowledge necessary to adapt to change.

Employment has declined in the banking industry. At their peak in 1991, the six major banks employed 173,000. Today, that number is 165,000—a 4 to 5 percent reduction. This reduction has been handled not by downsizing, but primarily by attrition and by redeploying people in new areas of business, such as telephone banking and trust services.

The main reason for this approach is that banking is a service business—a people business which consists of mutually beneficial relationships. Structural change always affects people—employees, employers, and customers—and it affects behaviour. So, structural change only succeeds to the extent that people are able and willing to adapt. In other words, it involves attitude and motivation.

Downsizing can hardly be called motivational. When a company turns to downsizing as a restructuring technique, it's making a conscious but short-sighted choice. Because there is little evidence to show downsizing improves performance, and much evidence to the contrary (see, for example, the articles by Wayne Cascio and Todd Hostager et al. in this volume).

Downsizing focuses very narrowly on costs, not people, skills or performance. Costs and people are viewed as one and the same. When this happens, restructuring becomes a quick financial fix, not a long-term business plan.

Almost every organization talks about people being their most important asset, but not every organization acts that way. In a service business, like a bank, when downsizing is used to address business problems, the negative impact is huge. It destroys the loyalty between the company and its employees. The emotional and psychological contract is broken, and that affects behaviour.

Evidence shows that downsizing severely damages the employment relationship and ultimately the customer service relationship. And when service suffers, the business suffers. Research also shows that when the employment relationship is healthy, employees are better motivated, more committed, and generally have a better attitude. They provide good service. And good service is profitable.

So what's the alternative to downsizing?

It's planning. A well-managed company manages the size and needs of its workforce well. I'm not talking about an acquisition, where duplication often leads to redundancies; I'm talking about the crucial planning a company needs to do to determine what human, technological, and financial resources are needed to meet the needs of all its stakeholders—customers, employees, shareholders, and suppliers. Planning is key.

Companies that avoid downsizing do so because they are better planners, and do five things well:

- They avoid one-time, short-sighted fixes. Business improvement is a process—a continuous process—not a transaction.
- They know their core competencies or strengths and they build their business decisions around them. They position and prepare their workforce to deliver on those strengths. Change that flows from business strategies is more acceptable to employees, because it makes sense and isn't viewed as a knee-jerk reaction to short-term trends in the marketplace.
- They support skills training. The impact of new technology I discussed earlier is not destroying jobs, it's changing work. Managing change is really about managing changing work. Training must be forward-looking, and it should help employees acquire skills that are adaptable to the new work environment.
- They make a commitment to employment. Leading companies put employee satisfaction on an equal footing with satisfying customers and shareholders. At Scotiabank, for example, we don't guarantee jobs, but we do everything possible to keep staff employed and to provide a stable work environment. This is crucial to maintaining loyalty, which is one of our core values. Our goal is to provide quality jobs with long-term career potential.
- They communicate. At Scotiabank, we make every effort to inform employees about our bank's strategy and its strengths. Communication helps provide employees with a context for what is going on in

their workplace. It helps cultivate a positive attitude toward change, because employees understand the business reasons for what is going on around them.

I think that if you use these five guidelines, you avoid mistaking people for costs. You avoid the expedient "grow and shrink" approach to business, where you add resources to handle increasing workloads, then cut them back when work slows. Instead, you focus not only on handling the immediate work, but on managing it in consideration of all your stakeholders, with a longer-term view in mind.

We know this works. During the 1970s, Scotiabank's assets increased by thirty-seven billion dollars, while our staffing increased by 9,500, or 68 percent. In the decade that followed, our assets grew by fifty-four billion dollars, but we required a net addition of only five hundred staff. The difference was that although our bank was growing rapidly, we were aggressively managing the work. We centralized functions. We created new ways of doing things so staff could focus on the customer. Our staff didn't stop working, but they did stop some of the work they were doing in the past, and started doing different work.

During the nineties, we've continued with this approach. And we've grown consistently, with no need for retrenchment. The result has been a steady record of job stability, providing high-quality, high-value jobs. In 1995, Scotiabank created four hundred positions in Canada. So far in 1996, we've added 875 employees. This is growth coming in new areas of business, such as telephone banking and mutual funds, but also in the traditional branch network.

Massive downsizing is not a legitimate means of managing over the long term. It's irresponsible and it's damaging. It's short-term thinking for short-term, and often questionable, gains. As the saying goes, no one ever shrunk to greatness. Grow your business wisely, manage change carefully day to day, and stay focused on the big picture.

PART IX
Overview

In the final section of this book, Wesley Cragg, one of North America's leading ethicists, provides a summation and an overview of the ethical issues raised by restructuring and by the other articles in this book. In his account of the ethical dimension of restructuring and the restructuring economy, he identifies the obstacles, opportunities, and challenges they present when they are considered from an ethical point of view.

24

Ethics and Restructuring: Obstacles, Challenges, and Opportunities

Wesley Cragg

My assigned task in this concluding chapter is to provide an overview of challenges and opportunities that the phenomenon of restructuring has created for ethics. Before addressing that task directly, however, I propose to begin with an examination of two obstacles that need to be overcome if ethics is to achieve a significant role in current debates. First, consider a recent article from the Business section of the *Globe and Mail* entitled "The big picture" by Donald Cox, a regular *Globe and Mail* investment columnist and the chairman of Harris Investment Management Incorporated of Chicago and Toronto-based Jones, Hourd Investments Incorporated (Cox 1997). The column in question records Cox's reaction to the news that the Dow Jones had just passed 6000 with no end to a rising stock market in sight. At issue was whether the bull market could be expected to continue, or whether stock prices then current represented a speculative excess that was bound to end in a spectacular stock market collapse of the sort experienced at the beginning of the Great Depression. Cox comments:

> The stagflationary 1970s brought three people to power who quite literally ushered in a new era. Paul Volker, who became the US Federal Reserve board chairman in 1979, the year of Margaret Thatcher's first victory in Britain and Ronald Reagan, who first won in 1980. These people insisted that central banks should follow US economist Milton Friedman's approach: the goal was price stability, not manipulating the economy. As for economic policy, they agreed with Austrian economist Joseph Schumpeter, who said that the greatest extension of wealth creation in

history was capitalism, *a system based on creative destruction*. He even
said that stable capitalism was a contradiction in terms. (Cox 1997, B21,
emphasis added)

These comments strike me as an intriguing place to begin my discussion of ethics and restructuring. Much of the discussion in this book
focuses on the destructive character of restructuring which, as the editor
notes in his introduction, has taken the form of downsizing, lay-offs,
government cutbacks, the closing and amalgamation of hospitals, boards
of education, schools and health services, and the "rationalization" of
higher education. Though some of the contributors to this volume advocate particular kinds of restructuring (Chrominska, Cascio, Leo Groarke,
etc.), none of the contributors to this book endorse it in the same unre-
strained spirit as Donald Cox. The process of restructuring—and the
restructuring economy—has not, from their point of view, been particularly creative in the positive sense of that term.

The strongest supporters of restructuring—economists, politicians,
and their supporters in the electorate—are of a different view. For some
of them at least, creative destruction is what restructuring is all about.
"Working smarter," "providing more with less" and similar slogans are
commonplaces in private and public sector management circles. What is
equally important is that these slogans imply a hidden ethical justification
for the pain and dislocation involved. Capitalism is destructive. But what
it destroys is inefficiency in the form of feather-bedding, exploitation of
privilege or political favour, fatigue, and loss of initiative. The result is a
market able to provide goods and services efficiently, and at the lowest
possible price. Since we are all consumers, we all gain in the long run.

This is an economic justification of restructuring that rests on dis-
guised ethical foundations. It constitutes an obstacle to a systematic discussion of ethics and restructuring, however, because its ethical parameters normally remain implicit and unaddressed. Nonetheless, the current
underlying justification of restructuring as carried out through most of this
decade is what is believed (implicitly) by its advocates to be its fundamentally creative character. It is an obstacle in the way of a discussion of
ethics and restructuring because, for the most part, those opposed to the
process rarely address this justification for restructuring directly, while
those who support restructuring that has an obviously destructive character rarely make the assumptions that underlie that support explicit.

The second example I want to mention by way of introduction centres on comments by Dr. Elaine Todres, deputy minister of the Solicitor

General and Correctional Services, Ontario. The comments were made at a conference entitled "Community Corrections: Making It Work in Ontario," organized by the John Howard Society. Dr. Todres was a keynote speaker. Various papers in this book discuss the growing impact of restructuring on the nature and quality of social and health services in the 1990s. The Honourable Edmond Blanchard specifically addresses the implications of restructuring for corrections.

Prisons should be of special interest to those interested in ethics and restructuring because the people who are allotted prison sentences are for the most part the least privileged members of our society. The proportion of people with disabilities of one kind or another is much higher in prison populations than in the population at large. Most inmates are very poor and badly educated. Their chances for succeeding under current economic conditions are about as slim as any other group in our society.

Elaine Todres has a very distinguished record of achievement as a public servant. She sits on the editorial committee of the Canadian Institute for Public Administration; she was appointed editor-at-large of the journal of the Agency for Instructional Technology, a non-profit, US–Canadian organization, and her writings have been widely published. They include an article on "Ethics and Government" in the *Journal of Canadian Public Administration*.

In her address, Dr. Todres described the mandate of her ministry and the mandate of the government. The first goal of the government of Mike Harris and her ministry was to reinvent the justice system. The second goal was "to deliver justice," particularly in the case of serious crimes. (Note that in the Canadian justice system, the provincial solicitor general is responsible only for people sentenced to less than two years.) The third objective of her ministry, she said, was to restructure with a view to reducing costs.

The impact of these priorities has been rather remarkable. Dr. Todres was speaking to a room full of people involved in community services. Many of them would likely lose their jobs because of the restructuring aimed a cost reductions that the policy of the government implied. For the inmates of provincial correctional institutions, the picture was even bleaker. Since the current government has taken office, there has been a 45 percent reduction in temporary absences in Ontario, all the provinces half-way houses have been closed, and the numbers of inmates released on parole have been reduced by more than 50 percent.

I offer these developments as an example of "creative destruction" at work in the public sector. It is clearly destructive, yet those responsible for making and implementing the policies in question profess to believe that they are creative. Similar policies are at work in health and education. Nor is Ontario an exception in this regard. Similar forces are at work in Western liberal democracies around the world.

The gap between "creative destruction" and ethics might seem to be enormous, but one thing that impressed me about Dr. Todres's presentation was her absolute conviction that the Conservative government was driven by a commitment to re-establish integrity in the political process. The government had taken office absolutely determined they were going to re-establish the public's perception of politicians as people of integrity, she claimed. They were going to do so by demonstrating that politicians were capable of keeping their promises. And that, she proposed, was exactly what Mike Harris, the premier of the province of Ontario, was doing.

I mention this because the people whose actions and policies are so much the focus of attention in a discussion of ethics and restructuring believe that what they are doing is ethical. It is important not to overlook this fact. For those who see the destruction and not the creativity, the fact that restructuring is seen as ethically justifiable by those directing its course is an obstacle to communication. Yet, if it is true, both sides should welcome a discussion of ethics and restructuring. These two examples point to several obstacles to a discussion of ethics and restructuring that must be addressed if progress is to be made and communication, with or without consequent agreement, is to be achieved.

Obstacles

It is important that those of us who believe deeply that ethics has a role to play in business and in public policy, should not overlook the obstacles that stand in the way of injecting ethics into the economic debates that are currently taking place. There are four of them that it is particularly important to identify and discuss.

The first obstacle to a meaningful analysis of the ethics of restructuring lies in the rhetoric of ethics itself. The problem with that rhetoric is that in our society it is as easily used by people trying to disguise the unethical character of what they are doing as it is by those whose motives are more pristine. There are many examples that illustrate this problem. Pyramid sales schemes are promoted for the benefit of their participants. Tobacco companies have no trouble using ethical paradigms—an appeal to individual freedoms, for example—in justifying their marketing activities. Politicians of all stripes use the vocabulary of ethics to castigate their opponents while at the same time frequently demonstrating a willingness to cut ethical corners when doing so seems to their benefit. The most recent presidential election in the United States is replete with examples of this phenomenon.

The ease with which people in public life appeal to ethics to justify their activities or criticize their opponents has left many people sceptical about the value of introducing ethical criteria into the examination of public issues in any form. As a consequence, debates about ethics carry a good deal of unwelcome baggage. For many, appeals to ethics have strongly negative connotations.

Ironically, the rhetoric of ethics can create obstacles to the task of examining restructuring from an ethical perspective even where ethics is understood positively. The problem is that a commitment to ethics as something potentially constructive and worthwhile is for people in the business community and elsewhere a double-edged sword. Companies and organizations that articulate clear ethical standards are often exposed to severe criticism that questions both their motivation and their conduct. Because of this, there is considerable risk in articulating high standards against which your behaviour can then be evaluated. For these standards can become weapons in the hands of opponents and competitors who are frequently not reluctant to attack those espousing them as hypocritical because of their failure to live up to their own standards in all respects. It is not surprising, therefore, that many organizations, both in the public and the private sector, set up codes of ethics which are designed to govern their employees, or members, for example, but refuse to reveal what those codes are. Thus, while the current prime minister of Canada made ethics a cornerstone of his campaign for office earlier this decade, the code of ethics he put in place to guide his ministers in the exercise of their responsibilities has never been made public. The same is true of the code of ethics to which the Real Estate Board of Toronto claims to hold its members responsible but which it also refuses to make public. (Mark Schwartz, a business ethics PhD student at York University, had enormous difficulties trying to obtain a copy of that code.)

The irony in this state of affairs is obvious. By articulating ethical standards, people expose themselves to criticism for failing to meet self-imposed standards that others are not expected to meet just because they have avoided espousing ethical commitments publicly. In unscrupulous hands, this double standard can become a weapon that can be used to achieve goals that are themselves frequently not in the public interest. This then constitutes a second obstacle to attempts to inject ethics into the debate on restructuring.

A third obstacle to useful discussion of the role of ethics in restructuring is the realization that ethics is no panacea. In the heat of debate, this fact is easily forgotten. Ethics, that is to say, has a limited reach in a number of senses. Virtue is no guarantee of success. The fact that you are well motivated ethically does not mean that you are going to be successful in your business dealings, whether in the public or the private sectors. There is more to business management and public and voluntary sector administration than ethics. Ethics is a *component* of effective leadership; but it is only one such component. Many other skills are required for success for which ethics is no substitute.

Another way of making this point is to observe that bad things do happen to good people and good organizations. Equally, good things sometimes happen to bad organizations. Hence, ethics is no panacea. Those of us arguing for its importance must be careful not to suggest otherwise.

The fourth obstacle faced by those wishing to advance the cause of ethics in restructuring is perhaps the most important one. It is the widely shared belief that ethics in reality has only a peripheral place in guiding and structuring economic activity, whether in business, health services, or education. That is to say, while many people regard ethics as something we should try to pay attention to if we can, ethical conduct is not seen as essential, and may indeed constitute a significant obstacle to success or the avoidance of failure. Often this view is accompanied by a related view that ethics is one of the things that must go if important financial issues, particularly survival, is at stake. Ethics is, on this view, a luxury. Alternatively, it is easier to be ethical if you are doing well than to be ethical if you are doing badly. These and similar views are deeply engrained in our modern culture. They constitute a significant obstacle to injecting ethics into current debates about the economy in a serious way.

I do not think that these four obstacles to injecting ethics into restructuring debates are insurmountable. Nevertheless, they are significant and they should be kept in mind if we are to engage that debate in a realistic fashion. The importance of so doing becomes even more apparent in the kinds of economic environments in which restructuring becomes a serious option. How then are these obstacles to be overcome?

Challenges

Two challenges face those who seek to evaluate restructuring and the new economy from an ethical perspective. Ignoring them will only create additional obstacles for those who believe that ethics should inform and structure business activity, public policy debate, and administrative procedures.

The first challenge is the relatively undeveloped state of business ethics. The reasons for this state of affairs are not particularly obscure. Until recently, the ethical values that people assume ought to guide business activity have gone largely unarticulated in contrast, for example, to law and economics.

The reason for this may lie in the fact that until recently shaping character and ethical beliefs was thought to be the job of the family and the school. In the world of business, this encouraged the idea that building an ethical business required simply hiring ethical employees. On this account, a business will be unethical if it employs unethical employees and ethical if it employs ethical employees. This view continues to dominate the thinking of many of the older generation of business leaders, which is one of the reasons why the study of business ethics and business ethics education has had such a difficult time getting off the ground in this country.

In deliberations about restructuring, the most explicit indication of the undeveloped nature of ethics is the many references to what commentators have described as the unwritten employment contract. Gary Graham of the Canadian Manufacturer's Association (in a presentation to the Laurier Conference on Ethics and Restructuring, 1996) described a central but informal tenet of that contract as the commitment on the part of an employer that "if you work hard and stay out of trouble, there will be a job for you while we stay in business," or alternatively, "while we remain profitable." David Drinkwalter identifies the same informal principle as the expectation of job security on the part of employees (Drinkwalter, 171).

Gary Graham suggests that this principle has played an important role in the evolution of employer–employee relationships over the years in countries like Canada. It's role in defining those relationships, however, has been largely informal. It is not enshrined in legislation in any explicit way. Nor will you find it explicitly articulated in collective agreements. For the most part and for most people, until recently, it was simply assumed and taken largely for granted.

In his presentation, Graham pointed out that this informal principle has become one of the significant casualties of an era of restructuring. What is slowly taking its place, he suggested, is an "employability" principle. A striking feature of the discussion that followed Graham's presentation was his reaction to a question asked by a member of the audience. Where and how, he was asked, should this implicit contract be articulated in labour relations? He evinced considerable surprise at the question and admitted he had no idea what the appropriate answer was.

This example illustrates how the ethical underpinnings of business activity still lie unarticulated even when people are committed to an ethical perspective. They provide foundations which, it is assumed, we don't need to probe, presumably because everybody knows what they are. On the other hand, if you listen carefully to the debate about ethics and restructuring, you will hear that assumption increasingly challenged, though only indirectly even by leaders who have been persuaded of the importance of business ethics.

One of the challenges facing those who want our society to examine restructuring and similar phenomena from an ethical perspective is to move the debate in the direction of an explicit evaluation of the need for formally articulated ethical values for the workplace. Workplace value frameworks need to be set out formally so that people can see them, evaluate them, and base their actions on them.

The second challenge is appropriately directed more specifically to the academic community. The challenge is to learn to balance "wrong analysis," the search for and critical evaluation of moral errors, with "right analysis," the search for and evaluation of sound ethical behaviour. It is a challenge for academics because their natural inclination is that of a critic. They look to see what is inadequate out there in the real world and then attempt to work out how to correct it. The result is that, typically, business ethics texts or cases focus on examples of mistakes or errors in judgment or moral wrongdoing. Hence, the attraction of cases like Dow Corning, or the Exxon *Valdez*, or Bophal, or Baring Bank, and so on. One of the favourite videos in current use in business schools is a thoughtful and articulate examination of the *Challenger* disaster. This video case study is a perfect example of wrong analysis, a particularly dramatic example of something going seriously wrong with disastrous consequences.

I am not suggesting that this type of analysis is inappropriate. What I am suggesting, however, is that the challenge to the academic community is to realize that critical analysis is not of great value in the field of ethics if there are no models which can substitute for, or at least provide an alternative approach to, the kinds of problems typically addressed in business ethics. Providing examples for study of commendable responses to challenging problems is what I describe above as "right analysis." We need to begin to look for those firms that have been guided by ethical considerations in the direction of ethically creative and courageous outcomes to contrast with cases describing organizational behaviour gone awry. Equally important is diagnosis that seeks to work out what was involved in getting it right.

One of the best examples of "right analysis" that I have seen recently is set out by Sylvia Chrominska in the previous chapter. It goes without saying that some people may disagree with this example. Nevertheless, it certainly is a very good example of an organization, or at least a part of an organization, trying to work its way through restructuring challenges from an ethical perspective with a view to getting things right before they go wrong. The second challenge is to place more emphasis on these kinds of examples.

I have suggested two challenges: the challenge of articulating those values that have remained inchoate in our culture but which need to surface and be examined, and the challenge of doing "right analysis" as well as "wrong analysis." If these are the key challenges, then what are the opportunities that these challenges present as we look at strategic planning, management, administration, and public policy development?

Opportunities

Challenges generate opportunities, in this case the opportunity to make clear what was previously unclear, and to set ethics on a solid footing for the future. I would suggest that there are four examples of opportunities that the challenges and obstacles discussed above give rise to.

The first opportunity, and in many respects the most fundamental, is to establish that ethics has a central role to play in policy development, strategic planning, and management. Central to accomplishing this task is bringing people to the realization that ethics is not *just* about rules. Ethics is about rules; that is undeniable. However, it is not *just* about rules—it is also about vision and envisioning. Ethics invites people to think about the future in creative ways.

Ethics brings into focus things that otherwise would go unnoticed. People who do not introduce an explicitly ethical dimension into their planning miss things that they ought to be paying attention to. That is to say, there are some things they are unlikely to see unless ethical values have an explicit and acknowledged role in strategic planning and management. It is not that they are necessarily evil or uncaring; they just don't see things that are important to what it is they are doing. Ethics requires that people move outside of the circle of their own interests and look at what they are doing through the eyes of others. Ethics also provides incentives and energy for the search for genuinely creative solutions.

Those who want to inject ethics into economic decision making must identify models that illustrate the envisioning character of ethics and its consequences. This is what makes right analysis so important to this kind of work.

The envisioning character of ethics can be illustrated and explained in many ways. One of those ways, in my view, is to convince people that building ethics into corporate decision making will result in better decisions from everyone's perspective, in the long run. That is not to say that things never go badly for ethical people; it is to say, rather, that in the long term, ethics can bring insight and understanding to management, strategic planning, and policy formation. The result will normally be a more sensitive and less damaging treatment of all those likely to be affected by economic decision making.

The first opportunity that restructuring makes possible is the opportunity to broaden the sense of vision in play where restructuring is under consideration. I have suggested that ethics is the key to this process. Much of what is said in this book illustrates this conclusion.

The second opportunity that restructuring generates is the opportunity to identify the values and principles that ought to guide ethical decision making in business, health, and education. Here, formally articulating the values by which an organization chooses to guide its operations and activities becomes crucial. In their contribution to this collection, Peggy Cunningham and Pamela Cushing illustrate the value of this activity for cause-related marketing. Cause-related marketing involves private sector support for a "good" cause like cancer research or the environmental protection of endangered species with a view to achieving a competitive advantage through the publicity generated.

Cause-related marketing is a valuable source of funding for hard-pressed, voluntary sector organizations. However, it also carries with it the implicit endorsement of the firm doing the marketing by the voluntary sector organization that stands to gain from the marketing arrangement. The same is true in the other direction; the firm engaged in cause-related marketing implies, by its partnership, endorsement of the cause and the organization being supported.

The moral complexity which cause-related marketing generates lies in the fact that both parties are entering the partnership for pecuniary reasons, with the consequent danger of exploitation, manipulation, and compromised principles. This makes cause-related marketing a good example of a development that calls for careful articulation of the values, rules, and principles that will ensure that damaging compromises are not made. In situations of this sort, creative ethical thinking is key if partners are to avoid potentially very damaging developments while opening the door to imaginative solutions to financially stressful pressures resulting from cutbacks in government funding.

Restructuring provides a third opportunity for ethics to which intellectually creative responses are needed if ethics is going to be taken seriously by our decision makers. The opportunity I have in mind here is the opportunity to bring empirical research into the service of ethical analysis. People from my particular background (I am a philosopher by training) often disparage the role of empirical research in applied ethics. This is perhaps not too surprising, given the quality of much of the research conducted to date. In spite of this fact, however, empirical research is vital, as a number of the contributions in this collection illustrate. One reason is the importance of testing the empirical dimensions of strategies which are justified by their advocates by reference to their anticipated beneficial consequences, much in the way of ethical defence in the business, health, education, and government communities has to do with outcomes. One of the tasks, then, of ethics is to ensure that the empirical foundations of ethical judgments are fair and balanced.

The role of empirical research in applied ethics is one of the themes that dominates this book. Wayne Cascio, for example, shows how empirical studies can test the claim that downsizing has beneficial, long-term effects for corporations. One of his own studies looks at Fortune 500 returns and the effect of downsizing on the stock market values of companies that have done so in dramatic ways. There is no doubt that an enormous spike in stock value can be the result of downsizing. Indeed, this can be the result of simply announcing a decision to downsize, whether the announcement is followed through on or not. Perhaps that, in itself, is enough to indicate that the downsizing itself does not have a key role to play in the evaluation of stocks, except insofar as it effects the psychology of short-term buying.

Other articles, for example Dewey and Groarke's piece on evidence-based decision making ("What Restructuring Can Learn from EBDM") raise ethically important empirical questions about restructuring in all sectors of the economy. An other example is Conrad Brunk's assessment ("Managing Risk in the Restructured Corporation") of the breast implant controversy, an issue that has touched the lives of many thousands of women and driven Dow Corning into bankruptcy.

There is a fourth opportunity that accompanies the challenges we face in the context of ethics and restructuring on which I wish to comment. That is the opportunity to test the ethical assumptions and reasoning underlying policies and strategies described by their advocates as ethical or ethically justified. The opportunities that restructuring in our economy provide in this regard are numerous, as illustrated throughout this collection. What is required is not only critical appraisal of promised or predicted outcomes, but also critical appraisal of the ethical coherence of the strategies for achieving those outcomes, as well as of the principles which underlie the proposals themselves. This is an extremely important work of a kind that ethicists are genuinely qualified to do. We can engage people in this kind of analysis even if we disagree with what they are proposing. If they are sincere in what it is they are trying to achieve, then they will want to respond to the analyses arrived at. Of course, not everyone who claims morally sound foundations for the agenda being advanced is sincere or will turn out to be sincere. However, in the end, sincerity can only be tested by inviting a dialogue, and those who are genuinely concerned with the ethical parameters of their proposals will respond. It is with these people that the discussion of ethics, restructuring, and the economy will begin.

One of the central difficulties we face in this endeavour is the extent to which debate can become polarized. Empirical claims are often seen to be unfair or biased. Those who identify themselves as ethicists have a special responsibility in this regard, if they are to encourage the best use of the opportunities for ethical inquiry that the current impulse toward restructuring makes possible. Once again, there are many examples of what is possible in this regard in this book. Barry Hoffmaster's essay ("The Ethics of Restructuring") is an example; Todd Hostager's account of corporate judo is similarly effective. A key element in all these analyses is the observation that the policies under examination are inconsistent with the stated goals of those who elaborate them.

We might apply this kind of analysis to the examples I began with by asking what ethical assumptions are implicit in theories like that of creative destruction. How does one know that the destruction is going to be creative? What kind of ethical parameters can one construct which will allow the thesis to be tested? If it is not tested, then the theory itself is seriously suspect, an expression of ideology or of intellectual fashion. Those who use expressions like "creative destruction" have an obligation to define the ethical parameters of their theories and concepts so that the public can discern what is creative and what is just destructive. Ethicists in their turn have an obligation to submit those justifications to careful examination. I think that this book (and the Wilfrid Laurier University conference from which it sprang), have gone some distance in that direction.

List of Contributors

David T. Bastien is an assistant professor of Organizational Communication in the College of Liberal Arts at Metropolitan State University and a project manager with Waypoint Associates of Wayzata, Minnesota.

Andrea Baumann is an associate dean of Health Sciences (Nursing) and co-principal investigator of the Nursing Effectiveness, Utilization and Outcomes Research Unit at McMaster University.

The Honourable Edmond P. Blanchard is the finance minister of the province of New Brunswick.

Derek Briton is a doctoral candidate in the Department of Educational Policy Studies at the University of Alberta.

Conrad G. Brunk is a professor of Philosophy at Conrad Grebel College, University of Waterloo.

A. Scott Carson is the dean of the School of Business and Economics at Wilfrid Laurier University.

Wayne Cascio is a professor of Management at the University of Colorado—Denver.

Sylvia D. Chrominska is the executive vice-president of Human Resources at Scotiabank.

Monica Collins is the director of Professional and Community Programs, University of Windsor.

Wesley Cragg is George R. Gardiner Professor of Business Ethics at the Schulich School of Business at York University.

Peggy Cunningham is an assistant professor in the School of Business, Queen's University.

Pamela J. Cushing is a graduate student in the Department of Anthropology at McMaster University.

Sharon Dewey is a graduate student in the Department of Religion and Culture at Wilfrid Laurier University.

Vince Di Norcia is a professor of Philosophy and chair of the Philosophy Department at Laurentian University.

David Drinkwalter is president of Resource Associates Canada, Inc.

Robert C. Evans is a senior partner in Evans Duff Associates.

Leo Groarke is a professor of Philosophy at Wilfrid Laurier University.

Louis Groarke is a professor in the Department of Philosophy at Humber College.

Ken Hanly is a former associate professor of Philosophy at Brandon University, and is recently retired.

Barry Hoffmaster is a professor of Philosophy and professor of Family Medicine at the University of Western Ontario.

Wayne Hooper is the chief executive officer of the newly formed Institute for Information and Education Technology.

Todd J. Hostager is an associate professor of Management in the College of Business at the University of Wisconsin—Eau Claire and a project manager with Waypoint Associates of Wayzata, Minnesota.

J.L. Kachur is a professor in the Department of Educational Policy Studies at the University of Alberta.

Nebojsa Kujundzic is a professor in the Philosophy Department at the University of Prince Edward Island.

Norma J. MacRae is the education and employment equity coordinator at Laurentian University.

Henry H. Miles is president of Waypoint Associates, Ltd., a Wayzata, Minnesota, consulting firm.

Darryl Reed is an instructor at York University and, formerly, at the Budapest University of Economics.

Barbara Silverman is the research projects coordinator for the Nursing Effectiveness, Utilization and Outcomes Research Unit at McMaster University.

Mary Sylver is the chief executive officer of the Willett Hospital.

John R. Williams is the director of Ethics, Canadian Medical Association.

Michael Yeo is an ethicist in the Research Directorate of the Canadian Medical Association.

Notes

Chapter 3

1 I thank Sylvie Lamer and Paddy Rodney for help in thinking about these matters.

2 I owe this distinction to Dr. John Dossetor.

3 The extreme of this approach is the pay package of Jerre L. Stead, the chief executive of Ingram Micro Inc., a computer distributor, which gives Mr. Stead nothing but stock options (Dobrzynski 1996, C1).

4 Ip 1996, B4: "the evidence that companies benefit from downsizing is mixed. There is little Canadian research, but the American Management Association found in a survey that among seven hundred companies that had downsized between 1989 and 1994, productivity rose in 34 percent of cases and fell in 30 percent, while profits rose in 51 percent of cases and declined in 30 percent. In 83 percent of cases, employee morale declined." For empirical information on the effects of restructuring, see the articles by Cascio and Hostager et al. in this volume.

5 In response to mounting criticism, the rhetoric and euphemisms devised by consultants are changing. The consulting industry now worries about "corporate anorexia" and promotes the goal of "growing the revenue line" (Uchitelle 1996, C1).

6 Canadian hospitals recently participated in a benchmarking study that allows hospital managers to compare how they are doing in hiring, firing, and managing employees (Gibb-Clark 1996, B9).

7 The points in this paragraph are taken from Armstrong et al. 1996.

8 The pressure to reduce costs exerted by managed care on hospitals in the United States also has led to smaller nursing staffs. In the New York area, for example, 1,316 nursing jobs, 3 percent of the total, were lost between February 1995 and February 1996 (Rosenthal, 1996 A16).

9 Nurses in New York City have even taken out an advertisement in the *New York Times* about the replacement of "RNs with unlicensed workers who insert catheters, replace IVs, and treat seriously ill patients after just a few weeks' training" and citing some "horrible results" of this "down skilling." ("Is Quality Patient Care Your Hospital's Top Priority? Don't Bet On It," *New York Times*, 12/06/96, A17). This was followed by an advertisement that raised questions such as: "What would you think of a hospital that hired people off the street, gave them *three weeks training*, and put them to work in the ER and intensive care units, caring for the most seriously ill patients? What would you think if that hospital allowed unlicensed workers to deliver care requiring expertise, like suctioning your lungs, putting in your IV, or inserting your

catheter?" (emphasis in original) ("Does Columbia–Presbyterian Put Patients' Health First?" *New York Times,* 31/07/96, A15).

10 See "OR redesign to benefit patients," *The Page* (Newsletter for the Staff of London Health Sciences Centre), Vol. 1, No. 7, 6 (August 1, 1996).

11 The introductory psychology "superclass" taught to 1,200 students at the University of Western Ontario certainly contributes to this goal. Moreover, it is said to be the "most popular" course at Western (Galt 1996, A1).

12 One hospital CEO agrees with that estimate, but he suspects that "perhaps another 40 percent is effective" and he has "no idea about the rest" (Hassen 1993, 181).

13 For an argument that health care is special, is not simply another consumer good, see Daniels 1985, ch. 1.

14 Another CEO agrees that TQM is a vehicle for preserving the health care system of which Canadians are so proud (Hassen 1993, 187).

15 One symptom of this is the worry that medical ethics is becoming no more than business ethics. See Douard 1996, 1, 5, 8.

Chapter 6

16 See R.A. Johnson 1996 for a useful three-way typology of restructuring forms: (1) *portfolio restructuring,* which includes divestitures, spinoffs, mergers, and acquisitions, (2) *financial restructuring,* which includes LBOs (leveraged buyouts), ESOPs (employee stock ownership plans), etc., and (3) *organizational restructuring,* which includes reorganizations and downsizings. The bottom line is that restructurings come in various forms and differ on numerous dimensions.

17 The historical record indicates that some learning may indeed be warranted. For instance, numerous studies have consistently shown that a significant percentage of M&As fail to perform up to expectations. See, for instance, Boyle and Jaynes 1972, Pritchett 1985, and Zweig et al. 1995.

18 In particular, Secretary R.B. Reich proposed a decrease or elimination of corporate income taxes for firms meeting the minimum requirements in the following areas: (1) upgrading employee skills, (2) profit sharing, (3) pensions, (4) health care, (5) retraining and placement of laid-off employees (Reich 1996).

Chapter 8

19 In personal conversation.

Chapter 9

20 This article is based on an earlier paper published by the three authors (Williams et al. 1996).

21 Our focus on the Queens Regional Board in this paper is not intended to convey the impression that it is the only regional body to deal explicitly with

ethical issues. We are aware of related initiatives in two other provinces, New Brunswick and Alberta, and a brief description of these will illustrate their similarities and differences with the Queens Regional Board's approach.

New Brunswick was one of the first Canadian provinces to regionalize health care. Recognizing the importance of ethics in health care, the Board of Trustees of the Region 3 established an Institutional Ethics Committee. Committee membership includes one staff representative from each of the major health care professions and an equal or greater number of community representatives. It meets at least ten times a year.

In addition to its Institutional Ethics Committee, the Region 3 Hospital Corporation has created a Bioethics Service. This is provided by a part-time bioethics advisor/consultant with formal training and experience in the field. His principal function is to implement, operate, and regularly review a bioethics education program for the region, including formal ethics rounds/seminars, staff development, and continuing education activities, and various informal teaching sessions. He provides staff support for the Institutional Ethics Committee, and undertakes clinical ethics consultations upon request.

The use of an ethics committee to provide advice on ethical issues is the favoured approach of one of Alberta's regional bodies, the Mistahia Regional Health Authority (based in Grande Prairie). A pre-existing bioethics committee at the region's main hospital has been given an expanded mandate to deal with ethical issues throughout the region.

22 Wayne Hooper was the founding CEO of the Queens Region Board. John Williams and Michael Yeo were contracted by the Queens Region Board to provide ethics education and advice.

Chapter 11

23 Smith 1995, 169: "Forms of evidence allowable in evidence based medicine, while now extending beyond the randomised controlled trial, remain heavily numerate. This encourages emphasis on the quantifiable and physical aspects of any clinical dilemma, which may be inappropriate. Denial of social and psychological aspects may be detrimental, and ignoring the less readily measured dimensions may be dangerous. Rich sources of evidence also include the anecdotal, which are so often slated, and the qualitative, which is not mentioned by this lobby yet has developed considerably and provides illuminative results. The search for justification continues."

24 "Ontario's Bill 26...received third and final reading Monday with a vote of 77 to 47.... The bill is the companion legislation to the government's Nov. 29 mini-budget, bringing the total cuts the Harris government has implemented to eight billion dollars, the largest in Ontario's history" (*Vancouver Sun*, 30/01/96).

Chapter 13

25 "True equal opportunity is a progressive way of doing business. It reflects excellence in human resource management and we are determined to continue our efforts in this area." (An official statement from The Royal Bank as quoted in Human Resources and Development Canada 1994, 4.)

Chapter 14

26 *Hopkins v. Dow Corning Corp.*, No. C-91-2132, 1991 US Dist. LEXIS 8580 (N.D. Cal. May 27, 1992). Appellate court judgment *(33 F. 3d 1116, 9th Cir. 1994)*.

27 The Supreme Court of Canada paved the way for liability claims against Dow Corning by upholding an award of ninety-five thousand dollars by a British Columbia court to Susan Hollis in *Hollis v. Dow Corning Corporation*. 4 S.C.R. 634, 1995. The Canadian court ruled that Dow Corning had a "duty to warn" the medical community and consumers of the risks posed by the implants, risks of which it had been aware. "Implant Makers Had 'Duty' to Warn," *Globe and Mail*, December 22, 1995, A1.

28 A second study at Brigham and Women's Hospital, Harvard Medical School by Sanchez-Guerrero (also published in the NEJM, 1995) examined the incidence of rheumatic disease among 121,700 American registered nurses from 1976 to 1990. The use of breast implants among those with confirmed rheumatic disease was compared to use in a randomly selected, age-matched control group. The authors "found no association between silicone breast implants and connective-tissue disease." Studies at the University of Michigan (1994), John Hopkins Medical Institutions (1992), and the University of Toronto also found no evidence of a connection between implants or silicone and scleroderma. For a summary and analysis of these studies, see Angell 1996, pp. 100 ff.

29 The Dow Corning implant case has been written up as a case study of unethical conduct in many business schools across North America, including the Harvard Business School. At a recent meeting of the Society of Business Ethics in Quebec City, Quebec, several panelists in a discussion of the Dow Corning case indicated that the scientific evidence brought forward in the period since the 1995 bankruptcy declaration by the company requires a revision of this widespread ethical analysis of the case.

30 Recent examples include the $180 million Agent Orange settlement against Dow Chemical, the $2.5 billion settlement against Johns–Manville for asbestos related claims, and the $2.5 billion against A.H. Robbins for the Dalkon Shield intrauterine birth control device.

31 Great Britain, for example, has not removed silicone implants from its market. Its Department of Health issued its own report in 1993 stating that it found no scientific reason for removing them, and it reiterated this conclusion in 1994. France imposed bans, lifted them, and imposed them again, seemingly unable to decide. Spain at first imposed a ban and then lifted it.

Chapter 16

32 As Badillo 1996, 155 observes, "To provide equal pay for equal work is a principle of all civilized humanity and should be particularly enforced within a university setting, where promotion of such ideals is a veritable commonplace."

33 The term "new appointment" is ambiguous. In 1990–91 16 percent of new appointees were hired at the two senior ranks, while 56 percent were hired at the assistant professor level. The group "Other," which accounted for 5 percent of new appointments, includes special lecturers, ungraded staff usually hired on a one-year contract basis, etc.

34 This is an actual remark from an interview with a part-timer.

35 Brehaut continues, "The effects of such a tenure policy are not likely to be as deleterious in a period when universities and colleges are expanding in number and size (e.g., in the 1960s in Canada) as in a period of limited growth or retrenchment (1970s and 1980s). To counter these effects, some people have supported the elimination of tenured positions and the introduction of three or five year contracts open for free competition, charging that because of the scarcity of academic jobs and the overbalance of qualified candidates, the standards required of new candidates have steadily escalated and tenure is denying the right to compete for jobs on the basis of equality."

36 This letter was published in *The South Carolina Post and Courier* in 1995. It was put on the Internet by the South Carolina Council of the American Association of University Professors as part of a policy discussion in defence of tenure.

Chapter 19

37 The following remarks are excerpted from a speech to the First Annual Laurier Conference on Business and Professional Ethics in October, 1996.

Chapter 22

38 The names of the Bell workers interviewed for this case study have been changed for the purposes of this article.

Bibliography

Abella, R.S. (1984). *Equality in Employment—A Royal Commission.* Ottawa: Minister of Supply and Services.

Aglietta, M. (1979). *A Theory of Capitalist Regulation.* London: Verso.

Agocs, C. and C. Burr (1996). "Employment Equity, Affirmative Action and Managing Diversity: Assessing the Differences." *International Journal of Manpower* 17 (4/5): 30–45.

Alberta Education (1995a). *90th Annual Report 1994–1995.* Edmonton: Author.

———— (1995b). *Regulatory Reform Action Plan.* Edmonton: Author.

———— (1996). *Charter School Handbook.* Revised. Edmonton: Author.

Allen, Robert E. (1996). "The Anxiety Epidemic." *Newsweek,* April 8.

American Management Association (1994). *AMA Survey on Downsizing and Assistance to Displaced Workers.* New York: American Management Association.

Andreasen, A.R. (1994). "Social Marketing: Its Definition and Domain." *Journal of Public Policy and Marketing* 13 (1): 108–114.

Andrews, H.A., L.M. Cook, J.M. Davidson, D.P. Schurman, E.W.Taylor, and R.H. Wensel (1994). *Organizational Transformation in Health Care.* Edmonton: University of Alberta Hospital.

Angell, Marcia (1994). "Do Breast Implants Cause Systemic Disease? Science in the Courtroom." *The New England Journal of Medicine.* 330 (24, June 16): 1748–1749.

———— (1996). *Science on Trial: The Clash of Medical Evidence and the Law in the Breast Implant Case.* New York: W.W. Norton & Co.

Appelbaum, Eileen (1997). "Close the Wage Gap Now." *USA TODAY,* August 7, NEWS, 12A.

Armstrong, P., J. Choiniere, G. Feldberg, J. White, and H. Rosenberg (1994). "Voices from the Ward." Occasional paper. Toronto: York University Centre for Health Studies.

Armstrong, Pat, Hugh Armstrong, Jacqueline Choiniere, Eric Mykhalovskiy, and Jerry P. While (1996). "The Promise and the Price: New Work Organizations in Ontario Hospitals." Toronto: Photocopy.

Arneson, Richard (1981). "What's Wrong With Exploitation?" *Ethics* 91 (1): 202.

Badillo, Robert (1996). "The Needs and Rights of Non-Tenured Faculty." *Proceedings of the American Philosophical Association* 69 (5): 152–156.

Barber, C. (1992). "Monetary and Fiscal Policy in the 1980's." In R. Allen and G. Rosenbluth (eds.), *False Promises*. Vancouver: New Star Books, 101–122.

Barlow, M. and H-J. Robertson (1994). *Class Warfare: The Assault on Canada's Schools*. Toronto: Key Porter.

Barnes, Nora Ganim (1991). "Philanthropy, Profits, and Problems: The Emergence of Joint Venture Marketing." *Akron Business and Economic Review* 22 (4): 78–86.

Bastien, D.T. (1987). "Common Patterns of Behaviour and Communication in Corporate Mergers and Acquisitions." *Human Resource Management* 26: 17–33.

―――― (1989). "Communication, Conflict, and Learning in Mergers and Acquisitions." In A.H. Van de Ven, H. Angle, and M.S. Poole (eds.), *Research on the Management of Innovation*. New York: Harper & Row.

―――― (1994). "A Feedback Loop Model of Post-Acquisition Performance: Customers and Competitors." *Management Communication Quarterly* 7: 46–69.

――――, T.J. Hostager, and H.H. Miles (1996). "Corporate Judo: Exploiting the Dark Side of Change When Competitors Merge, Acquire, Downsize, or Restructure." *Journal of Management Inquiry* 5: 261–275.

――――, R. McPhee, and K. Bolton (1995). "A Study and Extended Theory of Organizational Climate: A Structurational Approach." *Communication Monographs* 62: 132–151.

Baumann, A., L. O'Brien-Pallas, R. Deber, G. Donner, D. Semogas, and B. Silverman (1995). "The Process of Downsizing in Selected Ontario Acute Care Hospitals: Budget Reduction Strategies and Planning Process." Working paper series, March 1995 (No. 4). Hamilton: Quality of Nursing Worklife Research unit, McMaster University and University of Toronto.

―――― (forthcoming). "Downsizing in the Hospital System: A Restructuring Process." *Healthcare Management Forum*.

Bender, Eric (1996). "Downsizing Fuels White-collar Crime." *London Free Press*, July 26, D10.

Benner, P. (ed.) (1984). *From Novice to Expert*. Don Mills: Addison–Wesley Publishing Company.

Benoit, C. (1994). "Paradigm Conflict in the Sociology of Service Professions: Midwifery as a Case Study." *Canadian Journal of Sociology* 19 (3): 303–329.

Berle, A. and G. Means (1932). *The Modern Corporation and Private Property*. New York: Macmillan.

Bilik, A. (1992). "Privatization: Defacing the Community." *Labour Law Journal* 43 (6): 338–343.

Bloom, A. (1987). *The Closing of the American Mind*. Toronto: Simon & Schuster.

Boulding, Kenneth E. (1968). *Beyond Economics: Essays on Society, Religion and Economics*. Ann Arbor: University of Michigan.

Bowles, S. and Herbert Gintis (1976). *Schooling in Capitalist America*. New York, Basic Books.

Boyle, S.E. and P.W. Jaynes (1972). *Conglomerate Merger Performance*. Economic Report to the Federal Trade Commission. Washington: Federal Trade Commission.

Bradsher, Keith (1996). "Rich Control More of U.S. Wealth, Study Says, as Debts Grown for Poor." *New York Times*, June 22, 17.

Bragg, R., L. Uchtelle, N.R. Kleinfield, S. Rimer, E. Kolbert, K. Johnson, A. Kleimer, D.E. Sanger, and S. Lohr (1996). "The Downsizing of America." *New York Times*, March 3–9.

Braverman, H. (1964). *Labor and Monopoly Capital*. New York: Monthly Review.

Brehaut, W. (1995). "Tenure." *The Canadian Encyclopedia Plus*. Cd-Rom. Toronto: McClelland & Stewart Inc.

Brockner, J., S. Grover, T. Reed, R. De Witt, and M. O'Malley (1987). "Survivors' Reactions to Layoffs: We Get By with a Little Help From Our Friends." *Administrative Science Quarterly* 32: 526–541.

Brooks, Len (1996). "Downsizing versus Ethical Renewal." *Corporate Ethics Monitor* 8 (1): 1.

Bruton, G.D., J.K. Keels, and C.L. Shook (1996). "Downsizing the Firm: Answering the Strategic Questions." *Academy of Management Executive* 10: 38–45.

Bucklin, Louis P. and Sanjit Sengupta (1993). "Organizing Successful Co-Marketing Alliances." *Journal of Marketing* 57 (4): 32–46.

Byrne, John A. (1996). *Informed Consent*. New York: McGraw Hill.

Byham, W.C. (1993). *ZAPP! Empowerment in Health Care*. New York: Faucett Columbie.

Cameron, K.S., S.J. Freeman, and A.K. Mishra (1991). "Best Practices in White-Collar Downsizing: Managing Contradictions." *Academy of Management Executive* 5: 57–73.

Cameron, S., M. Horsburgh, and M. Armstrong-Stassen (1994a). "Effects of Downsizing on RNs and RNAs in Community Hospitals."

Working paper series, October 1994 (No. 6). Hamilton: Quality of Nursing Worklife Research Unit, McMaster University and University of Toronto.

———— (1994b). "Job Satisfaction, Propensity to Leave and Burnout in RNs and RNAs: A Multivariate Perspective." *Canadian Journal of Nursing Administration* 7: 43–61.

Campbell, A., M. Goold, and M. Alexander (1995). "Corporate Strategy: The Quest for Parenting Advantage." *Harvard Business Review* 73 (2): 120–132.

Canadian Nurses Association (1996). *Employment Cross Country Checkup.* (June). Ottawa: Author.

Card, D. and A. Krueger (1995). *Myth and Measurement.* Princeton: Princeton University Press.

Carson, A.S. (1984). "Education and Schooling." *International Review of Education* 30: 41–55.

Cascio, W.F. (1987). *Costing Human Resources: The Financial Impact of Behaviour in Organizations.* 2nd ed. Boston: Kent.

———— (1993). "Downsizing: What Do We Know? What Have We Learned?" *Academy of Management Executive* 7: 95–104.

———— (1995). *Guide to Responsible Restructuring.* Washington: US Department of Labor, Office of the American Workplace.

————, C.E. Young, and J.M. Morris (1996). "Financial Consequences of Employment-change Decisions in Major U.S. Corporations." Cincinnati: Paper presented at the annual conference of the Academy of Management.

Chomsky, Noam, and Edward Herman (1988). *Manufacturing Consent: The Political Economy of the Mass Media.* New York: Pantheon.

Clinton, W. (1995). "Remarks by the President on Affirmative Action." Washington: Office of the Press Secretary.

CMA (Canadian Medical Association), Working Group on Regionalization and Decentralization (1993). "The Language of Health System Reform." Ottawa: Author.

Conrad, D.A. and S.M. Shortell (1996). "Integrated Health Systems: Promise and Performance." *Frontiers of Health Services Management* (Cd-Rom).

Cook, Peter (1996). The Ungrateful Stock Market. *Globe and Mail,* April 9, B2.

Coombs, R.E. and J.D. Moorhead (1992). *Competitive Intelligence Handbook.* Metuchen, NJ: Scarecrow.

Council of Ontario Universities Status of Women Committee and the Committee on Employment and Educational Equity (1995). "Keeping Equity in the Decision-Making Process." Toronto: Council of Ontario Universities.

Coutts, Jane (1995). "Commission to Ease Pain of Mergers." *Globe and Mail*, Dec. 1, A8.

———— (1996). "Hospitals Replace Registered Nurses." *Globe and Mail*, April 2, A9.

Coward, Harold and Thomas Hurka (1993). *Ethics and Climate Change: The Greenhouse Effect*. Waterloo: Wilfrid Laurier University Press.

Cox, Donald (1997). "The Big Picture." *Globe and Mail*, Oct. 19, B21.

Cox, Robert (1987). *Production, Power, and World Order*. New York: Columbia University Press.

———— (1992). "Multilateralism and World Order." *Review of International Studies* 18: 161–180.

———— (1994). "Global Restructuring: Making Sense of the Changing International Political Economy." In Richard Stubbs and Geoffrey R.D. Underhill (eds.), *Political Economy and the Changing Global Order*. Toronto: McClelland & Stewart, 45–59.

Coyne, Andrew (1997). "Voice of the People, or the Last Gasps of Leftist Cranks?" *Toronto Star*, A27, March 6.

Cragg, Wes and Christine Koggel (1996). *Contemporary Moral Issues*. 4th ed. Toronto: McGraw–Hill.

Craig, A.W. and N.A. Solomon (1996). *The System of Industrial Relations In Canada*. 5th ed. Scarborough: Prentice–Hall.

Crane, David (1995). "We're Deep in a Job-creation Crisis." *Toronto Star*, Sept. 17, A24.

Crispo, John (1978). *Industrial Democracy in Western Europe*. Toronto: McGraw-Hill Ryerson.

Crossette, Barbara (1996). "U.N. Survey Finds World Rich-Poor Gap is Widening," *New York Times*, July 15, A3.

Cunningham, Peggy H. (forthcoming), "Dammed If You Do, Damned If You Don't: Understanding Ethical Pitfalls in Cause-Related Marketing." In *Essays on Philanthropy*. Indiana University: Center on Philanthropy.

Daniels, Norman (1985). *Just Health Care*. New York: Cambridge University Press.

De Meuse, K.A.P., P.A. Vanderheiden, and T.J. Bergmann (1994). "Announced Layoffs: Their Effect on Corporate Financial Performance." *Human Resource Management* 33: 509–530.

DeMara, Bruce (1997). "Megacity Bill Stands But Tories Faulted." *Toronto Star*, July 25, A2.

———— and Paul Moloney (1997). "Cities Uniting for $300,000 Legal Challenge." *Toronto Star*, March 5, A8.

———— and William Walker (1997). "The Pros and Cons of a Merger." *Toronto Star*, March 1, A7.

———— and Lisa Wright (1997). "North York Opts Out of Bill 103 Challenge." *Toronto Star*, March 6, A9.

Den Tandt, Michael (1996). "Are CEOs Apologies Enough?" *Globe and Mail*, May 28, B1.

Department of National Health and Welfare (Long Range Health Planning Branch) (1974). *Regionalization of Health Services in Canada*. Ottawa: Author.

Di Norcia, V. (1994). "Ethics, Technology Management and Innovation." *Business Ethics Quarterly* 3 (3): 235–252.

Dobrzynski, Judith H. (1996). "Top Post at Rock-bottom Wage." *New York Times*, October 4, C1.

Domini, E. (1977). *Teach Yourself Self-Defense*. Buchanan, NY: Emerson.

Douard, John (1996). "Are Medical Ethics Becoming Business Ethics?" *The Chronicle* (Newsletter of the Institute for the Medical Humanities, University of Texas Medical Branch at Galveston) 14 (1): 1–10.

Douglas, R. (1993). *Unfinished Business*. Auckland: Random House.

Dowdall, J. and M. Bahr (1994). *Responsible Restructuring: A Town Hall Forum*. Sept. 29. Philadephia: Conference sponsored by the US Dept. of Labor.

Downs, A. (1995). *Corporate Executions: The Ugly Truth About Layoffs–How Corporate Greed is Shattering Lives, Companies and Communities*. New York: AMACOM.

———— (1996). "The Wages of Downsizing." *Mother Jones* 20 (4, July–August).

Drucker, P. (1993). *Post-Capitalist Society*. New York: HarperBusiness.

Duffy, Ann, Nancy Mandell, and Norene Pupo (1989). *Few Choices: Women, Work and Family*. Toronto: Garamond Press.

Duncan, T. (1995). "Why Mission Marketing is More Strategic and Long-Term than Cause Marketing." *Proceedings of the Winter Marketing Educators' Conference*. San Diego: Winter Marketing Educators' Conference, 469–475.

Dunlap, A. (1996). *Mean Business*. New York: Random House, 1996.

Edgar, D. (1995). March 8. Personal communication.

Edmonton Logos Society (1996). *Logos School—A Program with a Difference*. Edmonton: The Author.

Elliott, B. and D. MacLennan (1994). "Education, Modernity and Neo-conservative School Reform in Canada, Britain and the US." *British Journal of Sociology of Education* 15 (2): 165–85.

Emberley, P.C. (1996). *Zero Tolerance: Hot Button Politics in Canada's Universities*. Toronto: Penguin.

Evidence-Based Medicine Working Group (1988). "Evidence-Based Medicine: A New Approach to Teaching the Practice of Medicine." *Journal of the American Medical Association* 268 (17): 2420.

Fahey, T., S. Griffiths, and T.J. Peters (1993). "Evidence Based Purchasing: Understanding the Results of Clinical Trials and Systematic Reviews." *British Medical Journal* 311: 1059–1060.

Feder, Barnaby J. (1996). "Quaker Oats and Iced Tea Just Won't Mix." *New York Times*, Aug. 7, C1.

Ferrell. O.C. and John Fraedrich (1991). *Business Ethics*. Boston: Houghton Mifflin Co.

Fine, Ben (1992). *Women's Employment and the Capitalist Family*. London: Routledge.

Ford Motor Co. (1994). "Ford to Realign Worldwide Automotive Processes and Organization to Manage Them." April 21. Dearborn, MI: Public Affairs Office, Ford Motor Co.

Freidson, E. (ed.) (1986). *Professional Powers. A Study of the Institutionalization of Formal Knowledge*. Chicago: The University of Chicago Press.

Freudenheim, Milt (1996). "Assessing H.M.O.s By New Standards: A Patient's Progress." *New York Times*, July 16, A1.

Friedman, M. and R. Friedman (1980). *Free to Choose*. New York: Avon.

Gabreil, Sherine E. et al. (1994). "Risk of Connective-Tissue Diseases and Other Disorders After Breast Implantation." *The New England Journal of Medicine* 330 (24, June 16): 1697–1702.

Galbraith, J.K. (1992). *The Culture of Contentment*. Boston: Houghton Mifflin.

Galt, Virginia (1996). "Lecture Rolls to Reggae Rhythm." *Globe and Mail*, Feb. 8, A1.

Gibb-Clark, Margot (1996). "Hospital Managers Gain Tool to Compare Notes." *Globe and Mail*, Sept. 11, B9.

Gideon, Péter (1995). "Hungary: Social Policy in Transition." *East European Politics and Societies* 9 (3): 433–458.

Gilder, G. (1981). *Wealth and Poverty*. New York: Basic Books.

Gill, D. (1996). "Generic/unregulated Care Provider." Fact Sheet. Hamilton: Nursing Effectiveness, Utilization and Outcomes Research Unit.

Gill, Stephen (1994). "Knowledge, Politics and Neo-Liberal Political Economy." In Richard Stubbs and R.D. Underhill (eds.), *Political Economy and the Changing Global Order*. Toronto: McClelland & Stewart.

Girard, Daniel (1997). "McGuinty Says Tories Wrong to Ignore Votes." *Toronto Star*, A7, March 2.

Gordon, R. (1987). *Macroeconomics*. 4th ed. Boston: Little, Brown and Company.

Greenhalgh, L., A.T. Lawrence, and R.I. Sutton (1988). "Determinants of Work Force Reduction Strategies in Declining Organizations." *Academy of Management Review* 13 (2): 241–254.

Groarke, Leo (1989). "Skepticism in International Affairs: Toward A New Realism." In Joseph C. Kunkel and Kenneth H. Klein (eds.), *Issues in War and Peace*. Wolfeboro: Longwood Academic.

———— (1996). "What's In a Number? Hall, Hurka, Sumner, Baker et al. on Consequentialism and Employment Equity." *Dialogue: The Canadian Philosophical Review* 30 (3): 359–373.

———— and Sally Scholz (1996). "Seven Principles for Better Practical Ethics." *Teaching Philosophy* 19 (4): 337–355.

Gurin, Maurice G. (1987). "Cause-related Marketing in Question." *Advertising Age*, Special Report, July 27, S-16.

Hagenlocker, E. (1994). *Think Global, Act Local—With Agility*. Aug. 3. Detroit: Speech presented at University of Michigan Automotive Management Briefing.

Hamburger, J. (1993). "Liberal Intolerance." In H. Dickman (ed.), *The Imperiled Academy*. New Brunswick, NJ: Transaction Press.

Hamilton Health Sciences Corporation (1996). *Your Health—A Newsletter for Patients and Families*. Hamilton: Chedoke–McMaster, Hamilton Health Sciences Corporation.

Hammer, M. and J. Champy (1994). *Re-engineering the Corporation*. New York: HarperBusiness.

Hardin, H. (1989). *The Privatization Putsch*. Halifax: Institute for Research on Public Policy.

Harrison, Marion L. et al. (1995). "Discharging Patients Earlier from Winnipeg Hospitals: Does It Adversely Affect Quality of Care?" *Canadian Medical Association Journal* 153: 745–751.

Hassen, Philip (1993). *Rx for Hospitals*. Toronto: Stoddart Publishing Co.

Hayek, F. (1944). *The Road to Serfdom*. Chicago: University of Chicago.

Health Transition Team (1993). *Partnerships for Better Health*. Charlottetown: Island Information Services.

Hebb, Tessa and Mike McCracken (1996). "Stakeholders vs. Shareholders." *Globe and Mail*, Aug. 15, B2.

Hendricks, C.F. (1992). *The Rightsizing Remedy: How Managers Can Respond to the Downsizing Dilemma*. Homewood, IL: Business One Irwin.

Herbert, Bob (1997). "A Workers' Rebellion." *Globe and Mail* (reprinted from the *New York Times*), Aug. 12, B2.

Herman E.S. and L. Lowenstein (1988). "The Efficiency Effects of Hostile Takeovers." In J.C. Coffee, L. Lowenstein, and S. Rose-Ackerman (eds.), *Knights, Raiders, and Targets*. New York: Oxford University Press.

Hitt, M.A., B.W. Keats, H.F. Harback, and R.D. Nixon (1994). "Rightsizing: Building and Maintaining Strategic Leadership and Long-Term Competitiveness." *Organizational Dynamics* 23: 18–32.

Hoffmaster, Barry (1991). "The Theory and Practice of Applied Ethics." *Dialogue: The Canadian Philosophical Review* 30 (3): 213–234.

Hogarty, T.F. (1970). "Profits from Merger: The Evidence of Fifty Years." *St. John's Law Review* 44: 378–391.

Holzmann, Robert (1992). "Social Policy in Transition from Plan to Market." *Journal of Public Policy* 12 (1): 1–35.

Human Resources Development Canada (1989). *Employment Equity: A Guide for Employers*. Ottawa: Author.

———— (1994). *Employment Equity: Creating a Diverse Workplace*. Ottawa: Author.

Hunt, Shelby D. and Scott Vitell (1991). "A General Theory of Marketing Ethics: A Retrospective and Revision." In N.C. Smith and J.A. Quelch (eds.), *Ethics in Marketing*. Homewood, IL: Irwin, 774–784.

Illich, I. (1970). *Celebration of Awareness: A Call for Institutional Revolution*. New York: Harper & Row.

———— (1971). *Deschooling Society*. New York: Harper & Row.

Ip, Greg (1996). "Shareholders vs. Job Holders." *Globe and Mail*, March 23, B1.

Israelson, D. (1996). "Corporate Backfiring." *Toronto Star,* June 2.

Jackall, R. (1988). *Moral Mazes*. New York: Oxford University Press.

Jencks, C. and D. Reisman (1968). *The Academic Revolution*. New York: Doubleday.

Jensen, Michael C. (1993). "Takeovers: Folklore and Science." In White (1993), 734–751.

Johnson, R.A. (1996). "Antecedents and Outcomes of Corporate Refocusing." *Journal of Management* 22: 439–483.

Jones, D. (1996). "Eaton: No Guarantees for Life." *USA Today*, March 20, 5B.

Jones, Del and John Waggoner (1997). "Strike Targets Two-tier Workforce: UPS Labor Efforts Could Reshape Flexible Workplace." *USA Today*, Aug. 5, 1B.

Kachur, J.L. (1995). *Hegemony and Anonymous Intellectual Practice.* PhD thesis. Edmonton: University of Alberta.

Keating, D. and J.F. Mustard (1993). *The National Forum on Family Security—Social Economic Factors and Human Development.* Aug. Working paper no. 5. Toronto: The Canadian Institute for Advanced Research Program in Human Development.

Keller, J.J. (1996). "AT&T Tries to Put New Spin on Big Job Cuts." *Wall Street Journal*, March 18, B1, B9.

Kelsey, J. (1995). *Economic Fundamentalism: The New Zealand Experiment.* Auckland: Auckland University Press.

Kerr, C. (1991). *The Great Transformation in Higher Education.* Albany, NY: SUNY Press.

King, D.S. (1987). *The New Right: Politics, Markets and Citizenship.* London: Macmillan.

Kotz, D., T. McDonough, and M. Reich (eds.) (1994). *Social Structures of Accumulation.* Cambridge: Cambridge University Press.

Ladd, E. Jr. and S.M. Lipset (1975). *The Divided Academy: Professors and Politics.* New York: McGraw–Hill.

Lakey, Jack (1997). "Voting Process Skewed, Tonks Says." *Toronto Star*, March 4, A9.

Landsberg, Michele (1997). "Megacity Fight Spawns Wave of Political Activism." *Toronto Star*, March 2, A2.

Lavis, John N. and Geoffrey M. Anderson (1996). "Appropriateness in Health Care Delivery: Definitions, Measurement and Policy Implications." *Canadian Medical Association Journal* 154: 321–328.

Lawsky, David (1997). "US Unions Unite Behind UPS Strikers." Reuters News Service. August 13, 6: 46 EDT.

Lawton, S., J. Freedman, and H.J. Robertson (1995). *Busting Bureaucracy to Reclaim Our Schools.* Montreal: Institute for Research on Public Policy.

Laxer, G. and T. Harrison (eds.) (1995). *The Trojan Horse: Klein's Alberta and the Future of Canada*. Montreal: Black Rose.

Le Grand, J. and W. Bartlett (1993). *Quasi-Markets and Social Policy*. London: Macmillan.

Leana, Carrie and D.C. Feldman (1992). *Coping with Job Loss: How Individuals, Organizations, and Communities Respond to Layoffs*. New York: Lexington Books.

Leana, Carrie (1996). "Downsizing's Downside." *Chicago Tribune Magazine*, April 14, 15–18.

Levac, Gaston, (1996). "Thunder Bay Regional Hospital: An Amalgamation." *Leadership*, May/June, 31–32.

Levy, Harold (1997). "Lastman Urges Calm Dialogue in Place of 'Catcalls, Jeering.'" *Toronto Star*, Feb. 22, A4.

Lieber, J.B. (1995). *Friendly Takeover: How an Employee Buyout Saved a Steel Town*. New York: Penguin.

Lin, Zhengxi (1995). *Jobs Excluded From the Unemployment Insurance System in Canada: An Empirical Investigation*. Ottawa: Human Resources Development Canada VI.

Lindgren, A. (1996a). "Remember, Behind Company Layoffs Lie Investors' Demands." *Globe and Mail,* March 31.

Lindgren, A. (1996b). "Layoffs Worrisome, But Who's to Blame?" *London Free Press*, March 29, D6.

Lipietz, A. (1987). *Mirages and Miracles: The Crisis of Global Fordism*. London: Verso.

Lipset, S.M. (1993). "The Sources of Political Correctness on American Campuses." In H. Dickman (ed.), *The Imperiled Academy*. New Brunswick, NJ: Transaction Press.

Lisac, M. (1995). *The Klein Revolution*. Edmonton: NuWest.

Lortie, Raynald (1994). "Part-time University Teachers—A Growing Group." *Educational Quarterly Review*, Statistics Canada, 1 (3).

Lyall, J. (1991). "Shut Out." *Nursing Times* 87: 19.

Lynn, B. (1996). "An Address Delivered to the Ontario University Education and Employment Equity Network." Hamilton: McMaster University.

———— and R. Bazile-Jones (1996). "Measuring the Impact of Diversity." *Management Accounting Issues,* No. 12. Toronto: Jointly Published by the Chartered Accountants of Canada and the Society of Management Accountants of Canada.

Mansfield, E. (1988). *Microeconomics*. 6th ed. New York: W.W. Norton.

Manzer, R. (1994). *Public Schools and Political Ideas: Canadian Educational Policy in Historical Perspective*. Toronto: University of Toronto.

Marks, M.L. and P.H. Mirvis (1985). "Merger Syndrome: Stress and Uncertainty." *Mergers and Acquisitions*, Summer, 50–55.

Marshall, Jonathan (1997). "Full-Time, Part-Time Facts and Fiction." *The San Francisco Chronicle*, Aug. 15, B1.

Martin, J. (1993). "The University as an Agent of Social Transformation: The Postmodern Argument Considered." In H. Dickman (ed.), *The Imperiled Academy*. New Brunswick, NJ: Transaction.

Maruyama, M. (1963). "The Second Cybernetics: Deviation-Amplifying Mutual Causal Processes." *American Scientist* 51 (2): 164–179.

Masuch, M. (1985). "Vicious Circles in Organizations." *Administrative Science Quarterly* 30: 14–33.

Maxwell, J. and S. Currie (1984). *Partnership in Growth*. Montreal: The Corporate Higher Education Forum.

McFarland, J. (1996). "Corporate Responsibility Stirs Ethical Debate." *Globe and Mail*, May 17, B8.

McGonagle, J. and C. Vella (1990). *Outsmarting the Competition: Practical Approaches to Finding and Using Competitive Information*. Napierville, IL: Sourcebooks.

McGregor, D. (1960). *The Human Side of Enterprise*. New York: McGraw Hill.

McMurtry, J. (1995). "The Social Immune System and the Cancer Stage of Capitalism." *Social Justice* 22 (4): 126.

McQuaig, L. (1995). *Shooting the Hippo*. Toronto: Viking.

Melaville, A.I., M.J. Blank, and G. Asayesh (1993). *Together We Can: A Guide for Crafting a Pro-family System of Education and Human Services*. Washington: US Departments of Education & Health and Human Services.

Meredith, Robyn (1996). "Executive Defends Downsizing." *New York Times*, March 19, C5.

Metropolitan Toronto District Health Council (1995). *Directions for Change: Toward a Coordinated Hospital System for Metro Toronto*. Final Report of the MTDHC Hospital Restructuring Committee. Willowdale, ON: Author.

Ministry of Health, Working Group on Health Services Utilization (1994). *When Less is Better:Using Canada's Hospitals Efficiently*. Ottawa: Author.

Mirvis, P.H. and M.L. Marks (1992). *Managing the Merger: Making it Work*. Englewood Cliffs, NJ: Prentice–Hall.

———— and S.E. Seashore (1979). "Being Ethical in Organizational Research." *American Psychologist* 34: 766–780.

Moorman, Christine, Rohit Deshpandé, and Gerald Zaltman (1993). "Factors Affecting Trust in Market Research Relationships." *Journal of Marketing* 57 (1): 81–101.

Morgan, Robert M., and Shelby D. Hunt (1994). "The Commitment-Trust Theory of Relationship Marketing." *Journal of Marketing* 58 (6): 20–38.

Morrow, R. and Carlos Torres (1990). "Ivan Illich and the De-schooling Thesis Twenty Years After." *New Education* 12 (3).

Newson, J. and H. Buchbinder (1988). *The University Means Business*. Toronto: Garamond.

Newton, Lisa H. (1993). "The Hostile Takeover: An Opposition View." In White (1993), 767–777.

Niblett, W.R. (1974). *Universities Between Two Worlds*. London: University of London Press.

Nightingale, D.V. (1982). *Workplace Democracy*. Toronto: University of Toronto.

Nitkin, David (1991). "Layoffs, Loyalty, Life and Labour." *Corporate Ethics Monitor* 3(1): 1

Noer, David M. (1993). *Healing the Wounds: Overcoming the Trauma of Layoffs and Revitalizing Downsized Organizations*. San Francisco: Jossey–Bass Publishers.

Norman, Patricia (1995). "Downsizing and Organizational Performance: Empirical Evidence." Vancouver: Presented at the annual Academy of Management Meeting.

O'Neill, H., P. Norman, and A.T. Ranft (1995). *Workforce Reductions and Market Valuation*.Vancouver: Presented at the annual Academy of Management Meeting.

Ontario Hospital Association (OHA), Small Hospitals Interim Steering Committee (1993). *Small Hospitals in Ontario: Towards the Year 2000*. Executive Summary. Toronto: Author.

Ontario Hospital Association (OHA), Small Hospitals Provincial Advisory Group (1994). *Role of Small Hospitals in Long-Term Care*. Toronto: Author.

Ontario Ministry of Community and Social Services (1996). *Business Plan*. May. Toronto: Author.

Osborne, D. and T. Gaebler (1992). *Reinventing Government: How the Entrepreneurial Spirit is Transforming the Public Sector*. New York: Plume.

PEI Health Task Force (1992). *Health Reform: A Vision for Change*. Charlottetown: PEI Cabinet Committee on Government Reform.

Packard, David (1995). *The HP Way*. New York: HarperBusiness.

Paquette, J. (1994). *Publicly Supported Education in Post-Modern Canada: An Imploding Universe*. Toronto: OSOS.

Pence, Gregory (1995). "Case Study in the Ethics of Teaching Philosophy." *Teaching Philosophy* 18, June (3): 165–166.

Perkins, D.S. (1987). "What Can CEOs Do for Displaced Workers?" *Harvard Business Review* 67 (6): 90–93.

Perry, L.T. (1986). "Least-Cost Alternatives to Layoffs in Declining Industries." *Organizational Dynamics* 14 (1): 48–61.

Peters, Tom and Robert Waterman (1982). *In Search Of Excellence*. New York: Harper.

Petzinger, T. Jr. (1996). "Does Al Dunlap Mean Business, or Is He Just Plain Mean?" *Wall Street Journal*, Aug. 30, B1.

Pickens, T.B. (1988). "The Stockholder Revolution." In M.L. Weidenbaum and K.W. Chilton (eds.), *Public Policy Toward Corporate Takeovers*. New Brunswick, NJ: Transaction.

Polanyi, K. (1944). *The Great Transformation*. New York: Farrar and Rinehart.

Porter, M.E. (1980). *Competitive Strategy*. New York: Free Press.

Pritchett, P. (1985). *After the Merger: Managing the Shockwaves*. Homewood, IL: Dow–Jones–Irwin.

Queens Region Health and Community Services (1994). *Governance Policies of Queens Regional Authority. Health and Community Services Prince Edward Island*. Charlottetown: Author.

_____ (1995). *Strategic Planning: An Information Guide for Employees, Physicians and Board Members*. Charlottetown: Author.

_____ (1995). *Community Needs Assessment: Final Report*. Charlottetown: Author.

Rachlis, M. and C. Kushner (1994). *Strong Medicine*. Toronto: HarperCollins.

Rawls, John (1971). *A Theory of Justice*. Cambridge: Harvard.

Reich, R.B. (1996). *Pink Slips, Profits, and Paychecks: Corporate Citizenship in an Era of Smaller Government*. Feb. 6. Speech delivered to the School of Business and Public Management, George Washington University.

Reicheld, F. (1996). "Loyalty Crisis Linked to Bottom Line." *Globe and Mail*, March 6.

Reisman, D. (1980). *On Higher Education*. San Francisco: Jossey–Bass.

Richardson, B. (1996). "Surviving the 'Miracle.'" *Canadian Forum* 86 (3): 1215.

Rifkin, Jeremy (1995). *The End of Work*. New York: Putnam's.

Right Associates (1992). *Lessons Learned: Dispelling the Myths of Downsizing*. 2nd ed. Philadelphia, PA: Right Associates.

Riseborough, Rosalind (1993). "Statistics Canada Data Reveal Teaching Employment Pattern." *CAUT Bulletin* 45 (11): 4.

Robertson, Gordon W. and Silas Braley (1973). "Toxicologic Studies, Quality Control, and Efficacy of the Silastic Mammary Prosthesis." *Medical Instrumentation* 7: 100–103.

Robertson, Susan, Victor Soucek, Rajinder Pannu and Daniel Schugurensky (1995). "'Chartering' New Waters: The Klein Revolution and the Privatization of Education in Alberta." *Our Schools Our Selves* 7 (2, March).

Robinson, M., Corporate Redeployment Manager, Intel (March 1995). Personal communication, plus briefing materials.

Rochon, M. (1995). Stakeholders Panel. Presentation at Hospital Restructuring: The Changing Face of the Hospital Sector conference, Ontario Hospital Association, May 15 and 16.

Roemer, John (1982). "What is Exploitation? Reply to Jeffery Reiman." *Philosophy and Public Affairs* 11 (4): Fall, 281–313.

Rosenbluth, G. (1992). "The Political Economy of Deficitphobia." In R. Allen and G. Rosenbluth (eds.), *False Promises: The Failure of Conservative Economics*. Vancouver: New Star Books, 61–79.

Rosenthal, Elizabeth (1996). "Once in Big Demand, Nurses Are Now Targets for Hospital Cutbacks." *New York Times*, August 19, A16.

Rothman, S. (1993). "Tradition and Change: The University Under Stress." In H. Dickman (ed.), *The Imperiled Academy*. New Brunswick, NJ: Transaction Press.

Rousseau, D.M. (1995). *Psychological Contracts in Organizations: Understanding Written and Unwritten Agreements*. Thousand Oaks, CA: Sage.

———— (1996). "Changing the Deal While Keeping People." *Academy of Management Executive* 10: 50–58.

———— and S. Tijoriwala (1996). *Managing Trust While Managing Change*. San Diego: Paper presented at the Annual Meeting of the Society for Industrial and Organizational Psychology.

Rusk, J. (1997). "Plebiscites a Tory Public-relations Disaster." *Globe and Mail*, March 3, A3.

Sackett, David L. and William M.C. Rosenberg, J.A. Muir Gray, R. Brian Hayes, and W. Scott Richardson (1994). "Evidence Based Medicine: What It Is and What It Isn't." *British Medical Journal* 312 (13): 71.

Sahney, V.K. and Gail L. Warden (1996). "The Quest for Quality and Productivity in Health Services." *Frontiers of Health Services Management* (Cd-Rom).

Salutin, Rick (1996). "Ethics Issues Raised by the Copps Conundrum." *Globe and Mail*, May 10, C1.

Samuelson, Robert (1996). "Capitalism Under Siege." *Newsweek* 104 (May 6), 51.

Schneier, C.E., D.G. Shaw, and R.W. Beatty (1992). "Companies Attempt to Improve Performance While Containing Costs: Quick Fix Versus Lasting Change." *Human Resources Planning* 15: 1–25.

Seabourne, T. and E. Herndon (1983). *Self-Defense: A Body–Mind Approach*. Scottsdale, AZ: Gorsuch Scarisbruck.

Sedgwick, D. (1994). "Fixing Ford." *Detroit News,* Sept. 18, 1–5.

Sehl, Mary (1996). "Long and Short Term Planning in Children's Mental Health." Paper presented to "Ethics and Restructuring: The First Laurier Conference on Business and Professional Ethics." Waterloo: Wilfrid Laurier University.

Shapiro, Eileen (1995). *Fad Surfing in the Boardroom*. Reading, MA: Addison Wesley.

Shaw, William H. (1996). *Social and Personal Ethics*. 2nd ed. Belmont: Wadsworth.

_____ and Vincent Barry (1995). *Moral Issues in Business*. Belmont: Wadsworth.

Silverman B.G., S.L. Brown, R.A. Bright, R.G. Kaczmarek, J.B. Arrowsmith-Lowe, and D.A. Kessler (1996). "Reported Complications of Silicone Gel Breast Implants: an Epidemiologic Review." *Annals of Internal Medicine* 124 (8): 744–756.

Sloan, A. (1996). "The Hit Men." *Newsweek* 104 (February 26): 44–48.

Smith, Blair (1995). Letter to *British Medical Journal* 313 (2): 169.

Smith, C. (1994). "The New Corporate Philanthropy." *Harvard Business Review* 94 (7): 107.

Smith, G. and R. Stodghill (1994). "Are Good Causes Good Marketing?" *Business Week,* March 21, 64.

Spears, John (1997). "'No' to Megacity if Taxes Unprotected: Poll." *Toronto Star*, March 1, A1.

Stambaugh, D.M. (1992). "Productivity Lost in Bids to Cut Costs." *National Underwriter* 96 (June 22): 39, 41, 48.

Statistics Canada (1991). *Perspectives on Labour and Income*. Vol. 3, No. 3.
――― (1996). Catalogue 81–227–XPB. Ottawa: Author.

Stein, Lewis David (1996). "Display of Discount Democracy Could Backfire." *Toronto Star*, March 4, A8.

Strange, Susan (1994). "Rethinking Structural Change in the International Political Economy: States, Firms and Diplomacy." In Richard Stubbs and Geoffrey R.D. Underhill (eds.), *Political Economy and the Changing Global Order*. Toronto: McClelland & Stewart, 103–115.

Stuller, J. (1993). "Why Not 'Inplacement'?" *Training* 30 (6, June): 37–41.

Sun Tzu (translated by S.B. Griffith) (1963). *The Art of War*. London: Oxford University Press.

Suris, O. (1994). "Retooling Itself, Ford Stresses Speed, Candor." *Wall Street Journal*, Oct. 27, B1, B10.

Sutherland, R.W. and M.J. Fulton (1992). *Health Care in Canada*. Ottawa: Health Group.

Sutton, H. (1988). *Competitive Intelligence*. Research Report No. 913. New York: The Conference Board.

Teeple, G. (1995). *Globalization and the Decline of Social Reform*. Toronto: Garamond.

Thanh Ha, Tu (1996). "Quebeckers Get First Taste of Bitter Deficit Pill." *Globe and Mail*, April 2, A9.

Thierry, Lauren and Christine Negroni (1997). "Part-Time Vs. Full-Time Workers." *CNN Inside Business*, August 9, 4:00 PM ET, transcript no-970809002V36.

Thurow, Lester (1980). *Zero Sum Society*. New York: Penguin.

Toronto Star (1997a). "Megacity: Our Best Hope For the Future." March 1, Editorial, B2.
――― (1997b). "It's Mega No to Megacity." March 4, A1.
――― (1997c). "Spendthrift Councils Squander City's Future." Aug. 5, Editorial, A14.

Toynbee, A. (1962). *A Study of History*. Abridged ed. Ed. D.C. Somerville. London: Oxford University Press.

Trotman, Alex (1994). *1994 Ford Facts*. Dearborn, MI: Author.

Uchitelle, Louis (1996). "Layoffs Are Out; Hiring is Back." *New York Times*, June 18, C1.
――― (1997). "Strike Points to Inequality In 2-Tier Job Market." *New York Times*, Aug. 8, A22.

Valpy, M. (1996). "Suffer the Murdered Babies." *Globe and Mail,* Aug. 3, D1.

Van Deusen, Cheryl (1996). "Downsizing: A Model for Collective Effort Among Community, Government Management and Labor." In Jeanne M. Logsdon and K. Rehbein (eds.), *Proceedings of the 7th annual International Association of Business and Society conference.* Sante Fe: University of New Mexico.

Van Rijn (1997). "Post Office Bounces Back Badly Addressed Ballots." *Toronto Star,* Feb. 22, A4.

Varadarajan, P. Rajan and Anil Menon (1988). "Cause-Related Marketing: A Coalignment of Marketing Strategy and Corporate Philanthropy." *Journal of Marketing* 52 (6): 58–74.

Vella, C.M. and J.J. McGonagle, Jr. (1987). *Competitive Intelligence in the Computer Age.* Westport, CT: Greenwood.

Villeneuve, M. (1996). Personal communication.

Villeneuve, M., D. Semogas, E. Peereboom, D. Irvine, L. McGillis Hall, S. Walsh, L. O'Brien-Pallas, and A. Baumann (1995). "The Worklife Concerns of Ontario Nurses." Working paper 1995 no. 11. Hamilton: Quality of Nursing Worklife Research Unit, University of Toronto and McMaster University.

Vitiello, J. (1994). *Technical and Skills Training.* Alexandria, VA: American Society for Training and Development.

Waldie, Paul (1996). "Horsham Chief Apologizes for Results." *Globe and Mail,* May 10, B9.

Wanagas, Don. "Why the Dodos on Council are Endangered." *Toronto Sun,* Jan. 31, p. 12.

Weick, K.E. (1979). *The Social Psychology of Organizing.* 2nd ed. Reading, MA: Addison–Wesley.

Werhane, Patricia H. (1993). "Two Ethical Issues in Mergers and Acquisitions." In White (1993), 752–757.

Westphal, Merold (1996). "The Role of Non-Tenured Faculty in the Academy." *Proceedings and Addresses of the American Philosophical Association* 69 (5): 150–161.

White, Thomas I. (1993). *Business Ethics.* New York: Mamillan.

Whitty, G. (1996). "Creating Quasi-Markets in Education: A Review of Recent Research on Parental Choice and School Autonomy in Three Countries." *Review of Research in Education* 23 (annual): 22.

Williams, J., M. Yeo, and W. Hooper (1996). "Ethics for Regional Boards." *Leadership in Health Services* 5 (4): 22–26.

Williams, L. (1993). *Workplace of the Future: A Report of the Conference on the Future of the American Workplace*. July 26. Washington: US Department of Commerce and US Department of Labor.

Wilson, M.C., S. Robert, A. Hayward, Sean R. Gunis, Eric B. Bass, and Gordon Guyatt for the Evidence-Based Medicine Working Group (1995). "VIII. How to Use Clinical Practice Guidelines: B. What Are the Recommendations and Will They Help You in Caring for Your Patients?" *Journal of the American Medical Association* 274 (20): 1631.

Winter, Elmer (1961). *A Woman's Guide to Earning a Good Living*. New York: Simon and Schuster.

Wolff, R.P. (1969). *The Ideal of the University*. Boston: Beacon.

Wright, James (1996). "Dartmouth's Productivity." *Dartmouth Alumni Magazine* 88 (6): 35–38.

Zweig, P.L., J.P. Kline, S.A. Forest, and K. Gudridge (1995). "The Case Against Mergers." *Business Week* Oct. 30: 122–130.

Index

affirmative action, 179;
    see employment equity
Alberta education, 261–271
Algoma Steel, 153–154
Allen, Robert, 144
amalgamation, 111–124; see merger(s)
American Express, 97
Angell, Marcia, 192–193
anorexia, corporate, 7, 146, 234
applied ethics, 5–6, 245; see ethics;
    university education
Aristotle (on proportional value), 224
Avon, 97

Bank of Montreal, 120
banking, 279–283
Barber, John, 117
Bell Canada, Bell Mobility, 96, 150,
    273–277
Bill 26 (Ontario), 166
Bill 41 (Alberta), 267
Bill 57 (Alberta), 267
Bill C91, 47, 48, 49
Bloom, Alan, 12–13
Body Shop, 99
British Columbia Resources and
    Investment Corporation
    (BCRIC), 56

Cadet Cleaners, 152
Canadian Auto Workers (CAW), 169
Canadian Tire, 152
capital/wealth accumulation, 43, 51,
    57; privatization as a form of
    capital accumulation, 52–56
cause-related marketing (CRM),
    95–110
charter schools, 262–268
Chase Manhattan Bank, 145

Chemical Bank, 145
Chevron USA, 67
Chrétien, Jean, 144
Chrysler, 169
communication, 62, 65, 72, 176–177,
    282–283
Communication Workers of America
    (CWA), 70–71
community, 57, 73, 133, 137,
    231–237, 253, 257, 275
comparable worth, 227
competitive intelligence, 79, 83, 84
conflict of interest, 120–124, 140, 165
continuous learning, 174
Continuous Quality Improvement
    (CQI), 29
corporate judo, 75–92
corporate raiding, 89–90
Cox, Donald, 287–288
Craig, Jenny, 234
"creative destruction," 288, 289

Daniels, Norman, 39
debt, 3, 4, 44–49, 56–57
deficits, 3, 25, 26, 44, 52
de-layering, 63–66
Deming, W. Edwards, 30
deontology, 101–102
deprofessionalization, 112, 203–211
deregulation, 43, 47, 266
deskilling, 144; see multi-skilling
diversity, 181
discrimination, 228–229
downsizing, 3, 7, 25, 43, 61–63,
    143–146, 151, 169, 175, 205,
    208, 233, 256, 273, 281;
        downsizing vs. restructuring,
        63, 279
Dow Corning, 189–201, 294

Dunlap, Albert, 73, 85, 144
Drucker, Peter, 151

early retirement, 173
Eaton, Robert J., 27, 85
education, 85–87, 88, 182;
    see Alberta education;
    liberal education; universities
efficiency, 33–34, 43, 75, 148, 168;
    see productivity
Emberley, Peter, 10, 11, 13
equity, 40, 127, 164; employment
    equity, 179–185; see
    discrimination
ethics, 290–299; the privatization of
    ethics, 25–26, 40; see applied
    ethics
EthicScan, 105
European Union, 244
evidence-based decision making
    (EBDM), 157–166
executive compensation, 144
exploitation, 225–227

Ford Motor Company, 30, 63–66,
    163–164
Friedman, Milton, 232–233

General Agreement on Tariffs and
    Trade (GATT), 167
General Motors, 280
General Electric, 280
Generation X, 227, 228
Gerard, Leo, 154
Gilder, George, 45
globalization, 4, 25; see 239–244
Golden Age of Capitalism, 44, 50, 51
governance, 130, 136, 151–154
government intervention, 87–89
guiding principles approach, 137–138

Harris, Mike, 119, 166, 261, 289, 290
Hayek, Friedrich, 58

Health Services Restructuring
    Commission (Ontario), 123
Hewlitt Packard, 148, 149
Hobbes, 112
"hyper-liberalism," 240, 241, 242;
    see New Right

IBM, 30
Illich, Ivan, 268–269, 270–271
IMF, 243
Intel, 66–67
integrity, 198
invisible hand, 85

Johnson & Johnson, 99
Juvenile Diabetes Foundation of
    Canada, 96

Kellogg, W.K., 149
Kentucky Fried Chicken (KFC), 97
Keynes, John Maynard, 58
Klein, Ralph, 51, 166, 261, 262, 268,
    269–270

Laffer, Arthur (the Laffer Curve), 45
Landsberg, Michelle, 117
language, 38, 106; see 204–205;
    see communication; Newspeak
lay-offs, 3, 25, 64, 252
"lean and mean," 70, 75, 168
liberal education, 11–22;
    see education
Lincoln Electric, 152
literacy, 248
London Life, 172

Manley, John, 144
Marx, Marxists, 58, 112
McKenna, Frank, 166
McMurtry, John, 50–51, 57
McQuaig, Linda, 48–49, 51
merger(s), 3, 75, 77; see amalgamation
Mill, John Stuart, 13–15

Minnesota Mining and Manufacturing Co. (3M), 30, 67–68
minimum wage, 46, 164–165
morale, employee, 206, 207, 223; *see* community; efficiency; productivity; uncertainty
Motorola, 30
multi-skilling, 32, 207; *see* deskilling

New Brunswick, 247–253
New Left, 269–270
New Right, 261–262, 268, 269–270; *see* "hyper-liberalism"; welfare state
New Zealand, 49, 51
Newfoundland outports, 231–232
Newspeak, 43
Nietzsche, 112
NYNEX Corporation, 70–71

Ontario Hydro, 172
outcomes research/measurement, 36–37, 207
outplacement, 61, 173–174

part-time work, 143, 234, 235, 236; involuntary part-time work, 220; *see* underemployment
Pepsi, 97, 106
Plato, 11–12
Polanyi, Karl, 50, 244
privatization, 52–56; *see* 250; *see* privatization of ethics
prevention, 162, 201, 252
productivity, 33–34, 61, 68, 75, 146, 147, 209; *see* efficiency

quality in health care, 34–35, 203, 207
Queens Region Board, 128–140

Rawls, John, 224
Reagan, Ronald, 45
realism, 112–113, 115, 124
redeployment, 66–68, 205–206

Reflexite, 68–70
regional health boards, 125–141
regionalization, 125–127
regulation, 51
regulation theory, 43
Reich, Robert, 85, 87
rich and poor, 28, 45
"right analysis" (in ethics), 294–295
risk assessment/management, 189–201

Scotiabank, 283
stakeholder(s), 7, 73, 80–81, 83, 104, 105, 123, 134, 135, 147, 151–152, 165
state capitalism, 240, 241
Stroh's, 148

technology, technological change, 3, 143, 167, 173, 240, 280; *see* 248–249
teleology, 101–102
tenure, 229–230
Theory X, 145, 150
Thunder Bay Regional Hospital, 113, 122
Todres, Elaine, 288–289
Total Quality Management (TQM), 29–34, 37–38
Toronto amalgamation, 111, 115–120, 121
Toronto Board of Education, 97, 106
Trotman, Alex, 63–65

unemployment insurance, 52, 203
uncertainty, 80–81, 155, 172, 193; *see* 222–223, 274–275
underemployment, 206–207, 213–230; *see* part-time work
union(s), 55, 57, 68, 148, 169, 206; *see* Communication Workers of America, Canadian Auto Workers
United Nations, 244

universities, university education, 8,
    9–23, 47–48, 183–185; university
    hiring, 216–230; the university's
    role as social critic, 13; *see*
    education
University of British Columbia, 97
unwritten contract(s), 170–172
UPS strike, 213–214, 216

values, 5–6, 37, 132, 137–138, 182
Voluntary Leaves of Absence (LOA),
    68–70

welfare, 52, 242–243; *see* welfare
    state
welfare state, 43–58
Westinghouse, 97
Willet Hospital, 255–259
World Bank, 243
World Trade Organization (WTO),
    167
"wrong analysis" (in ethics), 294–295

Xerox, 30